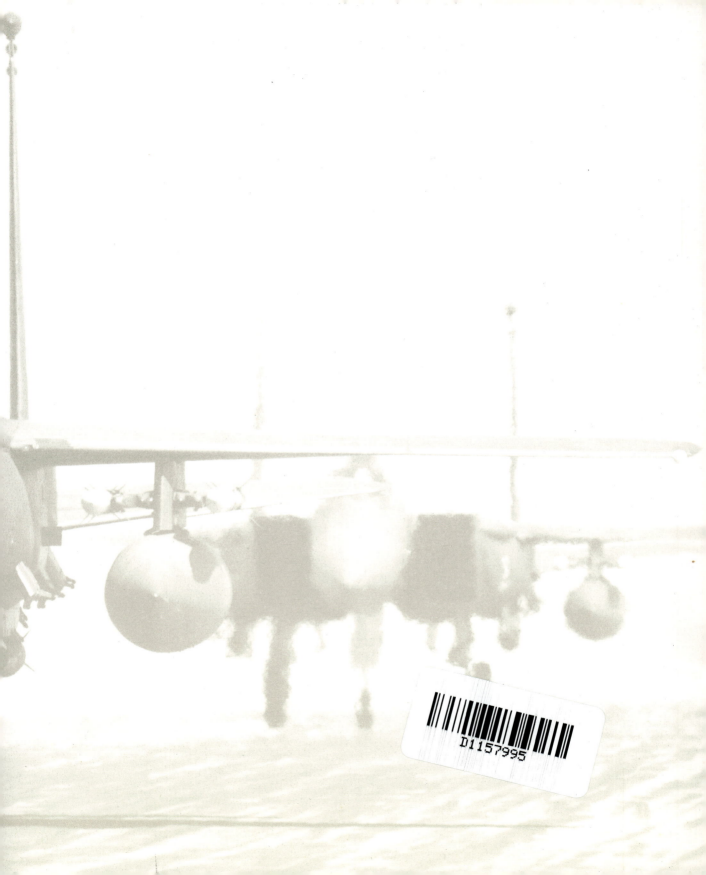

THE ESSENTIAL
AIRCRAFT IDENTIFICATION GUIDE

MODERN MILITARY AIRPOWER

1990–PRESENT

THOMAS NEWDICK
AND TOM COOPER

amber
BOOKS

This edition published in 2010 by
Amber Books Ltd
Bradley's Close
74–77 White Lion Street
London N1 9PF
United Kingdom
www.amberbooks.co.uk

A catalogue record for this book is available from the British Library.

ISBN: 978-1-907446-27-6

Distributed in the UK by
Casemate Ltd
17 Cheap Street
Newbury
RG14 5DD
www.casematepublishing.co.uk

Project Editor: James Bennett
Design: Brian Rust
Picture Research: Terry Forshaw
Additional Illustrations: Ugo Crisponi

Printed in Thailand

Picture Credits

All photographs courtesy of U.S. Department of Defense except for the following:
Air Team Images: 99
Australian Department of Defence: 183, 184
BAE Systems: 142
Bui Tuan Kheim: 159
Canadian Air Force: 32
Corbis: 87 (Matko Biljac/Reuters)
Czech Ministry of Defence: 88 (Jan Kouba)
Thomas Merkl: 121
Press Association Images: 157 (Chiang Ying-Ying)
Wikimedia Creative Commons License & GNU Free Documentation License: 101 (Boksi), 109 (Self Q), 138 (Retxham), 177 (Danie Van Der Werwe)

Contents

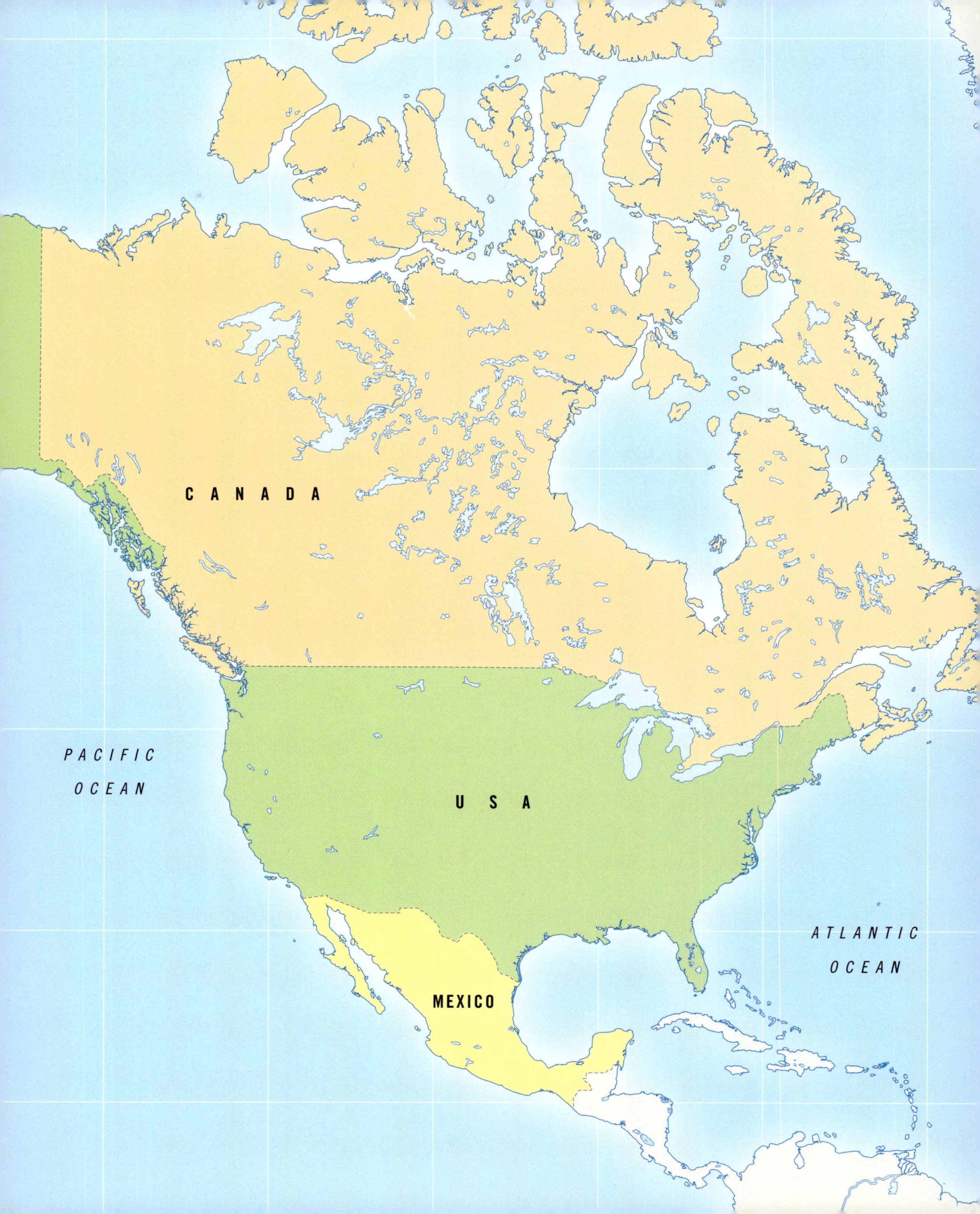
CANADA
PACIFIC OCEAN
USA
MEXICO
ATLANTIC OCEAN

Chapter 1

North America

Comprising elements from Canada, Mexico and the United States, North American airpower is dominated by the air arms of the U.S. While the U.S. Air Force is the world's most powerful air arm, the aviation components of the U.S. Navy, Marine Corps and U.S. Army are each, in turn, far larger and more capable than the air forces of most other nations. As well as these formations, the U.S. can also call upon additional airpower and personnel held by the Air Force Reserve Command, Air National Guard and other reserve organizations. Both Canada and the U.S. deploy air power in support of the North Atlantic Treaty Organization (NATO) and its various overseas missions, and the two countries also combine to provide air defence of the North American continent through North American Aerospace Defence Command (NORAD).

United States

United States Air Force

The world's largest air arm, the United States Air Force (USAF) is also the most potent, capable of executing a diverse range of missions anywhere in the world, at a moment's notice.

ANY GIVEN DAY, around 40 per cent of the USAF fleet can be expected to be involved in operations. Currently, the focus is on the Global War on Terror, involving 25,000 USAF personnel deployed to U.S. Central Command. Outside of this, combat operations involve around 213,000 airmen, including 30,000 from the Air National Guard (ANG) and Air Force Reserve Command (AFRC). Deployed units are organized within 10 Air and Space Expeditionary Forces (AEF), which complete 120-day tours in rotation. Two AEFs are deployed at a time, each with around 175 aircraft and 17,500 personnel.

One of five Joint Chiefs of Staff, the Air Force Chief of Staff is responsible for 10 Major Commands (MAJCOM): Air Force Global Strike Command (AFGSC); Air Combat Command (ACC); Air Education and Training Command (AETC); Air Force Material Command (AFMC); Air Force Space Command (AFSPC); Air Force Special Operations Command (AFSOC); Air Mobility Command (AMC); Pacific Air Forces (PACAF); United States Air Force in Europe (USAFE); and Air Force Reserve Command (AFRC). The major commands are divided into one or more numbered air forces, six of

BOMBER UNITS

USAF Warfare Center / Nellis AFB, Nevada		
53rd Wing / Eglin AFB, Florida		
53rd TEG Nellis AFB, Nevada		
31st TES	B-1B, B-2A, B-52H	Edwards AFB, California
72nd TES	B-2A	Whiteman AFB, Missouri
49th TES	B-52H	Barksdale AFB, Louisiana
337th TES	B-1B	Dyess AFB, Texas
57th Wing / Nellis AFB, Nevada		
USAFWS / Nellis AFB, Nevada		
77th WPS 'War Eagles'	B-1B	Dyess AFB, Texas
325th WPS	B-2A	Whiteman AFB, Missouri
340th WPS	B-52H	Barksdale AFB, Louisiana
Eighth Air Force / Air Force Global Strike Command / Barksdale AFB, Louisiana		
2nd BW / Barksdale AFB, Louisiana		
11th BS 'Mr. Jiggs'	B-52H	
20th BS 'Buccaneers'	B-52H	
96th BS 'Red Devils'	B-52H	

5th BW / Minot AFB, North Dakota	
23rd BS 'Bomber Barons'	B-52H
509th BW / Whiteman AFB, Missouri	
13th BS 'Devil's Own Grim Reapers'	B-2A
393rd BS 'Tigers'	B-2A
Twelfth Air Forces / Air Forces Southern Davis-Monthan AFB, Arizona	
7th BW / Dyess AFB, Texas	
9th BS 'Bats'	B-1B
28th BS 'Grim Reapers'	B-1B
28th BW / Ellsworth AFB, South Dakota	
34th BS 'Thunderbirds'	B-1B
37th BS 'Tigers'	B-1B
ARFC Tenth Air Force / NAS JRB Forth Worth / Carswell Field Texas	
917th Wing / Barksdale AFB, Louisiana	
93rd BS 'Indian Outlaws'	B-52H
Air Force Material Command	
412th TW / Edwards AFB, California	
419th FLTS 'Silent Sting'	B-1B, B-2A, B-52H

these being organized on a geographical basis, and four with functional duties. In addition to MAJCOMs and numbered air forces, the USAF includes smaller agencies reporting to headquarters in Washington DC. These agencies include the Air Force Flight Standards Agency, responsible for air traffic control and flight inspection; the Air Force District of Washington, which undertakes homeland and ceremonial duties around the capital; the USAF Academy, providing cadet training; and the USAF Auxiliary, with 52 mainly volunteer wings that undertake non-combat support missions in the U.S.

Air Force Global Strike Command

As its contribution to the U.S. nuclear deterrent, AFGSC possesses a fleet of 74 B-52Hs and 19 B-2As. Eventually, a new bomber is to be fielded, but this will be some time after the originally slated date of 2018. AFGSC commands the Eighth Air Force and the Twentieth Air Force, the latter operating ICBMs, and includes three bomber and four intelligence, surveillance and reconnaissance (ISR) wings.

As the largest MAJCOM, ACC maintains three numbered air forces and over 60 flying wings, including active, ANG and AFRC assignments, and the Air Warfare Center, responsible for tests and evaluation, and the USAF Weapons School. ACC equipment includes non-nuclear bombers, and all U.S.-based fighters, ISR and C2 assets. Numbered air forces are the First Air Force, with 10 ANG fighter wings that mainly support NORAD; the Ninth Air Force, responsible for the eastern U.S. and with five fighter wings; and the Twelfth Air Force, responsible for Central and Southern America, with seven active-duty wings, including the 65-strong fleet of B-1Bs.

With the F-22A in service and the F-35A waiting in the wings, the fighter arm is in an era of transition. By October 2012 the USAF intends to field 187 F-22s, with the first of 1763 F-35As coming on line.

▲ **Rockwell B-1B Lancer**

A formation of four B-1B bombers operated by the now-defunct 116th Bomb Wing from Robins AFB, Georgia. The Lancer force has now been streamlined, with two operational wings assigned to the Twelfth Air Force, and based at Dyess AFB, Texas, and Ellsworth AFB, South Dakota.

STRATEGIC RECONNAISSANCE UNITS

USAF Warfare Center / Nellis AFB, Nevada		
53rd Wing / Eglin AFB, Florida		
53rd TEG / Nellis AFB, Nevada		
Det 2	RQ-4A/B, U-2S	Beale AFB, California
31st TES	RQ-4A/B	Edwards AFB, California
Eighth Air Force / Air Force Global Strike Command / Barksdale AFB, Louisiana, 9th RW / Beale AFB, California		
Det 1	U-2S	RAF Akrotiri, Cyprus
1st RS	U-2S, TU-2S, T-38A, RQ-4A	Beale AFB, California
5th RS 'Black Cats'	U-2S	Osan AB, Korea
12th RS 'Blackbirds'	RQ-4A/B	Beale AFB, California
99th RS	U-2S, T-38A	Beale AFB, California
55th Wing / Offutt AFB, Nebraska		
1st ACCS 'First Axe'	E-4B	Offutt AFB, Nebraska
38th RS 'Fighting Hellcats'	RC-135V/W, TC-135W	Offutt AFB, Nebraska
45th RS 'Sylvester'	WC-135W, OC-135B, RC-135S/U, TC-135S	
Det 1	RC-135S	Eielson AFB, Alaska
82nd RS 'Hog Heaven'	RC-135V/W	Kadena AB, Okinawa
95th RS 'Kickin' Ass'	RC-135V/W	RAF Mildenhall, England
Det 1	RC-135V/W	Souda Bay, Crete
343rd RS 'Ravens'	RC-135V/W, TC-135W	Offut AFB, Nebraska
41st ECS AFB, 'Scorpions'	EC-130H	Davis-Monthan AFB, Arizona
42nd ECS	TC-130H	Davis-Monthan AFB, Arizona

F-22 FIGHTER SQUADRONS

NINTH AIR FORCE / AIR FORCES CENTRAL / SHAW AFB, SOUTH CAROLINA		
1st FW / Langley AFB, Virginia		
27th FS 'Fightin' Eagles'	F-22A	Langley AFB, Virginia
94th FS 'Hat in the Ring'	F-22A	Langley AFB, Virginia
192nd FW / Langley, Virginia		
149th FS 'Rebel Riders'	F-22A	Langley, Virginia
Twelfth Air Forces / Air Forces Southern Davis-Monthan AFB, Arizona		
49th FW / Holloman AFB, New Mexico		
7th FS 'Screamin' Demons'	F-22A	Holloman AFB, New Mexico
ARFC Tenth Air Force NAS JRB Forth Worth Carswell Field Texas		
477th FG		
302nd FS 'Sun Devils'	F-22A	Elmendorf AFB, Alaska
926th Group / Nellis AFB, Nevada		
706th FS	F-22A	Nellis AFB, Nevada
Air Education and Training Command		
325th FW / Tyndall AFB, Florida		
43rd FS 'American Hornets'	F-22A	
PACIFIC AIR FORCES		
Eleventh Air Force Elmendorf AFB, Alaska		
3rd Wing / Elmendorf AFB, Alaska		
90th FS 'Pair O'Dice'	F-22A	
525th FS 'Bulldogs'	F-22A	

The F-35 will eventually replace the F-16, numbers of which will drop from 1245 to 1086 in the year 2012. The 2012 fighter fleet will be completed by 178 F-15C/Ds and 217 F-15Es. Another type to be replaced by the F-35 is the A-10, of which 368 will remain in use in October 2012.

The USAF has moved with haste to field UAVs, and their operators are now permitted to graduate straight from undergraduate pilot training rather than first having to gain experience in a manned aircraft. The USAF's most numerically important UAVs are the MQ-1 and MQ-9, the latter with an attack capability.

AETC, headquartered at Randolph AFB, Texas, provides all aspects of flight and military training for USAF, via two numbered air forces, the Second (four wings and one group, but no flying units) and Nineteenth (five active component wings, five ANG wings and one AFRC wing). Headquartered at Peterson AFB, Colorado, AFSPC controls the Fourteenth Air Force, responsible for other space-based missions, and the Twenty-Fourth Air Force, the

Specifications

Crew: 1

Powerplant: 2 x 160kN (35,000lb) thrust Pratt & Whitney F119-PW-100 thrust-vectoring afterburning turbofan engines

Maximum speed: 2410km/h (1500mph)

Range: 2977km (1850 miles)

Service ceiling: 15,524m (50,000ft)

Dimensions: span 13.6m (44ft 6in); length 18.9m (62ft 1in); height 5.1m (16ft 8in)

Weight: 38,000kg (83,500lb) loaded

Armament: 1 x 20mm (0.78in) M61A2 Vulcan cannon; internal weapons bays for two AIM-9 Sidewinder and six AIM-120 ASRAAM air-to-air missiles

Lockheed Martin F-22A Raptor, 7th Fighter Squadron, 49th Fighter Wing, Holloman AFB

Although orders for the stealthy, fifth-generation F-22A have been slashed, in the Raptor the USAF possesses the world's premier air defence fighter.

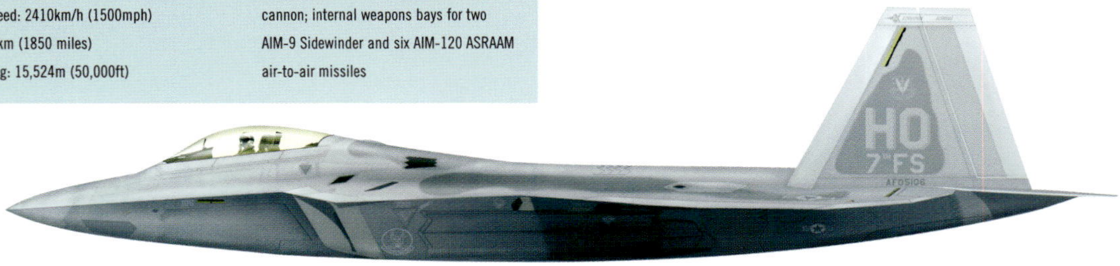

F-15 FIGHTER SQUADRONS

AIR COMBAT COMMAND / LANGLEY AFB, VIRGINIA		
65th AGRS	F-15C/D	Nellis AFB, Nevada
First Air Force / Air Forces Northern / Tyndall AFB, Florida		
120th FW / Great Falls International Airport, Montana		
186th FS 'Vigilantes'	F-15C/D	
125th FW / Jacksonville International Airport, Florida		
159th FS 'Jaguars'	F-15A/B/C/D	
Det 1	F-15A/C	Homestead ARB, Florida
142nd FW / Portland International Airport/ANGB, Oregon		
123rd FS 'Red Hawks'	F-15A/B/C/D	
Ninth Air Force / Air Forces Central / Shaw AFB, S. Carolina		
1st FW / Langley AFB, Virginia		
71st FS 'Ironmen'	F-15C/D	
4th FW / Seymour Johnson AFB, North Carolina		
333rd 'Lancers'	F-15E	
334th FS 'Eagles'	F-15E	
335th FS 'Chiefs'	F-15E	
336th FS 'Rocketeers'	F-15E	
33rd FW / Eglin AFB, Florida		
58th FS 'Gorillas'	F-15C/D	
104th FW / Westfield Barnes Airport/ANGB, Massachusetts		
131st FS 'Death Vipers'	F-15C/D	
Twelfth Air Forces / Air Forces Southern Davis-Monthan AFB, Arizona		
366th FW / Mountain Home AFB, Idaho		
389th FS 'Thunderbolts'	F-15E	
390th FS 'Wild Boars'	F-15C/D	
391st FS 'Bold Tigers'	F-15E	
131st FW / Lambert-St Louis International Airport, Missouri		
110th FS 'Lindbergh's Own'	F-15C/D	
159th FW / NAS JRB New Orleans, Louisiana		
122nd FS 'Cajuns'	F-15C/D	

ARFC Tenth Air Force / NAS JRB Forth Worth/Carswell Field Texas		
307th FS 'Stingers'		Langley AFB, Virginia
Det 4	F-15C/D	Eglin AFB, Utah
926th Group / Nellis AFB, Nevada		
706th FS	F-15C/D/E	
Air Education and Training Command		
325th FW / Tyndall AFB, Florida		
2nd FS 'American Beagles'	F-15C/D	
95th FS 'Boneheads'	F-15C/D	
173rd FW / Klamath Falls International Airport/Kingsley Field, Oregon		
114th FS 'Eager Beavers'	F-15B/C/D	
PACIFIC AIR FORCES		
Fifth Air Force / Yokota AB, Japan		
18th Wing / Kadena AB, Japan		
44th FS 'Vampires'	F-15C/D	
67th FS 'Fighting Cocks'	F-15C/D	
Eleventh Air Force Elmendorf AFB, Alaska		
3rd Wing / Elmendorf AFB, Alaska		
12th FS 'Dirty Dozen'	F-15C/D	
19th FS 'Gamecocks'	F-15C/D	
Thirteenth Air Force		
154th Wing / Hickam AFB, Hawaii		
199th FS	F-15A/BC/D	
UNITED STATES AIR FORCE IN EUROPE		
Third Air Force / Air Forces Europe / Ramstein AB, Germany		
48th FW / RAF Lakenheath, England		
492nd FW 'Madhatters'	F-15E	
493rd FS 'Grim Reapers'	F-15C/D	
494th FS 'Panthers'	F-15E	

F-16 FIGHTER SQUADRONS

Air Combat Command Langley AFB, Virginia

USAF Warfare Center / Nellis AFB, Nevada

57th Wing / Nellis AFB, Nevada

USAF ADS 'Thunderbirds'	F-16C/D	Nellis AFB, Nevada
64th AGRS	F-16C/D	Nellis AFB, Nevada

First Air Force / Air Forces Northern / Tyndall AFB, Florida

601st AOC / Tyndall AFB, Florida

125th FS Det 1	F-16C/D	Ellington Field/ANGB, Texas
112th FS Det 1	F-16C/D	Selfridge Field ANGB, Michigan

144th FW / Fresno-Yosemite International Airport/ANGB, California

194th FS 'Griffins'	F-16C	
Det 1	F-16C	March ARB, California

148th FW / Duluth International Airport/ANGB, Minnesota

179th FS 'Bulldogs'	F-16C	
Det 1	F-16C	Tyndall AFB, Florida

158th FW / Burlington IAP/Ethan Allen ANGB, Vermont

134th FS 'Green Mountain Boys'	F-16C	
Det 1	F-16C	Langley AFB, Virginia

177th FW / Atlantic City International Airport/ANGB, New Jersey

119th FS 'Jersey Devils'	F-16C	

Ninth Air Force / Air Forces Central / Shaw AFB, S. Carolina

20th FW / Shaw AFB, South Carolina

55th FS 'Lancers'	F-16C/D	
77th FS 'Gamblers'	F-16C/D	
79th FS 'Tigers'	F-16C/D	

113th Wing / Andrews AFB, Maryland

121st 'Capital Guardians'	F-16C/D	

122nd FW / Fort Wayne International Airport, Louisiana

163rd FS 'Marksmen'	F-16C	

127th Wing / Selfridge ANGB, Michigan

107th FS 'Red Devils'	F-16C/D

169th FW / McEntire JNGS, South Carolina

157th FS 'Swamp Fox'	F-16C/D

174th FW / Syracuse Hancock International Airport, New York

138th FS 'Cobras'F-16C	

180th FW / Toledo Express Airport, Ohio

112th FS 'Stingers'	F-16C/D

187th FW / Montgomery Regional Airport/Dannelly Field, Alabama

100th FS 'Panthers'	F-16C/D

Twelfth Air Forces / Air Forces Southern Davis-Monthan AFB, Arizona

388th FW / Hill AFB, Utah

4th FS 'Fightin' Fujins'	F-16C/D
34th FS 'Rude Rams'	F-16C/D
421st FS 'Black Widows'	F-16C/D

114th FW / Sioux Falls Regional Airport/Joe Foss Field, South Dakota

175th FS 'Lobos'	F-16C/D

115th FW / Dane County Regional Airport/Truax Field, Wisconsin

176th FS 'Badgers'	F-16C

132nd FW / Des Moines International Airport, Iowa

124th FS 'Hawkeyes'	F-16C/D

138th FW / Tulsa International Airport, Oklahoma

125th FS 'Tulsa Vipers'	F-16C/D

140th Wing / Buckley AFB, Colorado

120th FS 'Cougars'	F-16C

150th FW / Kirtland AFB, New Mexico

188th FS 'Tacos'	F-16C/D

F-16 FIGHTER SQUADRONS

ARFC Tenth Air Force / NAS JRB Forth Worth/Carswell Field Texas

307th FS 'Stingers' / Langley AFB, Virginia

Det 1	F-16C/D	Shaw AFB, South Carolina
Det 2	F-16C/D	Hill AFB, Utah
Det 4	F-15C/D	Eglin AFB, Utah

926th Group / Nellis AFB, Nevada

706th FS	F-16C/D	Nellis AFB, Nevada

301st FW / NAS JRB Forth Worth/Carswell Field, Texas

457th FS 'Spads'	F-16C/D	

419th FW / Hill AFB, Utah

466th FS 'Diamondbacks'	F-16C/D	

482nd FW / Homestead ARB, Florida

93rd FS 'Makos'	F-16C/D	

Air Education and Training Command

56th FW Luke AFB, Arizona

21st FS 'Gamblers'	F-16A/B	
61st FS 'Top Dogs'	F-16C/D	
62nd FS 'Spikes'	F-16C/D	
63rd FS 'Panthers'	F-16C/D	
308th FS 'Emerald Kings'	F-16C/D	
309th FS 'Wild Ducks'	F-16C/D	
310th FS 'Top Hats'	F-16C/D	
425th FS 'Black Widows'	F-16C/D	

149th FW / Kelly Field, Lackland AFB, Texas

182nd FS 'Lone Star Gunfighters'	F-16C/D	

162nd FW / Tucson International Airport, Arizona

148th FS 'Kickin' Ass'	F-16E/F	
152nd FS 'Tigers'	F-16C/D	
195th FS 'Warhawks'	F-16C/D	

178th FW / Springfield-Beckley Municipal Airport, Ohio

162nd FS 'Sabres'	F-16C/D, F-16AM/BM

944th FW / Luke AFB, Arizona

301st FS 'Red Tail Devils'	F-16C/D

PACIFIC AIR FORCES

Fifth Air Force / Yokota AB, Japan

35th FW / Misawa AB, Japan

13th FS 'Panthers'	F-16C/D
14th FS 'Samurais'	F-16C/D

Seventh Air Force Osan AB, Korea

8th FW / Kunsan AB, Korea

35th FS 'Pantons'	F-16C/D
80th FS 'Juvats'	F-16C/D

51st FW / Osan AB, Korea

36th FS 'Flying Fiends'	F-16C/D

Eleventh Air Force Elmendorf AFB, Alaska

354th FW / Eielson AFB, Alaska

18th AGRS 'Blue Foxes'	F-16C/D

UNITED STATES AIR FORCE IN EUROPE

Third Air Force / Air Forces Europe / Ramstein AB, Germany

31st FW / Aviano AB, Italy

510th FS 'Buzzards'	F-16C/D
555th FS 'Triple Nickel'	F-16C/D

52nd FW / Spangdahlem, Germany

22nd FS 'Stingers'	F-16C/D
23rd FS 'Fighting Hawks'	F-16C/D

▲ **Fairchild A-10 Thunderbolt II**

An A-10 takes off from Bagram Airfield, Afghanistan. The USAF maintains two Air Expeditionary Wings in Afghanistan: the 445th AEW at Bagram and the 451st AEW at Kandahar Airfield, with most assigned units deploying for four-month periods.

cyberspace combat component. Development, test and evaluation is the work of AFMC, its diverse test fleet headquartered at Wright-Patterson AFB, Ohio.

Special operations

Tasked with supporting unconventional warfare through the two wings of its Twenty-Third Air Force, AFSOC is headquartered at Hurlburt Field, Florida. Two special operations groups are additionally forward-deployed at bases in Japan and the UK.

AMC's 12 major air bases support its Eighteenth Air Force, providing airlift, tanker and aeromedical support. 18AF includes two Expeditionary Mobility Task Forces plus 13 active duty wings and one group, and 45 ANG and 24 AFRC wings.

Organic air support for overseas commands is handled by PACAF, headquartered at Hickam AFB, Hawaii, with four numbered air forces, and USAFE, headquartered at Ramstein AB, Germany, with two numbered air forces, one responsible for Africa.

Finally, ANG provides 87 flying wings across the U.S., units being assigned to ACC, AETC, AFSOC, AMC and PACAF, and also being committed to global operations. ANG aircraft represent around one-third of total strength, and cover a range of missions. AFRC, headquartered at Robins AFB, Georgia, controls three numbered air forces and 39 flying wings. It includes 'associate' units that operate aircraft in the possession of active duty units.

Specifications

Crew: 1

Powerplant: 2 x 106kN (23,810lb) thrust Pratt & Whitney F100-PW-100 turbofans

Maximum speed: 2655km/h (1650mph)

Range: 1930km (1200 miles)

Service ceiling: 30,500m (100,000ft)

Dimensions: span 13.05m (42ft 9.75in); length 19.43m (63ft 9in); height 5.63m (18ft 5in)

Weight: 25,424kg (56,000lb) loaded

Armament: 1 x 20mm (0.79in) M61A1 cannon, pylons with provision for up to 7620kg (16,800lb) of stores

▼ **McDonnell Douglas F-15A Eagle, 199th Fighter Squadron, 154th Fighter Wing, Hickam AFB**

F-15A 77-083 wears the colours of the Hawaii ANG's 199th FS, and was upgraded to near-F-15C standard under the Multi-Stage Improvement Program (MSIP-II), which adds AIM-120 AMRAAM, among other upgrades.

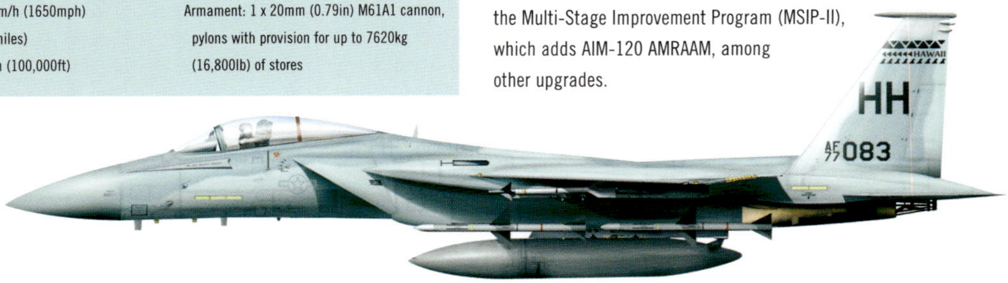

Specifications

Crew: 1
Powerplant: 1 x 126.7kN (28,500lb) thrust Pratt & Whitney F100-PW-229 afterburning turbofan
Maximum speed: 2177km/h (1353mph)
Range: 3862km (2400 miles)
Service ceiling: 15,240m (49,000ft)
Dimensions: span 9.45m (31ft); length 15.09m (49ft 6in); height 5.09m (16ft 8in)
Weight: 19,187kg (42,300lb) loaded
Armament: 1 x General Electric M61A1 20mm (0.79in) multi-barrelled cannon, wingtip missile stations; 7 x external hardpoints with provision for up to 9276kg (20,450lb) of stores

General Dynamics F-16C Fighting Falcon, 510th Fighter Squadron, 31st Fighter Wing, Aviano AB

F-16A 89-2137, seen here assigned to the 'Buzzards' of the 510th FS, was responsible for destroying three Serbian J-21 Jastrebs while serving with the 526th FS, 86th FW, over Bosnia on 18 February, 1994.

A-10 FIGHTER SQUADRONS

AIR COMBAT COMMAND / LANGLEY AFB, VIRGINIA		
Ninth Air Force / Air Forces Central / Shaw AFB, South Carolina		
23rd Wing / Moody AFB, Georgia		
74th FS 'Flying Tigers'	A/OA-10C	Moody AFB, Georgia
75th FS 'Sharks'	A/OA-10C	
110th FW / W.K. Kellog Airport/Battle Creek ANGB, Michigan		
172nd FS 'Mad Ducks'	A/OA-10C	
111th FW / NAS JRB Willow Grove, Pennsylvania		
103rd FS 'Black Hogs'	A/OA-10A/A+	
175th Wing / Martin State Airport/Warfield ANGB, Maryland		
104th 'Fighting Orioles'	A/OA-10C	
Twelfth Air Forces / Air Forces Southern Davis-Monthan AFB, Arizona		
355th FW / Davis-Monthan AFB, Arizona		
354th FS 'Bulldogs'	A/OA-10C	Davis-Monthan AFB, Arizona
357th FS 'Dragons'	A/OA-10C	Davis-Monthan AFB, Arizona
358th FS 'Lobos'	A/OA-10C	Davis-Monthan AFB, Arizona
124th Wing / Boise Airport / Gowen Field, Idaho		
190th FS	A/OA-10A	
188th FW / Fort Smith Regional Airport/Ebbing ANGB, Arkansas		
184th FS 'Flyin' Razorbacks'	A/OA-10A+	
ARFC Tenth Air Force / NAS JRB Forth Worth/Carswell Field Texas		
926th Group / Nellis AFB, Nevada		
706th FS	A/OA-10C	Nellis AFB, Nevada
422nd FW / Whiteman AFB, Missouri		
303rd FS 'KC Hawgs'	A/OA-10+	Whiteman AFB, Missouri
76th FS 'Hell's Angels'	A/OA-10C	Moody AFB, Georgia
917th Wing / Barksdale AFB, Louisiana		
47th 'Dogpatchers'	A/OA-10A+	
PACIFIC AIR FORCES		
Seventh Air Force / Osan AB, Korea		
51st FW / Osan AB, Korea		
25th FS 'Assam Dragons'	A/OA-10A	
UNITED STATES AIR FORCE IN EUROPE		
Third Air Force / Air Forces Europe / Ramstein AB, Germany		
52nd FW / Spangdahlem, Germany		
81st FS 'Panthers'	A/OA-10A/C	

United States

U.S. Navy

Fielding the world's largest and most powerful naval air arm, the U.S. Navy includes some 1300 carrier-based aircraft and helicopters, as well as over 200 land-based aircraft and 700 trainers.

BASIC ORGANIZATION OF the U.S. Navy divides assets between the Operating Forces and the Shore Establishment, each branch having a commander reporting to the Chief of Naval Operations, who in turn reports to the Joint Chiefs of Staff.

The Commander, U.S. Fleet Forces Command (COMUSFLTFORCOM), headquartered at NS Norfolk, Virginia, is part of the U.S. Joint Forces Command structure. Various commands report directly to COMUSFLTFORCOM, and cover the breadth of air, surface and submarine functions. The chief air components are the Commander, Naval Air Forces; Commander, Naval Air Force U.S. Atlantic Fleet (COMNAVAIRLANT); and the Naval Strike and Air Warfare Center (NSAWC).

COMNAVAIRLANT units are normally assigned to the Second, Fifth or Sixth Fleet. On the western coast, Commander, Naval Air Force U.S. Pacific Fleet (COMNAVAIRPAC) reports directly to the Commander, U.S. Pacific Fleet (COMPACFLT), also a component of U.S. Joint Forces Command, headquartered at Pearl Harbor, Hawaii, and primarily responsible for support of U.S. Pacific Command naval forces.

COMNAVAIRLANT and COMNAVAIRPAC maintain various functional air wings (including Airborne Command, Control, Logistics; Electronic Attack; Helicopter Maritime Strike; Helicopter Sea Combat; Strike Fighter; and Patrol and Reconnaissance), fleet carrier air wings, and the fleet carriers themselves.

With an HQ at NAS North Island, California, Commander, Naval Air Forces (COMNAVAIRFOR) also serves as COMNAVAIRPAC, with administrative control of both COMNAVAIRLANT and the Chief of Naval Air Training (CNATRA). COMNAVAIRFOR/COMNAVAIRPAC air assets are generally assigned to the Second, Third, Fifth, Sixth or Seventh Fleet.

The centrepiece of the U.S. Navy's airpower is the fleet of aircraft carriers, and their embarked air wings. The U.S. Navy has a total of 11 nuclear-powered carriers, comprising 10 'Nimitz'-class vessels and the USS *Enterprise*. The next generation of carriers is already being built, with the USS *Gerald R. Ford* due to enter service in 2015. *Enterprise* will retire in 2013, and the U.S. Navy hopes to fund construction of 10 'Gerald R. Ford'-class carriers by 2040.

Specifications

Crew: 1
Powerplant: 2 x 97.90kN (22,000lb) thrust General Electric F414-GE-400 afterburning turbofan engines
Maximum speed: 1190 km/h (1190mph)
Range: 722km (449 miles)
Service ceiling: 15,000m (50,000ft)
Dimensions: span 13.62m (60ft 1in); length 13.62m (44ft 9in); height 4.88m (16ft)
Weight: 29,900kg (66,000lb) loaded
Armament: 1 x 20mm(0.79in) M61A1 Vulcan cannon; 11 external hardpoints for up to 8050kg (17,750lb) of stores

Boeing F/A-18E Super Hornet, VFA-81 'Sunliners', USS *Carl Vinson*

Spearheading U.S. Navy carrier airpower is the F/A-18 series, which serves as a strike fighter and, following the retirement of the S-3, as a refuelling tanker. Armed with AIM-120 and AIM-9X air-to-air missiles, this F/A-18E wears the colourful markings associated with the commander of VFA-81.

STRIKE FIGHTER SQUADRONS

Strike Fighter Wing, Pacific – NAS Lemoore, California		
VFA-2 'Bounty Hunters'	NAS Lemoore, California	F/A-18F
VFA-14 'Top Hatters'	NAS Lemoore, California	F/A-18E
VFA-22 'Fighting Redcocks'	NAS Lemoore, California	F/A-18F
VFA-25 'Fist of the Fleet'	NAS Lemoore, California	F/A-18C
VFA-27 'Royal Maces'	NAF Atsugi, Japan	F/A-18E
VFA-41 'Black Aces'	NAS Lemoore, California	F/A-18F
VFA-94 'Mighty Shrikes'	NAS Lemoore, California	F/A-18C
VFA-97 'Warhawks'	NAS Lemoore, California	F/A-18C
VFA-102 'Diamondbacks'	NAF Atsugi, Japan	F/A-18F
VFA-113 'Stingers'	NAS Lemoore, California	F/A-18C
VFA-115 'Eagles'	NAS Lemoore, California	F/A-18E
VFA-122 (FRS) 'Flying Eagles'	NAS Lemoore, California	F/A-18E/F
VFA-125 (FRS) 'Rough Raiders'	NAS Lemoore, California	F/A-18B/C/D
VFA-137 'Kestrels'	NAS Lemoore, California	F/A-18E
VFA-146 'Blue Diamonds'	NAS Lemoore, California	F/A-18C
VFA-147 'Argonauts'	NAS Lemoore, California	F/A-18E
VFA-151 'Vigilantes'	NAS Lemoore, California	F/A-18C
VFA-154 'Black Knights'	NAS Lemoore, California	F/A-18F
VFA-192 'Golden Dragons'	NAF Atsugi, Japan	F/A-18C
VFA-195 'Dambusters'	NAF Atsugi, Japan	F/A-18C
Strike Fighter Wing, Atlantic – NAS Oceana, Virginia		
VFA-11 'Red Rippers'	NAS Oceana, Virginia	F/A-18F
VFA-15 'Valions'	NAS Oceana, Virginia	F/A-18E
VFA-31 'Tomcatters'	NAS Oceana, Virginia	F/A-18E
VFA-32 'Swordsmen'	NAS Oceana, Virginia	F/A-18F
VFA-34 'Blue Blasters'	NAS Oceana, Virginia	F/A-18C
VFA-37 'Bulls'	NAS Oceana, Virginia	F/A-18C
VFA-81 'Sunliners'	NAS Oceana, Virginia	F/A-18E
VFA-83 'Rampagers'	NAS Oceana, Virginia	F/A-18C
VFA-86 'Sidewinders'	MCAS Beaufort, South Carolina	F/A-18C
VFA-87 'Golden Warriors'	NAS Oceana, Virginia	F/A-18A+
VFA-103 'Jolly Rogers'	NAS Oceana, Virginia	F/A-18F
VFA-105 'Gunslingers'	NAS Oceana, Virginia	F/A-18E
VFA-106 (FRS) 'Gladiators'	NAS Oceana, Virginia	F/A-18B/C/D/E/F
VFA-131 'Wildcats'	NAS Oceana, Virginia	F/A-18C
VFA-136 'Knighthawks'	NAS Oceana, Virginia	F/A-18E
VFA-143 'Pukin' Dogs'	NAS Oceana, Virginia	F/A-18E
VFA-211 'Checkmates'	NAS Oceana, Virginia	F/A-18F
VFA-213 'Blacklions'	NAS Oceana, Virginia	F/A-18F

ELECTRONIC ATTACK SQUADRONS

Electronic Attack Wing, Pacific – NAS Whidbey Island, Washington		
VAQ-129 (FRS) 'Vikings'	NAS Whidbey Island, Washington	EA-6B, F/A-18F, EA-18G
VAQ-130 'Zappers'	NAS Whidbey Island, Washington	EA-6B
VAQ-131 'Lancers'	NAS Whidbey Island, Washington	EA-6B
VAQ-132 'Scorpions'	NAS Whidbey Island, Washington	EA-18G
VAQ-133 'Wizards'	NAS Whidbey Island, Washington	EA-6B
VAQ-134 'Garudas'	NAS Whidbey Island, Washington	EA-6B
VAQ-135 'Black Ravens'	NAS Whidbey Island, Washington	EA-6B
VAQ-136 'Gauntlets'	NAF Atsugi, Japan	EA-6B
VAQ-137 'Rooks'	NAS Whidbey Island, Washington	EA-6B
VAQ-138 'Yellowjackets'	NAS Whidbey Island, Washington	EA-6B
VAQ-139 'Cougars'	NAS Whidbey Island, Washington	EA-6B
VAQ-140 'Patriots'	NAS Whidbey Island, Washington	EA-6B
VAQ-141 'Shadowhawks'	NAS Whidbey Island, Washington	EA-6B
VAQ-142 'Gray Wolves'	NAS Whidbey Island, Washington	EA-6B

At any one time, 10 carriers are in service, provided with 10 Carrier Strike Groups (CSG) and Carrier Air Wings (CVW), five of each normally assigned to Atlantic and Pacific Fleets. One carrier, USS *George Washington*, is forward deployed in Japan.

A CVW normally comprises 67–68 aircraft. The fixed-wing component consists of four Strike Fighter Squadrons (VFA) equipped with the Hornet or Super Hornet (typically one squadron of F/A-18Es, one of F/A-18Fs, and two of F/A-18A/Cs), one Electronic Attack Squadron (VAQ) with either four EA-6Bs or five EA-18Gs, and one Airborne Command and Control Squadron (VAW) with four E-2Cs. In the CVW's latest configuration, the carrier's helicopters are now operated by one Helicopter Maritime Strike Squadron (HSM) with 11 MH-60Rs (six of which are generally embarked on other warships), and one Helicopter Sea Combat Squadron (HSC) with eight MH-60S (six on the the carrier and two on the CSG's logistic support ship). The HSC is responsible for search and rescue, CSAR, logistical support, vertical replenishment, special operations, anti-surface warfare and mine countermeasures. Finally, two C-2As serve carrier onboard delivery requirements.

Earlier 'legacy' F/A-18A/Cs are scheduled to give way to the F/A-18E/F by 2015, with 22 squadrons eventually to be equipped. The F/A-18E/F will remain in production until at least 2012, providing 493 examples by that date. The EA-18G entered service in 2009 and will replace the EA-6B by 2013,

Specifications

Crew: 6
Powerplant: 8 x 46.68kN (10,500lb) thrust Pratt & Whitney J57-P-29WA engines
Maximum speed: 1027km/h (638mph)
Range: 13,419km (8338 miles)
Service ceiling: 14,082m (46,200ft)
Dimensions: span 56.39m (185ft); length 47.73m (156ft 7in); height 14.73m (48ft 4in)
Weight: 204,116kg (450,000lb) loaded
Armament: 4 x 12.7mm (0.5in) M-3 MGs; up to 19,504kg (43,000lb) of bombs

Northrop F-5N Tiger II, VFC-111 'Sundowners', NAS Key West

F-5N Bu No. 761548 is a former Swiss air force jet that now serves with VFC-111, one of three full-time Fighter Squadron Composites that serve as adversary units for U.S. Navy 'aggressor' air combat training.

serving with 10 squadrons. In order to avoid a 'fighter gap', the U.S. Navy is upgrading 'legacy' Hornets in order to extend aircraft service life. Designated successor to the F/A-18A/C is the F-35C, which is planned to attain initial operational capability in 2015, eventually equipping 18 squadrons.

Further new equipment is represented by the E-2D, which will replace E-2Cs in VAWs beginning in 2011.

▲ Grumman E-2C Hawkeye

The U.S. Navy's 'eye in the sky', the E-2 serves with 10 front-line Airborne Command and Control Squadrons, including the 'Screwtops' of VAW-123, seen here embarked on board the aircraft carrier USS *Theodore Roosevelt*.

Rotary fleet rationalization

As the U.S. Navy's latest helicopters, the MH-60R and MH-60S began to be assigned directly to CVWs in 2009, and 10 squadrons of each deployed type are to be distributed among the CVWs by 2013. A further six 12-helicopter squadrons will be assigned to expeditionary duties and support of amphibious operations. These will operate from the new fleet of Littoral Combat Ships. Current Helicopter Anti-submarine Squadrons (HS) will become HSCs by 2012, adopting the MH-60S. Meanwhile, Helicopter Anti-submarine Light Squadrons (HSL) are becoming HSMs as they adopt the MH-60R.

AIRBORNE COMMAND AND CONTROL SQUADRONS

Airborne Command, Control, Logistics Wing – Naval Base Ventura County/NAS Point Mugu, California		
VAW-112 'Golden Hawks'	NAS Point Mugu, California	E-2C
VAW-113 'Black Hawks'	NAS Point Mugu, California	E-2C
VAW-115 'Liberty Bells'	NAF Atsugi, Japan	E-2C
VAW-116 'Sun Kings'	NAS Point Mugu, California	E-2C
VAW-117 'Wallbangers'	NAS Point Mugu, California	E-2C
VAW-120 (FRS) 'Greyhawks'	Chambers Field, NS Norfolk, Virginia	E-2C
VAW-121 'Bluetails'	Chambers Field, NS Norfolk, Virginia	E-2C
VAW-123 'Screwtops'	Chambers Field, NS Norfolk, Virginia	E-2C
VAW-124 'Bear Aces'	Chambers Field, NS Norfolk, Virginia	E-2C
VAW-125 'Tigertails'	Chambers Field, NS Norfolk, Virginia	E-2C
VAW-126 'Seahawks'	Chambers Field, NS Norfolk, Virginia	E-2C

The backbone of the land-based U.S. Navy is a fleet of 17 squadrons that between them field around 150 P-3C maritime patrol aircraft, 16 EP-3E ISR aircraft and 16 E-6B strategic communications aircraft. The P-8A will replace P-3Cs, with 84 on order for use by 12 active duty Patrol Squadrons (VP) from 2013.

Naval Reserve airlift

The U.S. Navy keeps a fleet of transport aircraft for logistical support, comprising C-9s, C-40s, C-130s (with KC-130Js replacing older models), C-20s and C-37s. Flown by Naval Reserve squadrons, these types routinely support overseas operations.

Instruction training is handled by the five Training Air Wings of Naval Air Training Command, with its HQ at NAS Corpus Christi, Texas, while conversion and tactics training takes place within Fleet Readiness Squadrons (FRS) assigned to the Atlantic and Pacific Fleets. The training community is undergoing modernization, with upgrades and new types coming on line. The planned fleet of 221 T-45s will be attained by 2012. The T-6B entered service in 2009 and will replace the T-34C by 2014. The rotary-wing training fleet is being rationalized, with TH-57B/Cs to be upgraded to a common TH-57D by 2014.

▲ **Sikorsky MH-60S Seahawk**

A rescue diver jumps out of an MH-60S while conducting SAR training in the Persian Gulf. The helicopter was operated by HSC-28 'Dragon Whales', which was embarked in the amphibious assault ship USS *Kearsarge* in support of the 'global war on terror'.

Commander, U.S. Naval Forces Southern Command maintains aircraft detachments at bases located in Central and South America, while Commander, U.S. Naval Forces Europe operates from European bases in support of the Sixth Fleet. Commander, U.S. Naval Forces Central Command is responsible for aircraft detachments in the Middle East (Fifth Fleet).

HELICOPTER MARITIME STRIKE SQUADRONS

Helicopter Maritime Strike Wing, Pacific – NAS North Island, California

HSL-37 'Easyriders'	MCAF Kaneohe Bay, Hawaii	SH-60B
HSL-43 'Battle Cats'	NAS North Island, California	SH-60B
HSL-45 'Wolfpack'	NAS North Island, California	SH-60B
HSL-49 'Scorpions'	NAS North Island, California	SH-60B
HSL-51 'Warlords'	NAF Atsugi, Japan	SH-60B/F
HSM-41 (FRS) 'Seahawks'	NAS North Island, California	MH-60R
HSM-47 'Sabrehawks'	NAS North Island, California	MH-60R
HSM-71 'Raptors'	NAS North Island, California	MH-60R

Helicopter Maritime Strike Wing, Atlantic – Naval Station Mayport, Florida

HSL-40 (FRS) 'Airwolves'	NS Mayport, Florida	SH-60B
HSL-42 'Proud Warriors'	NS Mayport, Florida	SH-60B
HSL-44 'Swamp Fox'	NS Mayport, Florida	SH-60B
HSL-46 'Grandmasters'	NS Mayport, Florida	SH-60B
HSL-48 'Vipers'	NS Mayport. Florida	SH-60B
HSL-60 'Jaguars'	NS Mayport, Florida	SH-60B
HSM-70 'Spartans'	NAS Jacksonville, Florida	MH-60R

HELICOPTER SEA COMBAT SQUADRONS

Helicopter Sea Combat Wing, Pacific – NAS North Island, California

HS-4 'Black Knights'	NAS North Island, California	SH-60F, HH-60H
HS-6 'Indians'	NAS North Island, California	SH-60F, HH-60H
HS-8 'Eightballers'	NAS North Island, California	SH-60F, HH-60H
HS-10 (FRS) 'Warhawks'	NAS North Island, California	SH-60F, HH-60H
HS-14 'Chargers'	NAF Atsugi, Japan	SH-60F, HH-60H
HSC-3 (FRS) 'Merlins'	NAS North Island, California	MH-60S
HSC-12 'Golden Falcons'	NAS North Island, California	MH-60S
HSC-21 'Blackjacks'	NAS North Island, California	MH-60S
HSC-23 'Wildcards'	NAS North Island, California	MH-60S
HSC-25 'Island Knights'	Andersen AFB, Guam	MH-60S
HSC-25 Det. 6	MCAS Iwakuni, Japan	MH-60S
HSC-85 'Golden Gators'	NAS North Island, California	MH-60S

Helicopter Sea Combat Wing, Atlantic – Chambers Field, Naval Station Norfolk, Virginia

HM-14 'Vanguard'	Chambers Field, NS Norfolk, Virginia	MH-53E
HM-14 Det. 1	Pohang AB, Republic of Korea	MH-53E
HM-15 'Black Hawks'	NAS Corpus Christi, Texas	MH-53E
HS-3 'Tridents'	NAS Jacksonville, Florida	SH-60F, HH-60H
HS-5 'Night Dippers'	NAS Jacksonville, Florida	SH-60F, HH-60H
HS-7 'Shamrocks'	NAS Jacksonville, Florida	SH-60F, HH-60H
HS-11 'Dragonslayers'	NAS Jacksonville, Florida	SH-60F, HH-60H
HS-15 'Red Lions'	NAS Jacksonville, Florida	SH-60F, HH-60H
HSC-2 (FRS) 'Fleet Angels'	Chambers Field, NS Norfolk, Virginia	MH-60S
HSC-22 'Sea Knights'	Chambers Field, NS Norfolk, Virginia	MH-60S
HSC-26 'Chargers'	Chambers Field, NS Norfolk, Virginia	MH-60S
HSC-28 'Dragon Whales'	Chambers Field, NS Norfolk, Virginia	MH-60S
HSC-84 'Red Wolves'	Chambers Field, NS Norfolk, Virginia	HH-60H

Specifications

Crew: 5–8

Powerplant: 2 x 64.5kN (14,500lb) thrust Pratt & Whitney JT8D-9 turbofan engines

Maximum speed: 907km/h (562mph)

Range: 2388km (1480 miles)

Service ceiling: 11,000m (37,000ft)

Dimensions: span 28.47m (93ft 5in); length 36.37m (119ft 3in); height 8.38m (27ft 6in)

Weight: 50,000kg (114,000lb) loaded

Rate of climb: 900m per min. (3000ft per min)

▼ Douglas C-9B Skytrain II, VR-61 'Islanders', NAS Whidbey Island

Named City of Oak Harbor, C-9B BuNo. 164608 is assigned to Fleet Logistics Support Squadron 61 (VR-61), one of four such US Navy Reserve squadrons flying the Skytrain II.

Specifications

Crew: 3–4
Powerplant: 2 x 1210kW (1622hp) General Electric T700-GE-700 turboshaft engines
Maximum speed: 296km/h (476mph)
Range: 964km (600 miles)
Service ceiling: 5790m (19,000ft)
Dimensions: rotor diameter 16.36m (53ft 8in); length 17.38m (57ft); height 5.13m (16ft 9in)
Weight: 9979kg (22,000lb) loaded
Armament: MK-54 air-launched torpedoes, Hellfire misssiles and usually 2 x 12.7mm (0.5in) machine guns

Sikorsky MH-60R Seahawk, HSM-71 'Raptors', USS *John C. Stennis*

MH-60R BuNo. 166520 is seen assigned to USS *John C. Stennis*, serving as part of CVW-9. The unit is shore-based at NAS North Island, San Diego. HMS-71 was the first fleet squadron to receive the MH-60R.

PATROL AND RECONNAISSANCE SQUADRONS

Patrol and Reconnaissance Wing Two – MCB Hawaii/MCAF Kaneohe Bay, Hawaii		
VPU-2 'Wizards'	MCAF Kaneohe Bay, Hawaii	P-3C
VP-4 'Skinny Dragons'	MCAF Kaneohe Bay, Hawaii	P-3C
VP-9 'Golden Eagles'	MCAF Kaneohe Bay, Hawaii	P-3C
VP-47 'Golden Swordsmen'	MCAF Kaneohe Bay, Hawaii	P-3C
Patrol and Reconnaissance Wing Ten – NAS Whidbey Island, Washington		
VP-1 'Screaming Eagles'	NAS Whidbey Island, Washington	P-3C
VP-40 'Marlins'	NAS Whidbey Island, Washington	P-3C
VP-46 'Gray Knights'	NAS Whidbey Island, Washington	P-3C
VP-69 (FRU) 'Totems'	NAS Whidbey Island, Washington	P-3C
VQ-1 'World Watchers'	NAS Whidbey Island, Washington	EP-3E, P-3C
VQ-2 'Batmen'	NAS Whidbey Island, Washington	EP-3E, P-3C
Patrol and Reconnaissance Group – Naval Station Norfolk, Virginia		
VP-30 (FRS) 'Pro's Nest'	NAS Jacksonville, Florida	P-3C
Patrol and Reconnaissance Wing Five – NAS Brunswick, Maine		
VP-8 'Tigers'	NAS Brunswick, Maine	P-3C
VP-10 'Red Lancers'	NAS Brunswick, Maine	P-3C
VP-26 'Tridents'	NAS Brunswick, Maine	P-3C
VPU-1 'Old Buzzards'	NAS Brunswick, Maine	P-3C
Patrol and Reconnaissance Wing Eleven – NAS Jacksonville, Florida		
VP-5 'Mad Foxes'	NAS Jacksonville, Florida	P-3C
VP-16 'War Eagles'	NAS Jacksonville, Florida	P-3C
VP-45 'Pelicans'	NAS Jacksonville, Florida	P-3C
VP-62 (FRU) 'Broadarrows'	NAS Jacksonville, Florida	P-3C

United States

United States Marine Corps

With a long tradition of expeditionary warfare and integrated air, land and sea operations, the USMC maintains a fleet of more than 1200 fixed-wing aircraft and helicopters.

THE AIRCRAFT OF the USMC operate from both land bases and warships and are organized within four air wings as part of the U.S. Navy's operating forces and under the command of the Commandant of the Marine Corps. USMC air assets can be combined with Marine ground forces to create rapidly deployable Marine Air Ground Task Forces (MAGTF) for a variety of missions, with airpower the responsibility of the Aviation Combat Element (ACE).

The USMC is divided into Atlantic and Pacific Fleet Marine Forces, each headed by a Marine Forces Commander. Each MARFOR has three numbered Marine Expeditionary Forces (MEF) and component Marine Expeditionary Brigades (MEB). The MEF comprises one or more Marine Divisions, Marine Air Wings (MAW) and Marine Logistics Groups (MLG). The MEB is smaller, with a reinforced infantry regiment, Marine Air Group (MAG) and Combat Logistics Regiment (CLR). There is also a Marine Forces Reserve Commander, albeit without permanent MEFs or MEBs.

Reflecting the demands of overseas operations, the USMC is increasing in size, with the aim of

▲ **Sikorsky CH-53E Super Stallion**

A CH-53E from Marine Heavy Helicopter Squadron 464 (HMH-464) approaches a USAF HC-130P to refuel over Djibouti. In 2008 the USMC operated 152 CH-53Es, with plans to replace these with 200 CH-53Ks from 2015. The new CH-53K has double the lift capacity of the CH-53E.

I MARINE EXPEDITIONARY FORCE – MCB CAMP PENDLETON, CALIFORNIA

3rd Marine Aircraft Wing – MCAS Miramar, California

Marine Aircraft Group Eleven – MCAS Miramar, California	
VMFAT-101 (FRS) 'Sharpshooters'	F/A-18A/B/C/D
VMFA(AW)-121 'Green Knights'	F/A-18D
VMFA(AW)-225 'Vikings'	F/A-18D
VMFA-232 'Red Devils'	F/A-18A+
VMFA-314 'Black Knights'	F/A-18C
VMFA-323 'Death Rattlers'	F/A-18C
VMGR-352 'Raiders'	KC-130J

Marine Aircraft Group Thirteen – MCAS Yuma, Arizona	
VMA-211 'Avengers'	AV-8B/AV-8B+
VMA-214 'Black Sheep'	AV-8B/AV-8B+
VMA-311 'Tomcats'	AV-8B/AV-8B+
VMA-513 'Nightmares'	AV-8B/AV-8B+

Marine Aircraft Group Sixteen – MCAS Miramar, California	
HMM-161 'Grey Hawks'	MV-22B
HMM-163 'Ridgerunners'	CH-46E
HMM-165 'White Knights'	CH-46E
HMM-166 'Sea Elks'	CH-46E
HMH-361 'Flying Tigers'	CH-53E
HMH-462 'Heavy Haulers'	CH-53E
HMH-465 'Warhorses'	CH-53E
HMH-466 'Wolfpack'	CH-53E

Marine Aircraft Group Three Nine – MCAS Camp Pendleton, California	
HMM(T)-164 (FRS) 'Knightriders'	CH-46E
HMLA-169 'Vipers'	UH-1N, AH-1W
HMLA-267 'Stingers'	UH-1N/Y, AH-1W
HMM-268 'Red Dragons'	CH-46E
HMLA/T-303 (FRS) 'Atlas'	HH-1N, UH-1N/Y, AH-1W/Z
HMM-364 'Purple Foxes'	CH-46E
HMLA-367 'Scarface'	UH-1N/Y, AH-1W
HMLA-369 'Gunfighters'	UH-1N, AH-1W

▲ **Bell-Boeing MV-22B Osprey**

MV-22B Ospreys of Marine Medium Tilt-rotor Squadron 264 take part in a firepower demonstration. The Osprey first deployed to Iraq with VMM-263 in 2007. The latest Block C standard Osprey features weather radar, improved situational awareness and forward firing countermeasures.

establishing three Marine Expeditionary Forces (MEF) of a similar size by 2011.

Three active component MAWs are backed up by a reserve MAW. The MAW includes a Headquarters, various MAGs, a Marine Air Control Group and a Marine Wing Support Group (MWSG).

A MAW can deploy as an ACE for an MEF, or otherwise provide units to support the MAGTF. A MAW or MAG can be deployed alone, but is typically reinforced to provide balanced support to a MEB. Seven Marine Expeditionary Units (MEU) can deploy as Expeditionary Strike Groups (ESG) or Amphibious Ready Groups (ARG) and are assigned with an ACE based around a reinforced Marine Medium Tilt-rotor or Helicopter Squadron.

The USMC component of U.S. Joint Forces Command, Marine Corps Forces Command, headquartered at NS Norfolk, Virginia, incorporates the II MEF and the 2nd MAW. Marine Forces Pacific, with its headquarters at MCB H. M. Smith, Hawaii, includes the I MEF and III MEF and their respective 3rd MAW and 1st MAW. Headquartered at NAS New Orleans JRB, Louisiana, Marine Forces Reserve is responsible for the 4th MAW, with its four MAGs.

Tilt-rotor revolution

The most significant new aviation asset employed by the USMC is the MV-22B tilt-rotor, which has

II MARINE EXPEDITIONARY FORCE – MCB CAMP LEJEUNE, NORTH CAROLINA

2nd Marine Aircraft Wing – MCAS Cherry Point, North Carolina

Marine Aircraft Group Fourteen – MCAS Cherry Point, North Carolina

VMAQ-1 'Banshees'	EA-6B
VMAQ-2 'Death Jesters'	EA-6B
VMAQ-3 'Moon Dogs'	EA-6B
VMAQ-4 'Seahawks'	EA-6B
VMAT-203 (FRS) 'Hawks'	AV-8B, TAV-8B
VMA-223 'Bulldogs'	AV-8B
VMA-231 'Ace of Spades'	AV-8B
VMA-542 'Flying Tigers'	AV-8B
VMGR-252 'Otis'	KC-130J

Marine Aircraft Group Two Six – MCAS New River, North Carolina

HMLA-167 'Warriors'	UH-1N, AH-1W
VMMT-204 (FRS) 'Raptors'	MV-22B
VMM-261 'Raging Bulls'	MV-22B
HMM-264 'Black Knights'	MV-22B
VMM-266 'Fighting Griffins'	MV-22B
HMH-461 'Ironhorse'	CH-53E

Marine Aircraft Group Two Nine – MCAS New River, North Carolina

VMM-162 'Golden Eagles'	MV-22B
VMM-263 'Thunder Eagles'	MV-22B
VMM-365 'Blue Knights'	MV-22B
HMLA-269 'Gunrunners'	UH-1N, AH-1W
HMLA-467 'Sabre Rattlers'	UH-1N, AH-1W
HMT-302 (FRS) 'Phoenix'	CH-53E
HMH-366 'Hammerheads'	CH-53E
HMH-464 'Condors'	CH-53E

Marine Aircraft Group Three One – MCAS Beaufort, South Carolina

VMFA-115 'Silver Eagles'	F/A-18A+
VMFA-122 'Werewolves'	F/A-18C
VMFA(AW)-224 'Bengals'	F/A-18D/C
VMFA-251 'Thunderbolts'	F/A-18C
VMFA-312 'Checkerboards'	F/A-18A+
VMFA(AW)-533 'Hawks'	F/A-18D

Specifications

Crew: 2
Powerplant: 2 x 1300kW (1680hp) General Electric T700 turboshaft
Maximum speed: 352km/h (218mph)
Range: 587km (218 miles)
Service ceiling: 3720m (12,200ft)
Dimensions: rotor diameter 14.6m (46ft); length 13.6m (44ft 7in); height 4.1m (13ft 5in)
Weight: 4953kg (14,750lb) loaded
Armament: 1 x 20mm (0.78in) M196 cannon; 8 x 70mm (2.75in) Zuni rockets; 8 x TOW missiles; 2 x anti-aircraft missiles

▲ Bell AH-1W Super Cobra, U.S. Marine Corps

Armed with AGM-114 Hellfire missiles, this AH-1W is typical of the type in USMC service. While the older 'Whiskey' Cobras are being upgraded, the USMC is also due to receive the new AH-1Z, the first examples of which will serve with west coast squadrons at MCAS Camp Pendleton. Meanwhile, the USMC inventory includes just over 160 AH-1Ws, and the type has seen widespread combat use in Operations Iraqi Freedom and Enduring Freedom.

entirely replaced the CH-46E among east coast units. By 2017, the MV-22B will be in use with 19 active and four reserve squadrons, and the USMC hopes to acquire 360 examples. The USMC aims to introduce a new heavylift helicopter, the CH-53K, to replace the CH-53D/E in 10 active duty squadrons and one reserve squadron, with service entry planned for 2015.

The upgraded UH-1Y attained operational status in 2008. Developed alongside the UH-1Y, the AH-1Z is slated to enter operational service in 2011. The USMC hopes to field 226 AH-1Zs and 123 UH-1Ys in 10 active squadrons and one reserve squadron.

The arrival of the short take-off and vertical landing (STOVL) F-35B will see the USMC replace its fleet of F/A-18s, AV-8Bs and EA-6Bs. Of these 'legacy' types, the F/A-18 will remain in use until 2023, although of the fleet total of around 235 aircraft, the two-seat F/A-18D will be disposed of by

Specifications

Crew: 2–3
Powerplant: 2 x 1150kW (1546shp) GE T700-GE-401C turboshaft
Maximum speed: 304km/h (189mph)
Range: 241km (130 nautical miles)
Service ceiling 6100m (20,000ft)
Dimensions: rotor diameter 14.88m (48ft 10in); length 17.78m (58ft 4in); height 4.5m (14ft 7in)
Weight: 8390kg (18,500lb) loaded
Armament: 2 x 70mm (2.75in) Hydra 70 rockets, 2 x mounts for 7.62mm (0.3in) M240D MGs

▲ Bell UH-1Y, HMLA/T-303 'Atlas', MCAS Camp Pendleton

UH-1Y Bu No. 167796 is operated by Marine Light Attack Helicopter Training Squadron 303, which prepares Marine aviators for the 'Huey' and Cobra communities. Part of the 3rd Marine Air Wing, the California-based unit is equipped with examples of the HH-1N, UH-1N/Y and AH-1W/Z.

III MARINE EXPEDITIONARY FORCE – MCB CAMP COURTNEY, OKINAWA, JAPAN

1st Marine Aircraft Wing – MCB Camp Foster, Okinawa, Japan

Marine Aircraft Group Twelve – MCAS Iwakuni, Honshu, Japan

VMA-211	AV-8B
VMFA(AW)-242 'Bats'	F/A-18D
VMFA(AW)-224	F/A-18D
VMFA(AW)-225	F/A-18D
VMAQ-*	EA-6B

Marine Aircraft Group Three Six – MCAS Futenma, Okinawa, Japan

HMM-262 'Flying Tigers'	CH-46E
HMM-265 'Dragons'	CH-46E
HMH-*	CH-53
HMLA-*	AH-1W, UH-1N
VMGR-152 'The Sumos'	KC-130J

* UDP unit

Marine Aircraft Group Two Four – MCB Hawaii/MCAF Kaneohe Bay, Hawaii

HMH-362 'Ugly Angels'	CH-53D
HMH-363 'Red Lions'	CH-53D
HMH-463 'Pegasus'	CH-53D

▲ McDonnell Douglas F/A-18A+ Hornet

A Hornet from Marine Fighter Attack Squadron 115 lands at Korat in Thailand. Pending the arrival of the F-35, the USMC is upgrading around 25 Hornets to F/A-18C+ standard, with helmet-mounted sights, AIM-9X missiles, modernized cockpit displays, and improved countermeasures.

2018. Under the Tactical Air Integration initiative, USMC F/A-18 units deploy aboard U.S. Navy carriers. Around 145 AV-8s remain in use and a programme of upgrades will keep the survivors in service until 2021, although retirements are to begin in 2013. The EA-6B will continue in use until 2019.

The first of three F-35B fleet readiness squadrons was scheduled to take its first aircraft in September 2010, with initial operational capability to follow in 2012. However, the programme has suffered from serious delays. By 2024 the fighter will be in service with 21 operational, three fleet readiness and one test squadron. The USMC plans to acquire a total of 420 F-35Bs, some of which will receive the Next Generation Jammer in order to supersede the EA-6B.

The USMC is responsible for Presidential airlift, for which it was waiting on a replacement for its VH-3Ds and VH-60Ns, operated by HMX-1. The planned new helicopter, the VH-71, was cancelled in 2009. Existing equipment will instead be upgraded.

Specifications

Crew: 1
Powerplant: 1 x 105.8kN (23,800lb) Rolls-Royce Pegasus vectored thrust turbofan
Maximum speed: 1065km/h (661mph)
Range: 277km (172 miles)
Service ceiling: 15,240m (50,000ft)
Dimensions: span 9.25m (30ft 4in); length 14.12m (46ft 4in); height 3.55m (11ft 7.75in)
Weight: 14,061kg (31,000lb) loaded
Armament: 1 x 25mm (0.98in) GAU-12U cannon, six external hardpoints with provision for up to 7711kg (17,000lb) (Short take-off) or 3175kg (7000lb) (Vertical take-off) of stores

▼ Boeing AV-8B+ Harrier II, VMA-231 'Ace of Spades', MCAS Cherry Point

Marine Attack Squadron 231 is one of three front-line Harrier II units within Marine Aircraft Group 14 (MAG-14), and the 2nd Marine Aircraft Wing (2nd MAW), the major USMC aviation unit on the east coast.

United States

United States Army

Recent changes to the structure of the U.S. Army mean it is now better suited to expeditionary warfare, joint operations, 'plug and play' structuring, and long-term overseas deployments.

THE U.S. ARMY has been undergoing far-reaching changes since 2004, shifting from its previous divisional structure to one based on brigades.

U.S. Army Aviation consists of around 287,800 active and 26,900 reserve personnel. The basic force structure is the brigade, fielded either as a Combat Aviation Brigade (CAB) or a Theater Aviation Brigade (TAB), both of which can be tailored to meet particular operational demands. The CAB supports five battalions and can be used in support of up to four Brigade Combat Teams (BCT). The CAB is available in four configurations: heavy, medium, light and Aviation Expeditionary Brigade (AEB). The AEB is assigned to six of eight Army National Guard (ARNG) divisions.

The four different CAB configurations differ chiefly in their mix of reconnaissance and attack assets. Heavy division CABs have two attack/reconnaissance battalions (ARB), medium division CABs have one ARB and a cavalry squadron, the light variant has two cavalry squadrons, and the AEB maintains one ARB. Formations with only a single ARB are additionally equipped with a Security and Support Battalion (SSB), with a strength of three companies, although this is to be increased to four through the addition of an air ambulance company. Each CAB has a General Support Aviation Battalion (GSAB) attached, this including a command aviation company, a heavy helicopter company and an air ambulance company.

Under the new brigade structure, two Theater Aviation Commands (TACs) are each responsible for a pair of TABs primarily equipped with CH-47 and UH-60 transport helicopters, as well as fixed-wing aircraft and medevac helicopters. TABs also have GSABs attached, although the latter are provided with two, rather than one, air ambulance company.

The 160th Aviation (Special Operations) (Airborne) provides air support for unconventional warfare. Essentially equivalent to a brigade, the 160th SOAR has approximately 2100 personnel and 190 aircraft within four battalions, three of which are dedicated to airlift (each with two heavy helicopter companies and one assault helicopter company, or with three heavy helicopter companies), plus one battalion with single light attack and light transport companies and two assault companies.

U.S. ARMY AVIATION FIXED-WING INVENTORY

C-12C/D	14/12	C-31A	2
RC-12D	9	UC-35A	20
RC-12H	6	UC-35B	8
JRC-12G	1	C-37A	2
C-12J	2	C-37B	1
RC-12K	7	C-41A	2
RC-12N	14	O-2A	2
RC-12P	9	EO-5C	8
RC-12Q	3	TO-5C	1
C-12R/V	29	T-34C	4
C-12U	71	UV-18A	4
C-20E	1	Cessna 182	2
C-20F	1	Beech 1900D	1
C/JC-23A	3	DHC-7-102	1
C-23C	43	King Air 300	11
C-26B/E	13		

U.S. ARMY AVIATION HELICOPTER INVENTORY

UH-1H/V	123	HH-60L	31
AH/MH-6M	51	UH-60L	664
CH-47D	309	HH-60M	11
CH-47F	65	UH-60M	31
MH-47E	6	AH-64A	155
MH-47G	50	AH-64D (Block I)	252
OH-58A/C	276	AH-64D (Block II)	280
OH-58D	339	TH-67A	181
UH-60A	954		

Specifications

Crew: 3

Powerplant: 2 x 3460kW (4640hp) Rolls-Royce AE2100-D2A turboprop

Maximum speed: 602km/h (374mph)

Range: 1852km (1151 miles)

Service ceiling: 9144m (30,000ft)

Dimensions: span 28.7m (94ft 2in); length 22.7m (74ft 6in); height 9.64m (31ft 8in)

Weight: 30,500kg (67,241lb) loaded

Propellers: 6-bladed 4.15m (13ft 7in) Dowty Propeller 391/6-132-F/10

Alenia C-27J Spartan, Alaska ARNG, Redstone Arsenal, Alabama

Acquired as a replacement for the C-23C Sherpa among the U.S. Army's fleet of over 250 fixed-wing aircraft, the first C-27J was delivered in October 2008. The U.S. Army planned to purchase over 50 C-27Js, although the Department of Defense's 2010 budget request called for transfer of the C-27J to the USAF.

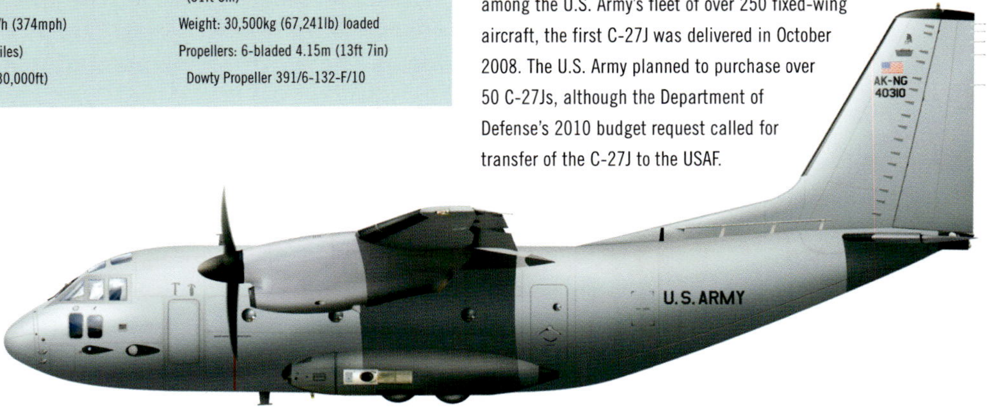

Specifications

Crew: 2

Powerplant: 1 x 1300kW (1800shp) Lycoming T53-L-703 turboshaft

Maximum speed: 277km/h (172mph)

Range: 510km (315 miles)

Service ceiling: 3720m (12,200ft)

Dimensions: rotor diameter 13.6m (44ft) length 16.1m (53ft); height 4.1m (13ft 5in)

Weight: 4500kg (10,000lb) loaded

Armament: 1 x 20mm (0.78in) M197 cannon; 7–19 x 70mm (2.75in) Hydra 70 rockets; 4 or 8 x TOW missiles

Bell AH-1F Cobra, N Troop, 4th Squadron, 2nd Armored Cavalry Regiment, Iraq

Named Sand Shark, 67-15643 was a modernized Cobra that served during Operation Desert Storm in 1991. In 1999 the U.S. Army retired the AH-1F from the active duty inventory, final operator being the 25th Infantry Division (Light).

Specifications

Crew: 3–4

Powerplant: 2 x 1210kW (1622hp) General Electric T700-GE-700 turboshaft engines

Maximum speed: 296km/h (476mph)

Range: 964km (600 miles)

Service ceiling: 5790m (19,000ft)

Dimensions: rotor diameter 16.36m (53ft 8in); length 17.38m (57ft); height 5.13m (16ft 9in)

Weight: 9979kg (22,000lb) loaded

Armament: MK-54 air-launched torpedoes, Hellfire misssiles and usually 2 x 12.7mm (0.5in) machine guns

Sikorsky EH-60A Quick Fix II, 1st Battalion, 212th Aviation Regiment 'Crusaders'

The EH-60A provided the U.S. Army with an organic electronic countermeasures (ECM) capability, the helicopter having an external antenna designed to intercept and jam enemy communications.

U.S. ARMY IN KOREA		
Eighth U.S. Army, Korea – Yongsan Barracks, Seoul, Korea		
2nd Infantry Division Camp Red Cloud, Uijeongbu, Korea		
2nd Combat Aviation Brigade Desiderio AAF, Camp Humphreys, Pyeongtaek, Korea		
1-2nd AVN	Butts AAF, Fort Carson, Colorado	AH-64D
2-2nd AVN	Seoul K-16 AB, Korea	UH-60A/L
3-2nd AVN	Desiderio AAF, Camp Humphreys, Pyongtaek, Korea	UH-60A, CH-47D, C-12J/U
4-2nd AVN	Desiderio AAF, Camp Humphreys, Pyongtaek, Korea	AH-64D

160TH AVIATION (SPECIAL OPERATIONS) (AIRBORNE), FORT CAMPBELL, KENTUCKY		
1-160th AVN	Campbell AAF, Fort Campbell, Kentucky	AH/MH-6M, MH-60K/L
2-160th AVN	Campbell AAF, Fort Campbell, Kentucky	MH-47G
3-160th AVN	Hunter AAF, Savannah, Georgia	MH-47G, MH-60K/L
4-160th AVN	Gray AAF, Fort Lewis, Washington	MH-47G, MH-60K/L

There are three Regimental Aviation Squadrons (RAS), two of which are configured as air cavalry squadrons (ACS). The latest ACS consists of three reconnaissance/attack troops (OH-58Ds or AH-64Ds) and an assault helicopter troop (UH-60s). Of the five Military Intelligence Battalions (MIBN), three are based around one company of RC-12s, and one of RQ-5 UAVs. Of the other two MIBNs, one is based in Korea with two fixed-wing companies, while the other is stationed in the U.S., with one company.

New equipment

The U.S. Army is forging ahead with various re-equipment programmes. The Armed Reconnaissance Helicopter programme to replace the OH-58D scout/attack helicopter was axed in 2008, and as many as 368 Kiowa Warriors will now have to be upgraded. More successful is the UH-72A, which entered service in 2006 in the Light Utility Helicopter role, replacing UH-1s and OH-58A/Cs. Meanwhile the AH-64D continues to be built and produced via upgrade of AH-64As, with a target of 718 D-models to be fielded by 2013. Both the UH-60 and CH-47 also remain in production. The latest MH-47G upgrade entered service in 2005, followed by the newly built CH-47F two years later. Until 2019 the U.S. Army will receive 262 remanufactured CH-47Fs and 190 new-production models. The latest UH-60M variant was introduced in 2006, followed by the HH-60M air ambulance in 2008. Plans call for 1235 M-models, including 303 HH-60Ms and 72 MH-60Ms to replace the MH-60K/L.

Over 250 fixed-wing aircraft serve in logistics support and electronic roles. Most numerous is the C-12 family, serving in a variety of roles. Eventually, both C-12 and C-26 will be replaced by 116 Future Utility Aircraft (FUA), while RC-12s and EO-5Cs will be replaced by an Aerial Common Sensor (ACS).

As a major operator of UAVs, the U.S. Army fields the RQ-7 and is replacing its RQ/MQ-5s with the MQ-1C. The U.S. Army also plans to operate MQ-8B vertical take-off and landing UAVs.

Beechcraft C-12 Huron

The C-12 transport fleet includes around 100 aircraft, among them C-12U, C-12R and upgraded C-12V aircraft. Some C-12R/Vs and C-12C/Ds have been modified for Reconnaissance, Surveillance, Targeting and Acquisition (RSTA) missions.

Canada

Canadian Armed Forces

The world's second-largest country, with the world's longest coastline, the defence of Canada is entrusted to the Canadian Armed Forces, established as a unified formation in February 1968.

Canada is a member of both NATO and the North American Aerospace Defense Command (NORAD) and is a regular participant in UN peacekeeping missions.

The air component of the Canadian Armed Forces is led by the Commander of Air Command and the Chief of the Air Staff, with headquarters in Ottawa. Operational command and control of the Air Command in Canada and overseas is the responsibility of the Commander of 1 Canadian Air Division (1 Cdn Air Div) and Canadian NORAD Region, who maintains headquarters in Winnipeg.

Air Command fields a total of 13 wings across Canada, equipped with over 330 aircraft.

1 Wing is responsible for the CH-146 helicopter and includes six tactical helicopter and training squadrons located at bases throughout Canada. 3 Wing is a multi-role formation, while 4 Wing combines combat forces, a helicopter unit, and also provides training for fighter pilots. Canada maintains a SAR squadron at 5 Wing, Goose Bay, where NATO tactical flying training is conducted and the same base also hosts regular CF-188 detachments.

Air mobility and SAR are the tasks of 8 Wing, while 9 Wing provides SAR assets for Newfoundland and Labrador, flying the CH-149 helicopter.

Naval assignments

Naval aviation is embodied in 12 Wing, which provides detachments of CH-124s for Canadian warships. The maritime mission is also undertaken by 14 Wing, whose CP-140s conduct surveillance missions over the Atlantic, and support SAR taskings. Similar duties are conducted by 19 Wing, responsible for maritime patrol over the Pacific Ocean, as well as SAR and tactical training.

15 Wing is home to the NATO Flying Training in Canada (NFTC) programme, as well as Canada's Snowbirds aerobatic demonstration team. 16 Wing is the largest training wing, but does not have aircraft assigned to its various schools. Another training formation, 17 Wing, includes three squadrons plus ground schools and provides facilities for the Central Flying School. Finally, 22 Wing at North Bay is responsible for surveillance and early warning support of the aerospace defence of North America.

Specifications

Crew: 1
Powerplant: 2 x 71.1kN (16,000lb) General Electric F404-GE-400 turbofans
Maximum speed: 1912km/h (1183mph)
Combat radius: 740km (460 miles)
Service ceiling: 15,240m (50,000ft)
Dimensions: span 11.43m (37ft 6in); length 17.07m (56ft); height 4.66m (15ft 3.5in)
Weight: 25,401kg (56,000lb) loaded
Armament: 1 x 20mm (0.78in) M61A1 Vulcan six-barrel rotary cannon with 570 rounds, nine external hardpoints with provision for up to 7711kg (17,000lb) of stores

McDonnell Douglas CF-188A Hornet, 425 Squadron, CFB Bagotville

The backbone of Canada's combat fleet is the CF-188, of which an original 138 examples were acquired. The force has been greatly reduced, and now serves with just three squadrons, 80 survivors having received a mid-life upgrade.

CANADIAN ARMED FORCES FLYING SQUADRONS

1 Wing CFB Kingston, Ontario

400 Squadron	CH-146 Griffon	CFB Borden, Ontario
403 Squadron	CH-146 Griffon	CFB Gagetown, New Brunswick
408 Squadron	CH-146 Griffon	CFB Edmonton, Alberta
427 Squadron	CH-146 Griffon	CFB Petawawa, Ontario
430 Squadron	CH-146 Griffon	CFB Valcartier, Quebec
438 Squadron	CH-146 Griffon	St Hubert, Quebec

3 Wing CFB Bagotville, Quebec

425 Squadron	CF-188 Hornet	CFB Bagotville, Quebec
439 Squadron	CH-146 Griffon	CFB Bagotville, Quebec

4 Wing CFB Cold Lake, Alberta

409 Squadron	CF-188 Hornet	CFB Cold Lake, Alberta
410 Squadron	CF-188 Hornet	CFB Cold Lake, Alberta
417 Squadron	CH-146 Griffon	CFB Cold Lake, Alberta
419 Squadron	CT-155 Hawk	CFB Cold Lake, Alberta

5 Wing CFB Goose Bay, Newfoundland

444 Squadron	CH-146 Griffon	CFB Goose Bay, Newfoundland

8 Wing CFB Trenton, Ontario

412 Squadron	CC-144 Challenger	Ottawa, Ontario
424 Squadron	CH-149 Cormorant, CC-130 Hercules	CFB Trenton, Ontario
426 Squadron	CC-130 Hercules, CC-144 Challenger	CFB Trenton, Ontario
429 Squadron	CC-177 Globemaster III	CFB Trenton, Ontario
436 Squadron	CC-130 Hercules	CFB Trenton, Ontario
437 Squadron	CC-150 Polaris	CFB Trenton, Ontario

9 Wing CFB Gander, Newfoundland

103 Squadron	CH-149 Cormorant	CFB Gander, Newfoundland

12 Wing CFB Shearwater, Nova Scotia

406 Squadron	CH-124 Sea King	CFB Shearwater, Nova Scotia
423 Squadron	CH-124 Sea King	CFB Shearwater, Nova Scotia
443 Squadron	CH-124 Sea King	Victoria IAP, British Columbia

14 Wing CFB Greenwood, Nova Scotia

404 Squadron	CP-140 Aurora/Arcturus	CFB Greenwood, Nova Scotia
405 Squadron	CP-140 Aurora/Arcturus	CFB Greenwood, Nova Scotia
413 Squadron	CC-130 Hercules, CH-149 Cormorant	CFB Greenwood, Nova Scotia

15 Wing CFB Moose Jaw, Saskatchewan

431 Squadron 'Snowbirds'	CT-114 Tutor	CFB Moose Jaw, Saskatchewan

17 Wing CFB Winnipeg, Manitoba

402 Squadron	CC-142 Dash 8	CFB Winnipeg, Manitoba
435 Squadron	CC-130 Hercules	CFB Winnipeg, Manitoba
440 Squadron	CC-138 Twin Otter	Yellowknife, Northwest Territories

19 Wing CFB Comox, British Columbia

407 Squadron	CP-140 Aurora	CFB Comox, British Columbia
442 Squadron	CC-115 Buffalo, CH-149 Cormorant	CFB Comox, British Columbia

Specifications

Crew: 3
Powerplant: 2 x 671 kW (900hp) Pratt & Whitney Canada PT6T-3D turboshafts
Maximum speed: 260km/h (160mph)
Range: 656km (405 miles)
Capacity: 10 troops or 6 stretchers
Dimensions: rotor diameter 14m (45ft 11in); length 17.1m (56ft 1in); height 4.6m (15ft 1in)
Weight: 5355kg (11,900lb)
Armament: 1 x 7.62mm (0.29in) C6 GPMG; 1 x 7.62mm (0.29in) Dillon Aero M134D 'Minigun'

Bell CH-146 Griffon, 430 Squadron 'Silver Falcon', CFB Valcartier

A military version of the Bell 412CF, the CH-146 provides the backbone of the Canadian Armed Forces' tactical helicopter capability. Quebec-based 430 Squadron supports the 5e Groupe Brigade Mécanisé du Canada.

Specifications

Crew: 8–15
Powerplant: 4 x 3700kW (4600hp) Allison T-56-A-14-LFE turboprops
Maximum speed: 750km/h (462mph)
Range: 9300km (5737 miles)
Service ceiling: 10,700m (35,100ft)
Dimensions: span 30.38m (99ft 8in); length 35.61m (116ft 10in); height 10.49m (34ft 5in)
Weight: 27,892kg (61,362lb) loaded
Armament: Mk 46 Mod V torpedoes, signal chargers, smoke markers, illumination flares

Lockheed CP-140 Aurora, 407 Squadron, CFB Comox

The CP-140 is essentially a P-3C built for Canada. Designed for anti-submarine warfare, the Aurora is also used to monitor illegal fishing, immigration, drug trafficking and pollution, as well as for search and rescue.

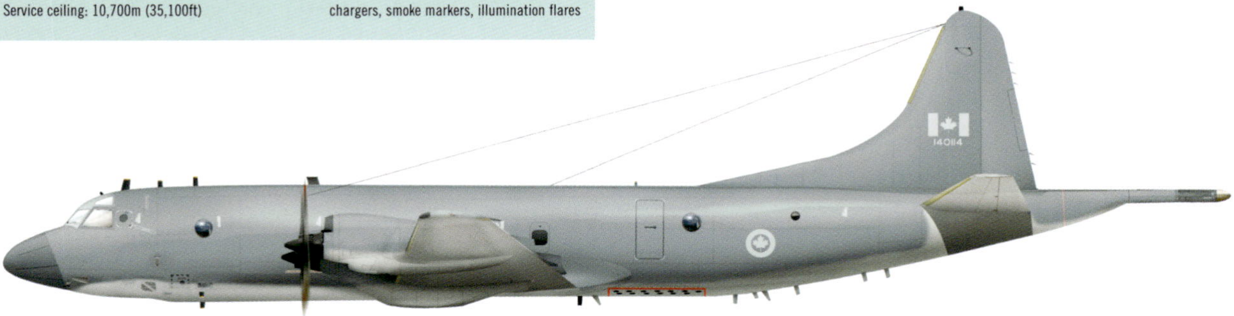

Boeing CC-177 Globemaster III

Trenton-based 429 Squadron operates the Canadian Forces Globemaster III fleet. Received in 2007-08, the four airlifters have been used for humanitarian relief operations as well as in support of Joint Task Force Afghanistan under Operation Athena, which involves maintaining the air bridge between Canada and Afghanistan.

Mexico

Méxican Air Force and Mexican Naval Aviation

The smallest North American nation, Mexico's modest air arm is a reflection of limited external threats, although its aircraft are increasingly involved in internal and anti-narcotics operations.

The organization of the Fuerza Aérea Méxicana is based around two combat wings, subdivided into groups, which in turn maintain fixed- and rotary-wing squadrons located at 18 bases around the country, some of these installations not having aircraft permanently assigned. The overarching command structure is arranged on a geographical basis (divided between the Central Air Region, Western Air Region and Southeastern Air Region). Squadrons provide aircraft for fighter, close support, transport, training and various second-line duties.

The Armada de México includes both land-based and aircraft and helicopters that embark on Mexican warships, as well as an independent training element.

Specifications

Crew: 1
Powerplant: 1 x 1342kW (1800shp) Pratt & Whitney Canada PT6T-3 or -3B turboshaft
Maximum speed: 223km/h (138mph)
Range: 439km (237 nautical miles)
Service ceiling: 5305m (17,400ft)
Dimensions: rotor diameter 14.6m (48ft); length 17.43m (57ft 1.7in); height 3.8m (12ft 7in)
Weight: 5080kg (11,200lb) loaded
Armament: not known

Bell 212, Escuadrón Aéreo 103, Oaxaca

Oaxaca-based Escuadrón Aéreo 103 of the Fuerza Aérea Mexicana is a mixed helicopter unit, also equipped with the Bell 206. Other rotary-wing types on strength with the Mexican Air Force include ex-Israeli CH-53s.

Specifications

Crew: 1
Powerplant: 2 x 22.2kN (5000lb) General Electric J85-GE-21B turbojets
Maximum speed: 1741km/h (1082mph)
Range: 306km (190 miles)
Service ceiling: 15,790m (51,800ft)
Dimensions: span 8.13m (26ft 8in); length 14.45m (47ft 4.75in); height 4.07m (13ft 4.25in)
Weight: 11,214kg (24,722lb) loaded
Armament: 2 x 20mm (0.79in) cannon; two air-to-air missiles, five external pylons with provision for 3175kg (7000lb) of stores, including missiles, bombs, ECM pods, cluster bombs, rocket launcher pods and drop tanks

Northrop F-5E Tiger II, Escuadrón Aéreo 401, Santa Lucia

Air Squadron 401 is responsible for Mexico's most potent fighter equipment, represented by the F-5E/F. Refitted in 2005 with AN/APQ-159 radar, and armed with AIM-9P air-to-air missiles, the Mexican Tiger IIs are based at Base Aérea Militar (BAM) No 1, at Santa Lucia, close to the capital, Mexico City.

CUBA
DOMINICAN REPUBLIC
GUATEMALA
HONDURAS
EL SALVADOR
NICARAGUA
COSTA RICA
PANAMA
VENEZUELA
COLOMBIA
ECUADOR
BRAZIL
PERU
BOLIVIA
PARAGUAY
PACIFIC OCEAN
URUGUAY
ARGENTINA
CHILE
ATLANTIC OCEAN

Chapter 2

Central America and South America

Having emerged from years of conflict, the air forces of Central America today typically operate modest fleets of transport aircraft and helicopters, with only Honduras being equipped with high-performance jet fighters. In the Caribbean, a seriously depleted Cuban air arm remains that region's only significant player. With a few exceptions, recent economic woes have had an adverse effect on the composition and serviceability of the combat fleets of air arms in both Central and South America. In South America, where Argentina and Brazil have traditionally maintained the most capable air arms, Chile and Venezuela are now positioned to challenge them as among the best-equipped air forces on that continent.

Argentina

Argentine Air Force, Army Aviation and Naval Aviation

Traditionally among the most powerful air arms in Latin America, Argentina's air force has suffered from a lack of funding in recent years and operates an ageing front-line fleet.

Argentina's three branches of the military each operate an independent aviation arm. There have been no major military actions since the Falklands War, but all three air arms participate in local crisis relief and counter-smuggling work.

Many Fuerza Aérea Argentina (FAA) aircraft are in need of replacement. Transport capability is provided by I Air Brigade, with various models of Hercules representing the main airlift assets, KC-130s also conducting aerial refuelling. Five 707s include one example equipped for electronic warfare – the others are outfitted for VIP and strategic transport. Lineas Aéreas del Estado (LADE), an FAA-operated airline, mainly uses five F28s.

II Air Brigade provides transport, liaison, photo-reconnaissance and other support missions. III Air Brigade is responsible for the fleet of around 40 Pucará counter-insurgency aircraft. Pucarás are widely used for countering drug-smuggling flights along the northern borders. As well as SAR helicopters and the Cruz del Sur aerobatic team (with Su-29s), IV Air Brigade operates 18 Pampas for training and light attack, with 12 more on order and older aircraft due to be upgraded.

V Air Brigade flies 33 OA/A-4AR Fightinghawk fighter-bombers, the FAA's most modern combat type, as well as the ageing Mirage interceptor fleet. Mirage survivors comprise nine Israeli-supplied Fingers and 10 Mirage IIIEAs, while a training unit operates seven Mirage 5A Mara, two Mirage IIIDAs and three two-seat Daggers.

FUERZA AÉREA ARGENTINA AIR BRIGADES

I Brigada Aérea	C-130B/H, KC-130H, L-100-30 Hercules, Fokker F28, Boeing 707	El Palomar
II Brigada Aérea	Learjet 31A, Fokker F27	Paraná
III Brigada Aérea	IA-58A/D Pucará	Reconquista
IV Brigada Aérea	IA-63 Pampa, SA315B Lama Su-29AR	Mendoza Morón
V Brigada Aérea	OA/A-4AR	Villa Reynolds
VI Brigada Aérea	Mirage IIIEA/DA, Mirage 5A Mara, Finger/Dagger	Tandil
VII Brigada Aérea	Chinook, Bell 212, UH-1N, Hughes 369/500	Moreno
IX Brigada Aérea	Saab 340, DHC-6	Comodoro Rivadavia

Specifications

Crew: 1
Powerplant: 1 x 41.97kN (9436lbf) (dry thrust) SNECMA Atar 09C turbojet
Maximum speed: Mach 2.2 (2350km/h; 1460mph)
Range: 4000km (2485 miles)
Service ceiling: 18,000m (59,055ft)
Dimensions: span 8.22m (26ft 11in); length 15.55m (51ft 0.25in); height 4.50m (14ft 9in)
Weight: 13,700kg (30,203lb) loaded
Armament: 2 x 30mm (1.18in) DEFA 552 cannons, bombload of 5774kg (12,730lb)

IAI Finger, I Escuadrón, VI Brigada Aérea, Tandil

An Israeli-upgraded Dagger (itself an IAI-built Mirage 5), the Finger is in service with Escuadrón I, alongside the Mirage and Dagger fleet at Tandil. Aircraft C412 wears markings to confirm its role in the damage of two Royal Navy warships during the 1982 Falklands War.

FAA helicopter activity is focused on VII Air Brigade, although its Chinooks are non-operational. IX Air Brigade flies on behalf of LADE and supports Argentina's Antarctic mission. A Military Aviation School is equipped with T-34s and EMB-312s.

The Comando de Aviación de Ejército (Argentine Army Aviation Command) is dominated by the UH-1H, and is centred upon Agrupación Aviación de Ejército 601, at Campo de Mayo, with smaller Aviation Sections located across the country. Fixed-wing assets include OV-1D battlefield reconnaissance aircraft and G222 turboprop transports.

The Comando de Aviación Naval Argentina (Argentine Naval Aviation Command) is headed by S-2Ts for anti-submarine warfare, Super Etendard attack fighters, a large fleet of helicopters, and P-3Bs and Beech 200s for maritime patrol. Other units provide aerial photography, training and transport.

Specifications

Crew: 1
Powerplant: 1 x 49kN (11,023lb) SNECMA Atar 8K-50 turbojet
Maximum speed: 1180km/h (733mph)
Range: 850km (528 miles)
Service ceiling: 13,700m (44,950ft)
Dimensions: span 9.6m (31ft 6in); length 14.31m (46ft 11.2in); height 3.86m (12ft 8in)
Weight: 12,000kg (26,455lb) loaded
Armament: 2 x 30mm cannon, provision for up to 2100kg (4630lb) of stores, including nuclear weapons and Exocet air-to-surface missiles

Dassault Super Etendard, 2° Escuadrilla Aeronaval de Caza y Ataque, Base Aeronaval Comandante Espora

Armed (as seen here) with Exocet anti-ship missiles, the Super Etendard is the Argentine Navy's most potent asset. The aircraft have also been deployed to Rio Grande in Tierra del Fuego.

Grumman S-2T Turbo Tracker

The Argentine Navy's Fuerza Aeronaval No. 2, based at Comandante Espora (Bahía Blanca), incorporates the Escuadrilla Aeronaval Antisubmarina, equipped with five S-2T Turbo Trackers for anti-submarine warfare missions, and a single PC-6 Turbo Porter utility transport.

COMANDO DE AVIACIÓN NAVAL ARGENTINA NAVAL AIR SQUADRONS

Escuadrilla Aeronaval Antisubmarina	S-2T, PC-6	Base Aeronaval Comandante Espora
2° Escuadrilla Aeronaval de Caza y Ataque	Super Etendard	Base Aeronaval Comandante Espora
1° Escuadrilla Aeronaval de Helicópteros	SA316B Alouette III, AS555 Fennec	Base Aeronaval Comandante Espora
2° Escuadrilla Aeronaval de Helicópteros	SH-3D, ASH-3D	Base Aeronaval Comandante Espora
2° Escuadrilla Aeronaval de Sostén Logístico Móvil	Fokker F28	Base Aeronaval Ezeiza
Escuadrilla Aeronaval de Exploración	P-3B	Base Aeronaval Almirante Zar
Escuadrilla Aeronaval de Vigilancia Marítima	Beechcraft 200	Base Aeronaval Almirante Zar

Bolivia

Bolivian Air Force

With only limited combat equipment, the Fuerza Aérea Boliviana (FAB) focuses on transport and training, with squadrons divided between three geographical regions (I, II and III Air Brigades).

THE BOLIVIAN AIR Force maintains major bases at La Paz, Colcapiro and Santa Cruz. Each base is assigned an Air Brigade, responsible for Air Groups with particular assignments. Air Groups are in turn equipped with squadrons. Transporte Aéreo Militar is the FAB's military airline and is based at La Paz.

Specifications

Crew: 1–4
Powerplant: 1 x 1044kW (1400hp) Avco Lycoming T53-L-13 turboshaft engine
Maximum speed: 204km/h (127mph)
Range: 511km (317 miles)
Service ceiling: 3840m (12,600ft)
Dimensions: rotor diameter 14.63m (48ft); length 12.77m (41ft 11in); height 4.41m (14ft 5in)
Weight: 4309kg (9500lb) loaded

Bell UH-1H, Grupo Aéreo 51, Chapacura
Primary rotary-wing unit in the FAB is Grupo Aéreo 51. This UH-1H serves with the 'Fuerza de Tarea' squadron at Chapacura air base.

Costa Rica

Air Section

Part of the Civil Guard, Costa Rica's small Air Section operates from three bases (Liberia, San José and a naval station at Golfito), with the centre of operations at San José, the capital.

KNOWN AS THE Servicio de Vigilancia Aerea of the Fuerza Pública (Air Section of the Civil Guard), Costa Rica's air arm lacks armed aircraft, but is routinely engaged on counter-narcotics work and is also capable of staging rescue, medical evacuation and VIP transport missions. Piper and Cessna light aircraft are supported by MD500 helicopters.

Specifications

Crew: 1–2
Powerplant: 1 x 236kW (316hp) Allison 250-C18A turboshaft engine
Maximum speed: 244km/h (151mph)
Range: 606km (375 miles)
Initial climb rate: 518m/min (1700 fpm)
Dimensions: rotor diameter 8.03m (26ft 4in); length 9.24m (30ft 4in); height 2.48m (8ft 2in)
Weight: 1361kg (2994lb) loaded

McDonnell Douglas Helicopters MD500E, Servicio de Vigilancia Aérea, San José/Juan Santamaria
San José is home to Costa Rica's Servicio de Vigilancia Aérea, within which the MD500 is the only helicopter asset, with two examples in use for surveillance duties. MSP018 also wears Police titles.

Brazil

Brazilian Air Force, Army Aviation and Naval Aviation

Part of the largest armed forces in the region, the Força Aérea Brasileira (FAB) comprises five commands, while further air power is provided by air elements of the Brazilian army and navy.

The Brazilian Air Force is eagerly awaiting a new fighter, which will be procured under the FX-2 programme as a replacement for existing Mirage 2000 and F-5 fighters, and eventually for the AMX.

Headquartered at Brasilia, the Terceira Força Aérea (3rd Air Force) includes the FAB's premier fighter unit, 1° Grupo de Defesa Aérea at Anápolis, with Mirage 2000B/Cs, plus EMB-326 Xavante jet trainers and EMB-312 Tucano turboprop trainers. 1° Grupo de Aviação de Caça at Santa Cruz has two squadrons, both with upgraded F-5 fighters and EMB-312s. 3° Grupo de Aviação (GAv) has three squadrons with mixed fleets of EMB-314 Super Tucanos, EMB-312s and Cessna 208s at Boa Vista, Porto Velho and Campo Grande. 5° GAv has an EMB-110 light transport squadron at Fortaleza. 6° GAv maintains a Learjet 35 and EMB-110 squadron at Recife, and a squadron with Cessna 208 and EMB-145SA/RS airborne early warning aircraft at Anápolis. 10° GAv at Santa Maria is a 3rd Air Force AMX wing, with two squadrons of the fighter-bombers. 14° GAv flies a unit of F-5s and EMB-312s from Canoas. Finally, 16° GAv operates a single AMX squadron at Santa Cruz.

The Quinta Força Aérea (5th Air Force), headquartered at Rio de Janeiro, is responsible for three transport groups, equipped primarily with C-130s, as well as the 9° GAv, with a squadron of C-295 transports at Manaus, and the 15° GAv, with a mixed EMB-110 and C-295 unit at Campo Grande.

The Segunda Força Aérea (2nd Air Force), also headquartered at Rio de Janeiro, comprises the 7° GAv with four EMB-111 squadrons at Salvador, Florianópolis, Belém and Santa Cruz. The last of these bases will receive P-3AM surveillance aircraft from 2010. The 2nd Air Force's helicopters are organized under the 8° GAv, with five squadrons operating a fleet of UH-1H, HB350 (locally manufactured AS350), AS332 and UH-60L (plus light fixed-wing types) from Belém, Recife, Afonsos, Santa Maria and Manaus. The 2nd Air Force also incorporates the 10° GAv, with a single UH-1H, EMB-110 and C-295 squadron at Campo Grande.

Training Command

The FAB's Comando Aéreo de Treinamento, with its HQ at Natal, includes 1°/4° GAv with EMB-326 jet trainers, 2°/5° GAv with EMB-314s, and 11° GAv with a squadron of HB350s. A separate Department of

Specifications

Crew: 1
Powerplant: 2 x 97kN (21,834lb) SNECMA M53-P2 turbofans
Maximum speed: 2338km/h (1453mph)
Range: 1480km (920 miles)
Service ceiling: 18,000m (59,055ft)
Dimensions: span 9.13m (29ft 11.5in); length 14.36m (47ft 1.25in); height 5.2m (17ft 0.75in)
Weight: 17,000kg (37,480lb) loaded
Armament: 1 x DEFA 554 cannon; nine external pylons with provision for up to 6300kg (13,889lb) of stores, including air-to-air missiles, rocket launcher pods, and various attack loads, including 454kg (1000lb) bombs

Dassault Mirage 2000C, 1° Esq, 1° Grupo de Defesa Aérea, Anápolis

Designated as the F-2000 in FAB service, the Mirage 2000 was acquired as a successor to the Mirage III. Flying from Anápolis, the Mirage fleet is chiefly tasked with the air defence of the capital, Brasilia.

Training handles initial flying training, with a varied fleet of light aircraft and gliders at Pirassununga. The public face of the FAB is the Esquadrão de Demonstração Aérea, or 'Esquadrilha da Fumaça' (Smoke Squadron), an aerobatic team equipped with EMB-312s and also based at Pirassununga.

With a vast territory, much of it yet to be opened up to land communications, the FAB maintains a considerable transport capability. The Comando Geral do Ar (General Air Command) is responsible for seven numbered Comandos Aéreos Regional, normally each with one Esquadrão de Transporte Aéreo equipped with EMB-110, EMB-120 and Cessna 208 aircraft. Bases are at Belém, Pernambuco, Galeão, São Paulo, Canoas and Santa Maria, Brasilia and Manaus (the latter bases houses the 7 Esquadrão de Transporte Aéreo, which also operates from additional bases at Boa Vista and Puerto Velho).

The Grupo de Transporte Especial consists of the 1°/1° GTE and 2°/1° GTE at Brasilia, with various VIP transport and governmental aircraft including the A319, ERJ-190, Boeing 737, AS332, EC635, HB355, Learjet 35/55, BAe 125 and Legacy 600.

The Comando Geral de Apoio (General Support Command) includes the Diretoria e Electrônica e Proteção, with its Grupo Especial de Inspeção em Vôo flying the BAe 125 and EMB-110 on navaids inspection duties from Santos Dumont AP.

The Força Aeronaval da Marinha do Brazil is responsible for Latin America's only carrier air group, which embarks on the NAe *São Paolo*. Esquadrão de Aviões de Interceptação e Ataque 1 is the sole fixed-wing naval unit, responsible for TA/A-4KU fighters. Naval aircraft are primarily based on shore at São Pedro da Aldeia, and also include helicopter units, comprising a squadron of SH-3s (to be replaced by SH-60s), one of Lynx, a squadron of AS355s and HB350s, a squadron of AS332s (to be replaced by AS532s), two squadrons of HB350s at Manaus and Ilha do Terrapleno de Leste, and two squadrons of Bell 206s at Ladário and São Pedro da Aldeia.

Brazilian army aviation

The Aviação do Exército (AvEx), formed in 1986, consists of the 1° Grupo AvEx, with four component brigades. Of these, the 4° Brigada de Aviação de Exército is based at Manaus in the Amazon and does counter-narcotics work. Other AvEx units are at Taubaté. With the arrival of the AS532, a new base will be set up in Mato Grosso do Sul, in the south of the country. Other types in AvEx service comprise the AS550, HB350, AS565 and HB565 and the S-70A.

FORÇA AÉREA BRASILEIRA COMBAT AND TRANSPORT UNITS

Esquadrão de Demonstração Aérea		
'Esquadrilha da Fumaça'	EMB-312	Pirassununga
Grupo de Transporte Especial Brasilia		
1°/1° GTE	A319, ERJ-190, Boeing 737, AS332, EC635, HB355	Brasilia
2°/1° GTE	Learjet 35/55, BAe 125, Legacy 600	Brasilia
Comando Geral de Apoio (General Support Command) Diretoria e Electrônica e Proteção		
Grupo Especial de Inspeção em Vôo	Santos BAe 125, EMB-110	Dumont AP
Comando Geral do Ar (General Air Command)		
Comandos Aéreos Regional		
1° Comando Aéreo Regional		
1 Esquadrão de Transporte Aéreo	EMB-110, Cessna 208	Belém
2° Comando Aéreo Regional Recife		
2 Esquadrão de Transporte Aéreo	EMB-110, EMB-120	Recife
3° Comando Aéreo Regional		
3 Esquadrão de Transporte Aéreo	EMB-110, EMB-120	Galeão
4° Comando Aéreo Regional		
4 Esquadrão de Transporte Aéreo	EMB-110, EMB-120	São Paulo
5° Comando Aéreo Regional		
5 Esquadrão de Transporte Aéreo	EMB-110	Canoas*
6° Comando Aéreo Regional		
6 Esquadrão de Transporte Aéreo	EMB-110, EMB-120, EMB-121	Brasilia
7° Comando Aéreo Regional Manaus		
7 Esquadrão de Transporte Aéreo	EMB-110, EMB-120, Cessna 208	Manaus

Chile

Chilean Air Force, Naval Aviation and Army Aviation

Acquisition of new fighters and upgrade programmes for older combat equipment mean that the Fuerza Aérea de Chile (FACH) is one of the most capable air forces in the region.

▲ Lockheed Martin F-16D Fighting Falcon

A Grupo 3 F-16D prepares to refuel from a USAF KC-135 over the Pacific. Chilean F-16C/Ds are equipped to a high standard, and are understood to use Israeli Python 4 and Derby missiles in addition to American weapons.

PREVIOUSLY A MUCH smaller and less capable force, the FACH is now perhaps the most powerful in Latin America. Modernization has seen the F-5E/F upgraded to Tigre III standard, and acquisition of the F-16C/D Block 50, 10 examples being delivered from March 2006. Mirage 5 Elkans have been replaced by 18 second-hand F-16AM/BMs acquired from the Netherlands in 2007, with a further 12 ex-Netherlands F-16s now arriving to replace the retired Mirage 50 Pantera. The EMB-314 Super Tucano has been acquired to begin replacement of the fleet of A/T-36 Halcón jet trainers. For initial pilot training, the T-35A/B remains in use with the Escuela de Aviación Militar (Military Aviation School).

The FACH transport fleet is based around three C-130Hs, as well as two Boeing 707s, one capable of aerial refuelling, the other electronic warfare. Ex-USAF KC-135E tankers supplement the latter. Other transports provide presidential transport, while light transport tasks are flown by the DHC-6 and C-212.

Five Beech 99A Petrels are equipped for maritime surveillance, although this role is now the preserve of Aviación Naval (Naval Aviation). Beech King Air and Learjet 35A aircraft are used for aerial photography. Other light aircraft in service include the Piper

FUERZA AÉREA DE CHILE	
I Brigada Aérea, Iquique	
Grupo de Aviación 1	A/T-36 Halcón, EMB-314
Grupo de Aviación 2	Beech 99A, C-212, SA315B Lama
Grupo de Aviación 3	F-16C/D
II Brigada Aérea, Santiago	
Escuela de Aviación Militar, El Bosque	T-35A/B Pillán
Grupo de Aviación 9	UH-1H, Bell 412, Bell 206, BK117, S-70A, PA-28 Dakota, O-2A
Grupo de Aviación 10	KC-135E, C-130H, Boeing 707, Boeing 737, Beechcraft 200, Gulfstream IV
Servicio Aerofotogramétrico	Learjet 35A, DHC-6, Beechcraft 100
Escuadrilla de Alta Acrobacia Halcones	Extra 300L
III Brigada Aérea, Puerto Montt	
Grupo de Aviación 5	DHC-6, C-212, Citation Jet
IV Brigada Aérea, Punta Arenas	
Grupo de Aviación 6	DHC-6, UH-1H
Grupo de Aviación 12	F-5E/F Tigre III
Grupo de Exploración Antártica 19, Eduardo Frei Base	UH-1H, BO105
Escuadrilla de Enlace	Bell 412
V Brigada Aérea, Antofagasta	
Grupo de Aviación 7	F-16AM/BM
Grupo de Aviación 8	F-16AM/BM
Escuadrilla de Enlace	Bell 412, C-212

Dakota, Cessna O-2A, Beech Super King Air and Cessna Citation. FACH helicopters include examples of the UH-1D/H, Bell 412 and SA315B Lama.

Aviación Naval

Responsible for over 5950 km (3,700 miles) of coastline, an Antarctic sector and various islands, Aviación Naval (Naval Aviation) is headed by Fuerza Aeronaval No. 1, heading most naval flying operations and including three operational squadrons (Vuelo de Patrulla 1/Patrol Flight 1, Escuadrón de Helicópteros de Ataque 1/1st Attack Helicopters Squadron, Helicópteros Utilitarios 1/Utility Helicopters 1, and Vuelo de Carga 1/Cargo Flight 1), as well as the Escuela de Aviación Naval (Naval Aviation School, VT-1) and Naval Aviation Maintenance Centre.

Fuerza Aeronaval No. 2 in the south of the country is headquartered at Punta Arenas, with smaller bases at Isla Dawson and Puerto Williams. Punta Arenas receives detachments from other squadrons, typically hosting one or two P-3As and a single EMB-111 patrol aircraft, a single C-212 utility transport, plus various helicopters.

A smaller Aviación Naval presence is maintained in the north of the country, at Iquique, and this normally hosts an EMB-111 and a BO105.

The Brigada de Aviación del Ejército de Chile (BAVE, Chilean Army Aviation Brigade), headquartered at Rancagua, consists of Regimiento de Aviación No. 1 plus five aviation sections, the latter typically attached to an army division. Alongside C-212, Cessna 208 and lighter fixed-wing types, the BAVE operates Ecureuil, Esquilo, Lama, Puma (which the BAVE hopes to replace with Cougars), Super Puma and MD530F helicopters.

SERVICIO DE AVIACIÓN DE LA ARMADA DE CHILE

Fuerza Aeronaval 1, Base Aeronaval Viña del Mar	
VT-1	O-2, PC-7
VC-1	C-212
VP-1	EMB-111, P-3ACH, UP-3A
HU-1	Bell 206, BO105, SA365
Escuadrón Embarcadero, Base Aeronaval Viña del Mar	
HA-1	AS332, AS532, SA365
Fuerza Aeronaval 2, Punta Arenas	
Aircraft from various squadrons	EMB-111, C-212, BO105, SA365, P-3ACH Punta Arenas, Puerto Williams and Isla Dawson

Aérospatiale AS532SC Cougar

The Chilean Navy's Super Puma and Cougar helicopters carry the local designation SH-32 and are operated by the Escuadrón de Helicópteros de Ataque 1 (HA-1, 1st Attack Helicopters Squadron). Six Cougars (as seen here) were delivered in the 1990s, along with a single AS332B1. HA-1 embarks on Chilean Navy frigates.

Specifications

Crew: 1
Powerplant: 1 x 126.7kN (28,500lb) thrust Pratt & Whitney F100-PW-229 afterburning turbofan
Maximum speed: 2177km/h (1353mph)
Range: 3862km (2400 miles)
Service ceiling: 15,240m(49,000ft)
Dimensions: span 9.45m (31ft); length 15.09m (49ft 6in); height 5.09m (16ft 8in)
Weight: 19,187kg (42,300lb) loaded
Armament: 1 x GE M61A1 20mm (0.79in) multi-barrelled cannon, wingtip missile stations; seven external hardpoints with provision for up to 9276kg (20,450lb) of stores

Lockheed Martin F-16D Fighting Falcon, Grupo de Aviación 3, Iquique

Assigned to I Brigada Aérea, the FACH's advanced F-16C/Ds are based at Iquique/Diego Aracena AB (also known as B.A. 'Los Condores').

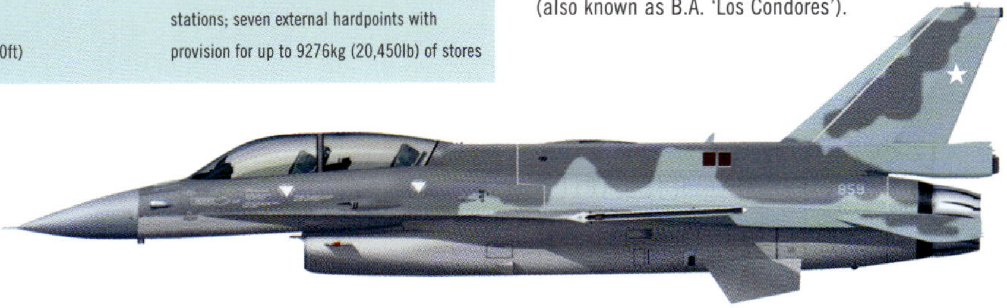

Colombia

Colombian Air Force

Subdivided into six major commands, the Fuerza Aérea Colombiana (FAC) is widely involved in the country's war on insurgents and is also active against narcotics production and trafficking.

The six commands of the FAC are the Comando Aéreo de Combate (CACOM), Comando Aéreode Apoyo Táctico (CAATA), Comando Aéreo de Transporte Militar (CATAM), Escuela Militar de Aviación (EMAVI), Comando Aéreo de Mantenimiento (CAMAN) and the Servicio de Aeronavigación a Territorios Nacionales (SATENA).

Each command is responsible for a Grupo, and a number of constituent Escuadrones. Of the combat commands, CACOM 1 at Palanquero is responsible for air defence, with Kfir and Mirage 5 fighters and T-37 trainers, while CACOM 2 at Apiay flies counter-insurgency and anti-narcotics missions with Tucanos, Super Tucanos, AC-47s and AH-60Ls, among others. CACOM 2 also maintains an OV-10 squadron at Yopal, while most bases incorporate a COIN/anti-narcotics squadron with fixed- and rotary-wing types on strength. CACOM 3 at Barranquilla operates OA-37s and Super Tucanos, CACOM 4 at Melgar flies various helicopters, CACOM 5 at Rionegro flies AH-60L gunships, and CACOM 6 at Tres Esquinas has Tucanos. CATAM at Bogotá is the FAC transport command, primarily operating C-130s, CN235s and C-295s.

Specifications

Crew: 1
Powerplant: 1 x 79.41kN (17,860lb thrust) (with afterburner) IAI/General Electric license-built J79-JIE turbojet engine
Maximum speed: 2440km/h (1516mph)
Range: 548 miles (882km)
Service ceiling: 17,690m (58,038ft)
Dimensions: span 8.22m (26.97ft); length 15.65m (51.35ft); height 4.55m (14.93ft)
Weight: 16,500kg (36,376lb) loaded
Armament: 2 x 30mm Rafael DEFA 533 cannons plus cluster bombs and missiles

IAI Kfir C7, Escuadrón de Combate 111, Grupo de Combate 11, Palanquero

As well as the Kfirs of Escuadrón de Combate 111, Palanquero air base hosts the Mirage 5s of Escuadrón de Combate 112 and the T-37B/C trainers of Escuadrón de Combate 116.

Specifications

Crew: 3
Powerplant: 2 x 1545kW (2225shp) Klimov TV3-117VM turboshafts
Maximum speed: 250km/h (156mph)
Range: 950km (594 miles)
Service ceiling: 6000m (19,690ft)
Dimensions: rotor diameter 21.35m (69ft 10in); length 18.42m (60ft 5in); height 4.76m (15ft 7in)
Weight: 11,100kg (24,470lb) loaded
Armament: Capable of carrying up to 1500kg (3300lb) of bombs, rockets and gunpods on six hardpoints

Mil Mi-17MD, Batallón de Aviacion No. 3 Carga y Transporte, Comando Operativo 25 de Aviacion, Fuerte Tolemaida

Batallón de Aviacion No. 3 utilizes a mixed fleet of Russian-supplied Mi-17MD, Mi-17-1V and Mi-17-5V helicopters, and the unit maintains numerous helicopter detachments around the country.

Cuba

Cuban Air Force

Once the most powerful air arm in Central America, the Defensa Anti-Aérea y Fuerza Aérea Revolucionaria (DAAFAR) is now in a parlous state, with limited funds and poor serviceability.

THE ORGANIZATION OF the DAAFAR is based around three air zones, each with squadrons that are operationally subordinated to Air Defence, Tactical Air, Logistic Support and Air Training Commands. In 2007, four major active bases supported an estimated 31 operational combat types.

Specifications

Crew: 1
Powerplant: 2 x 81.4kN (18,298lb) Sarkisov RD-33 turbofans
Maximum speed: 2443km/h (1518mph)
Range: 1500km (932 miles)
Service ceiling: 17,000m (55,775ft)
Dimensions: span 11.36m (37ft 3.75in); length (including probe) 17.32m (56ft 10in); height 7.78m (25ft 6.25in)
Weight: 18,500kg (40,785lb) loaded
Armament: 1 x 30mm (1.18in) GSh-30 cannon, provision for up to 4500kg (9921lb) of stores

Mikoyan MiG-29, 231° Escuadrón de Caza, 1779 Regimento, San Antonio de Los Baños
The most potent combat aircraft available to the DAAFAR is the MiG-29, which equipped a single squadron. In 2007, Western estimates suggested that only three examples were still airworthy.

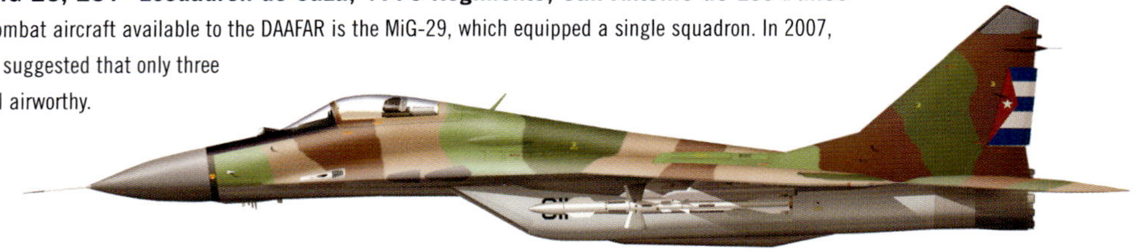

Dominican Republic

Dominican Air Force

The Fuerza Aérea Dominicana (FAD) divides the Dominican Republic into Southern and Northern Air Zones, with headquarters in San Isidro and Santiago de los Caballeros, respectively.

THE FLYING OPERATIONS of the FAD are handled by the Air Command, which supports air assets at eight bases, although most of the fleet is centred at San Isidro. Individual units include combat, transport, liaison, training and helicopter squadrons, with Super Tucanos being the most potent assets.

Specifications

Crew: 1–4
Powerplant: 1 x 1044kW (1400hp) Avco Lycoming T53-L-13 turboshaft engine
Maximum speed: 204km/h (127mph)
Range: 511km (317 miles)
Service ceiling: 3840m (12,600ft)
Dimensions: rotor diameter 14.63m (48ft); length 12.77m (41ft 11in); height 4.41m (14ft 5in)
Weight: 4309kg (9500lb) loaded

Bell UH-1H, FAD
Approximately 11 UH-1Hs serve alongside the FAD's diverse fleet of OH-58, Bell 430, Dauphin, OH-6 and Schweizer 333 helicopters.

Ecuador

Ecuadorian Air Force, Naval Aviation and Army Aviation

Tensions with neighbouring Peru mean that the Fuerza Aérea Ecuatoriana (FAE) has seen combat in the past, and the current force provides a balance of air defence and offensive assets.

THE BASIC STRUCTURE of the FAE consists of a headquarters in Quito responsible for two elements: I Zona Aérea for transport and communications, and II Zona Aérea responsible for three combat wings and a flying school.

I Zona Aérea is based at Quito, its aircraft being operated by Ala de Transporte 11's four transport squadrons, which include C-130s, BAe 748s, DHC-6s, and Dhruv helicopters. TAME, also at Quito, is the FAE-operated airline. II Zona Aérea's three wings are Ala de Combate 21 at Taura (one squadron of Mirage F1s and one of Kfirs), Ala de Combate 22 at Guayaquil (two squadrons with helicopters and liaison types), and Ala de Combate 23 at Manta (one squadron of A-37B – with a detachment at Lago Agrio – and one of Strikemasters).

The Servicio Aéreo del Ejército Equatoriano operates both fixed-wing aircraft and helicopters in support of the army, while Aviación Naval Equatoriana provides a small naval air component.

Specifications

Crew: 1
Powerplant: 2 x 37.3kN (8400lb) Rolls-Royce/Turbomeca Adour Mk 811 turbofans
Maximum speed: 1699km/h (1056mph)
Range: 537km (334 miles)
Service ceiling: Unavailable
Dimensions: span 8.69m (28ft 6in); length 16.83m (55ft 2.5in); height 4.89m (16ft 0.5in)
Weight: 15,700kg (34,613lb) loaded
Armament: 2 x 30mm (1.18in) Aden Mk.4 cannon; provision for 4763kg (10,500lb) of stores

SEPECAT Jaguar ES, Escuadrón de Combate 2111, Ala de Combate 21, Taura

Armed with Magic 2 missiles, and bombs, this Jaguar is depicted as it appeared during the 1995 conflict with Peru, when several were prepared for raids against targets deep inside Peru, although they did not participate in combat operations. The FAE Jaguar fleet is now in storage.

Specifications

Crew: 1
Powerplant: 1 x 100kN (15,873lb) SNECMA Atar 9K-50 turbojet
Maximum speed: 2350km/h (1460mph)
Range: 900km (560 miles)
Service ceiling: 20,000m (65,615ft)
Dimensions: span 8.4m (27ft 7in); length 15m (49ft 2.25in); height 4.5m (14ft 9in)
Weight: 15,200kg (33,510lb) loaded
Armament: 2 x 30mm (1.18in) 553 DEFA cannon with 135 rpg, five external pylons with provision for up to 6300kg (13,889lb) of stores

Dassault Mirage F1JA, Escuadrón de Combate 2112, Ala de Combate 21, Taura

Mirage FAE806 was one of two Mirage F1s to score an air-to-air victory against Peruvian Sukhoi Su-22s, during the 1995 War. Typical air-to-air weapons for the Mirage are the Magic 2 (as here) and Python 3 missiles.

Specifications

Crew: 1
Powerplant: 1 x 52.9kN (11,890lb st) IAI Bedek-built General Electric J-79-J1E turbojet
Maximum speed: 2440km/h (1516mph)
Range: 768km (477 miles)
Service ceiling: 17,680m (58,000ft)
Dimensions: span 8.22m (26ft 11.5in); length 15.65m (51ft 4.25in); height 4.55m (14ft 11.25in)
Weight: 11,603kg (25,580lb) loaded
Armament: 2 x Rafael-built 30mm (1.18in) DEFA 553 cannons and assortment of air-to-ground, air-to-air and air-to-surface missiles

IAI Kfir C2, Escuadrón de Combate 2113, Ala de Combate 21, Taura

Based at Taura (Guayaquil), this FAE Kfir wears the camouflage and markings used during the 1995 war with Peru. Captain Mata flew this jet on 10 February 1995, when he shot down a Peruvian A-37B.

El Salvador

Salvadorean Air Force

Equipped with a small force of light attack, utility transport and helicopter types, the Fuerza Aérea Salvadoreña (FAS) divides its assets between Brigada Aérea 1 and 2.

The first jet equipment for the FAS arrived in the 1970s and the combat fleet is today based upon the OA/A-37 jets of Brigada Aérea 2 at Comalapa, used for counter-insurgency and light attack, and operated alongside O-2s for forward air control.

The combat force is supported by BT-67 (turboprop C-47 conversions), Arava, UH-1 and MD500 aircraft of Brigada Aérea 1 at Ilopango, some of these types being outfitted as gunships or used in support of special forces. T-35 trainers are in use, while Bell 407 and 412 helicopters are employed for VIP and personnel transport.

Specifications

Crew: 1–2
Powerplant: 1 x 1342kW (1800hp) Pratt & Whitney Canada PT6T-3B-1 engine
Maximum speed: 259km/h (161mph)
Range: 695km (432 miles)
Service ceiling: 4970m (16,306ft)
Dimensions: rotor diameter 14.02m (46ft); length 12.92m (42ft 4in); height 4.32m (14ft 4in)
Weight: 5397kg (11,900lb) loaded

Bell 412EP Guardian, Escuadrón de Helicopteros, Brigada Aérea 1, Ilopango

Alongside the Bell 412EP, known locally as the Guardian, El Salvador's Escuadrón de Helicopteros operates examples of the UH-1H Guardian, UH-1M Cazador, the MD500 Guardiancillo and a single Bell 407.

Specifications

Crew: 1
Powerplant: 2 x 12.7kN (2850lbf) General Electric J85-GE-17A turbojets
Maximum speed: 816km/h (507mph)
Range: 1480km (920 miles)
Service ceiling: 12,730m (41,765ft)
Dimensions: span 10.93m (35ft 10.3in); length 8.62m (28ft 3.4in); height 2.7m (8ft 10.3in)
Weight: 6350kg (14,000lb) loaded
Armament: 1 x 7.62mm (.308in) GAU-2B/A minigun (mounted in nose), plus 8 underwing hardpoints with a capacity of 1230kg (2712lb)

▼ Cessna A-37B Dragonfly, Escuadrón Caza y Bombardeo, Brigada Aérea 2, B.A. Comalapa

The A-37B, known locally as the 'Dragón', serves with the FAS attack squadron at Comalapa. The same base also hosts the FAS forward air control squadron, equipped with the Cessna O-2A.

Guatemala

Guatemalan Air Force

The Fuerza Aérea Guatemalteca includes army, navy and air force elements and is led by A-37B jets, supported by PC-7 and T-35 trainers, as well as transport and rotary-wing assets.

Guatemala has emerged from a troubled era of guerrilla war, and its air force includes the Escuadrón de Aviones de Ataque (A-37), Escuadron de Reconocimiento y Ataque (PC-7) and Escuadrón de Transporte Aéreo at La Aurora. The latter unit is equipped with BT-67, F27 and Arava transports. Other units at La Aurora are the Aircraft Squadron (with Beech and Cessna utility transports), Presidential Squadron, and Helicopter Squadron (with Bell 205, 206, 212, 214 and UH-1). Squadrons are divided among three wings, responsible for fixed-wing aircraft, helicopters and maintenance. Aircraft operate primarily from La Aurora and Retalhuleu.

Specifications

Crew: 1–2
Powerplant: 1 x 1342kW (1800hp) Pratt & Whitney Canada PT6T-3B-1 engine
Maximum speed: 259km/h (161mph)
Range: 695km (432 miles)
Service ceiling: 4970m (16,306ft)
Dimensions: rotor diameter 14.02m (46ft); length 12.92m (42ft 4in); height 4.32m (14ft 4in)
Weight: 5397kg (11,900lb) loaded

▼ Bell 412, Escuadrón de Helicópteros, Ala Rotativa, La Aurora

The Helicopter Squadron is headquartered at La Aurora. As well as the Bell 412, equipment includes Bell 205A, Bell 206B, Bell 206L, Bell 212 and UH-1H types.

Honduras

Honduran Air Force

Aircraft of the Fuerza Aérea Hondureña (FAH) come under the command of their home base, with four major facilities located at Toncontin, Palmerola, Moncada and San Pedro Sula.

In common with other air arms in the region, the combat capability of the FAH rests on the OA/A-37B, supported by F-5E/F fighters for air defence, these being among the most advanced fighters in Central America. Toncontin is home to the transport and helicopter fleet, together with air force headquarters, assets including a single C-130, Bell 412s, a VIP fleet and various Cessna and Piper utility types. Palmerola is home to the FAH flight academy (the Academia Militar de Aviacion), with piston-engined T-41s and turboprop Tucanos (for which Honduras was the first export customer). Moncada houses the F-5 fighters, although serviceability of these is limited, while San Pedro Sula is home to the A-37s of 1 Grupo Aérotactico, around nine Dragonflies being operational.

Nicaragua

Nicaraguan Air Force

Emerging from a civil war that lasted throughout the 1980s, the air force of the Ejército de Nicaragua is today an integral component of Nicaragua's armed forces.

Previously known as the the Fuerza Aérea Nicaraguënse, Nicaragua's air arm is now designated as the Fuerza Aérea – Ejército de Nicaragua. The air force is based around just two operational squadrons, an Escuadrón de Transporte (with a handful of An-26, An-2, Beech 200 and Cessna 206 and 404 transports) and an Escuadrón de Ala Rotativa which operates the survivors of the once-powerful fleet of Mi-8/17 helicopters. Both units are based at Managua, although helicopter detachments can additionally be found at Bluefields, Montelimar, Puerto Cabezas, Punta Huete, San Carlos, Juigalpa, Matagalpa and Siuna.

The Escuela de Aviacion at Managua is responsible for training, with Cessna and Piper types on strength.

Specifications

Crew: 3
Powerplant: 2 x 1545kW (2225shp) Klimov TV3-117VM turboshafts
Maximum speed: 250km/h (156mph)
Range: 950km (594 miles)
Service ceiling: 6000m (19,690ft)
Dimensions: rotor diameter 21.35m (69ft 10in); length 18.42m (60ft 5in); height 4.76m (15ft 7in)
Weight: 11,100kg (24,470lb) loaded
Armament: Capable of carrying up to 1500kg (3300lb) of bombs and rockets on 6 hardpoints

Mil Mi-17, Escuadrón de Ala Rotatoria, Managua

Although marked as a Mi-17, serial 318 is actually a Mi-8MT. The 'Hip' family was mainstay of the Nicaraguan armed forces during the civil war, and today it is estimated that around a dozen are in service.

Panama

Panamanian Air Force

Previously the Fuerza Aérea Panameña, Panama's Servicio Nacional Aeronaval was resurrected in 1989 and today possesses a small force of fixed-wing aircraft and helicopters.

THE SERVICIO NACIONAL Aeronaval (SENAN) is a component of the Fuerzas Publicas Panameña. Tasked with coastal and border patrol, disaster relief and counter-narcotics, the SAN has three squadrons of aircraft at Tocumen, and a VIP flight at Balboa.

Specifications

Crew: 1–2
Powerplant: 1 x 1342kW (1800hp) Pratt & Whitney Canada PT6T-3B-1 Turbo Twin Pac turboshaft
Maximum speed: 259km/h (161mph)
Range: 695km (432 miles)
Service ceiling: 4970m (16,306ft)
Dimensions: rotor diameter 14.02m (46ft); length 12.92m (42ft 4in); height 4.32m (14ft 4in)
Weight: 5397kg (6470lb) loaded

Bell 412, 2nd Escuadrón de Helicópteros, Tocumen

The 2nd Escuadrón flies Bell 205, 212, 407 and 412 types, among others.

Paraguay

Paraguayan Air Force

The Fuerza Aérea Paraguaya (FAP) is headed by the first brigade controlling seven Grupo Aereos each with a different tasking. FAP combat assets are controlled by the Grupo Aerotáctico (GAT).

RESPONSIBLE FOR COMBAT equipment, the GAT operates the EMB-312, with the EMB-326 now withdrawn. Other groups are responsible for transport (Brigada Aerotransportada), training (with T-35s) and rotary-wing (Grupo Aéreo de Helicópteros) equipment. Major FAP bases are Silvio Pettirossi, Asunción, Ñu-Guazú and Concepción.

Specifications

Crew: 2
Powerplant: 1 x 11.1kN (2500lbf) Bristol Siddeley Viper Mk. 11 turbojet
Maximum speed: 806km/h (501mph)
Range: 1665km (1035 miles)
Service ceiling: 12,500m (41,000ft)
Dimensions: span 10.56m (34ft 8in); length 10.65m (34ft 11.25in); height 3.72m (12ft 2.5in)
Weight: 3765kg (8300lb) loaded
Armament: 2 x 12.7mm (0.5in) Browning MGs and up to 900kg (2000lb) of weapons on six hardpoints, including gun pods, bombs and rockets

Embraer EMB-326GB (AT-26) Xavante, 1 Escuadrón de Caza, Silvio Pettirossi IAP

Operated from Silvio Pettirossi IAP, this Xavante (now retired) was flown by 1 Escuadrón de Caza 'Guarani', within which it was assigned to one of two flights: Escuadrilla Orion or Escuadrilla Centauro.

Peru

Peruvian Air Force

The Fuerza Aérea del Peru (FAP) employs a wide variety of types, including Western and Russian designs, although current levels of serviceability and funding are poor.

STRUCTURE IS BASED on five numbered wings, most of which are responsible for up to three air groups with their own constituent squadrons. Types adopted by the FAP in the 1980s, and still in use, include Mirage 2000, MiG-29, MB339, Su-22M and Su-25 jets, and Bell 212, Mi-17 and Mi-25 helicopters.

Specifications

Crew: 1
Powerplant: 1 x 97.1kN (21,834lb) SNECMA M53-P2 turbofan
Maximum speed: 2338km/h (1453mph)
Range: 1480km (920 miles)
Service ceiling: 18,000m (59,055ft)
Dimensions: span 9.13m (29ft 11.5in); length 14.36m (47ft 1.25in); height 5.2m (17ft 0.75in)
Weight: 17,000kg (37,480lb) loaded
Armament: 2 x DEFA 554 cannon with 125rpg; 9 external pylons with provision for up to 6300kg (13,230lb) of stores

▼ Dassault Mirage 2000P, Escuadrón Caza-Bombardeo 412, Grupo Aéreo 4, La Doya-Mariano Melgar

The Mirage 2000 remains Peru's most capable fighter, with 12 examples in use.

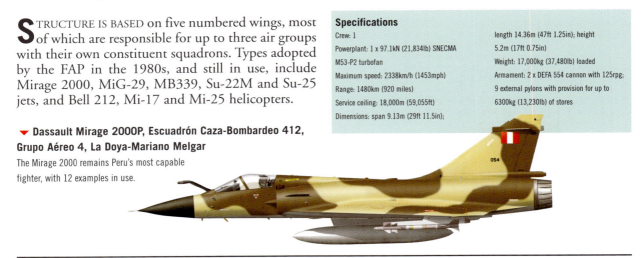

Uruguay

Uruguayan Air Force

The current Fuerza Aérea Uruguaya fleet was primarily acquired in the 1980s, and comprises transports, trainers, utility aircraft, helicopters, as well as a light attack force.

CANELONES IS HOME to Brigada Aérea I, with single transport and helicopter squadrons. At Durazno, Brigada Aérea II provides OA/A-37s and Pucará unit, a liaison squadron, and an advanced training squadron. Brigada Aérea III consists of an observation/liaison squadron at Montevideo.

Specifications

Crew: 1–4
Powerplant: 1 x 1044kW (1400hp) Avco Lycoming T53-L-13 turboshaft engine
Maximum speed: 204km/h (127mph)
Range: 511km (317 miles)
Service ceiling: 3840m (12,600ft)
Dimensions: rotor diameter 14.63m (48ft); length 12.77m (41ft 11in); height 4.41m (14ft 5in)
Weight: 4309kg (9500lb) loaded

▲ Bell UH-1H, Escuadón Aéreo No. 5 Helicópteros, Canelones

Part of Brigada Aérea I, this 'Huey' serves with EA5H's AS365s and Bell 212s.

Venezuela

Venezuelan Air Force

The Aviación Militar Venezolana (AMV) has emerged in recent years as one of the most powerful air arms in the region, pursuing an ambitious re-equipment programme.

COMBAT TYPES ACQUIRED in the 1970s and 1980s, including the F-16, VF-5, T-2, OV-10 and Tucano, remain in service, but are now being joined by new types, including the Su-30MKV multi-role fighter and K-8 Karakorum jet trainer. Much-needed transport and tanker capacity is due to arrive in the form of Il-76s and Il-78s. Primary fighter bases are Barcelona (home to the Su-30MKVs of Grupo 13), Maracay, home of Grupo 16 F-16s, and El Sombrero, where Su-30MKVs are replacing Grupo 11 Mirage fighters. Additional bases are at Boca del Rio (Grupo 14 training types), La Carlota (housing the presidential transport unit, Grupo 4, and transport units of Grupo 5), Barquisemeto (Grupo 12 VF-5s and K-8s), Maracaibo (Grupo 15 OV-10s and Tucanos) and Maracay (Grupo 6 transport operations and the helicopters of Grupo 10). Light transports are chiefly operated by Grupo 9 at Puerto Ayacucho. Both the army and navy also maintain air arms, as the Comando de la Aviación Naval and Aviación del Ejército. The army inventory includes A109, AS-61D, Mi-17, Mi-26 and Mi-35 helicopters.

Specifications

Crew: 2
Powerplant: 2 x 74.5kN (16,750lbf) AL-31FL low-bypass turbofans
Maximum speed: Mach 2.0 (2120km/h; 1320mph)
Range: 3000km (1864 miles)
Service ceiling: 17,300m (56,800ft)
Dimensions: span 14.7m (48ft 2.5in); length 21.94m (72in 11in); height 6.36m (20ft 9in)
Weight: 24,900kg (54,900lb) loaded
Armament: 1 x30mm (1.18n) GSh-3-1 gun, plus air-to-air and air-to-surface missiles

Sukhoi Su-30MKV, Escuadrón 131, Grupo Aéreo de Caza 13, Barcelona

Grupo Aéreo de Caza 13 'Libertador Simon Bolivar' was the debut operator of the AMV's two-seat Su-30MKV fighter. One of 24, this example, carrying a Kh-29T air-to-surface missile, is flown by Escuadrón 131 'Ases'.

Specifications

Crew: 2
Powerplant: 1 x 16.01kN (3600lb) Garrett TFE731-2A-2A turbofans
Maximum speed: Mach 0.75 (800km/h; 498mph)
Range: 2250km (1398 miles)
Service ceiling: 13,000m (42,651ft)
Dimensions: span 9.63m (31ft 7in); length 11.6m (38ft); height 4.21m (13ft 9in)
Weight: 4330kg (9546lb) loaded
Armament: 1x 23mm (0.90in) cannon pod, 5 hardpoints with a capacity of 1000kg (2205lb)

Hongdu K-8, Escuadrón 35, Grupo Aéreo de Caza 12, Barquisemeto

Deliveries of the K-8 to the Comando Aéreo de Instrucción (Training Command) began in 2010. The Chinese-built K-8 is replacing the T-2D Buckeye as primary jet trainer in service with the FAV.

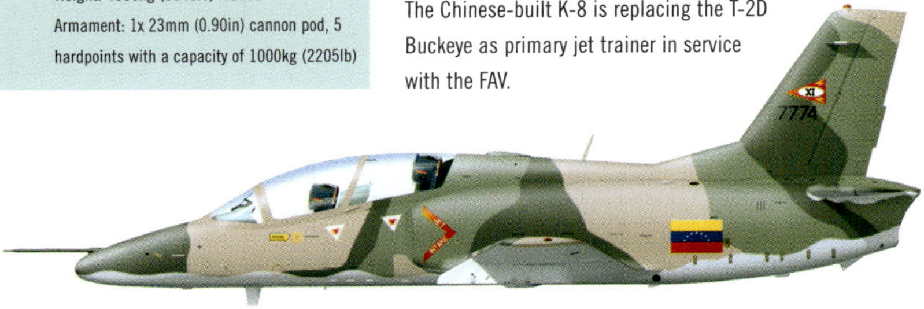

ARCTIC
OCEAN
NORWAY
SWEDEN
FINLAND
DENMARK
UNITED
KINGDOM
IRELAND
NETHERLANDS
GERMANY
BELGIUM
LUXEMBOURG
FRANCE
SWITZERLAND
AUSTRIA
ITALY
SPAIN
PORTUGAL
GREECE
TURKEY
CYPRUS

Chapter 3

Western Europe

With the exception of those of neutral Austria, Finland, Sweden and Switzerland – and a handful of smaller non-aligned air arms – the composition of the major air forces of Western Europe is characterized to a significant degree by their position within the NATO Alliance. Previously poised to fight a large-scale campaign against the forces of the Warsaw Pact, the air arms of Western Europe have had to adapt to the post-Cold War world, and this has involved severly reduced defence budgets, large-scale force reductions and the shift towards more deployable units applicable for peacekeeping duties as well as asymmetric warfare. Western European air arms are also notable for their pursuit of multi-national aircraft projects, typified by the Eurofighter, the A400M airlifter and the NH90 multi-role helicopter.

Austria

Österreichische Luftstreitkräfte

Entirely defensive in its posture, the Österreichische Luftstreitkräfte is a component of the Bundesheer, the armed forces of neutral Austria, and is primarily charged with air policing.

THE AIR ARM comes under the leadership of the Kommando Luftstreitkräfte, reporting to the defence ministry and responsible for a Surveillance Wing (equipped with EF2000s and Saab 105s), an Air Support Wing consisting of three squadrons, and a Helicopter Wing with various detachments. Eight bases are in regular use, with the most important at Zeltweg (fighters) and Langenlebarn (helicopters and light transports), while Schwaz/Tirol and Aigen/Ennstal both serve as helicopter bases. Alongside the EF2000 fighter, the types in use are three C-130K transports, armed Saab 105 jet and PC-7 turboprop trainers, AB212 and S-70A transport helicopters, PC-6 utility transports and Alouette III and OH-58 liaison/scout helicopters.

Specifications

Crew: 1
Powerplant: 2 x 90kN (20,250lbf) Eurojet EJ200 afterburning turbofans
Maximum speed: Mach 2 (2495km/h; 1550mph)
Range: 2900km (1840 miles)
Service ceiling: 19,810m (65,000ft)
Dimensions: span 10.95m (35ft 11in); length 15.96m (52ft 5in); height 5.28m (17ft 4in)
Weight: 16,000kg (35,300lb) loaded
Armament: 1 x 27mm (1.06in) Mauser BK-27 cannon; 13 hardpoints holding up to 7500kg (16,500lb) of payload

Eurofighter EF2000, 1. Staffel, Überwachungsgeschwader, Zeltweg
Austria ordered 15 EF2000s, comprising nine new Tranche 1 Block 5 aircraft and six ex-Luftwaffe Tranche 1 Block 2 aircraft, the latter upgraded to Block 5 standard. Primary weapon is the IRIS-T air-to-air missile.

Belgium

Belgium Air Component

A founder NATO member, Belgium's once-independent air arm has been rationalized with the end of the Cold War, and now operates as a branch of the unified Belgian Armed Forces.

BELGIAN AIR POWER is today represented by the Belgium Air Component (successor to the Belgische Luchtmacht/Force Aerienne Belge). As well as losing its independence in 2002, the force has experienced significant cutbacks since the early 1990s. The backbone of the combat fleet is the F-16,

Lockheed C-130H Hercules
Belgium's fleet of 11 C-130H transports are operated by the Flight Tactical Transport Squadron, part of 15 Wing at Brussels-Melsbroek.

operated by 2 Wing at Florennes and 10 Wing at Kleine Brogel. From an original total of 160 F-16s, 90 have been upgraded, but some of these have since been disposed of, and a force of 60 jets is planned for 2015. Transport capability is provided by the C-130H (due to be replaced by A400Ms) and single examples of the A330 and A310, while VIP transport is handled by Dassault 20/900 and ERJ-135/145 jets. Basic training is conducted by 1 Wing at Beauvechain, equipped with SF260s. Fighter pilots continue on the Alpha Jet in France, including Belgian-owned Alpha Jet 1B+ aircraft operated by the Belgium-French Alpha Jet School on permanent detachment at Cazaux. Transport and helicopter pilots also complete their training in France.

Naval helicopters

The Belgium Air Component is also responsible for maritime Sea King Mk48 helicopters and Alouette IIIs, the latter used for search and rescue. Both types operate from Koksijde and are to be replaced by 10 NH90 helicopters. Since 2004 the Belgium Air Component has also included former Army equipment, comprising the A109 attack/observation helicopter and Alouette II training/scout helicopter of the Heli Wing at Bierset.

Specifications

Crew: 2
Powerplant: 1 x 106kN (23,830lb) thrust Pratt & Whitney F100-PW-200 turbofan with afterburner
Maximum speed: Mach 2
Range: 925km (525 miles)
Service ceiling: above 15,240m (50,000ft)
Dimensions: span 9.45m (31ft); length 15.09m (49ft 6in); height 5.09m (16ft 8in)
Weight: 17,010kg (37,500lb) loaded
Armament: 1 x General Electric M61A1 20mm (0.78in) multi-barrelled cannon, wingtip missile stations; provision for up to 9276kg (20,450lb) of stores

SABCA F-16B Fighting Falcon, 2 Wing, Florennes

Built locally by SABCA, this F-16B was originally delivered as a Block 15AA OCU aircraft in the late 1980s. FB-21 was one of 90 Belgian F-16s that were put through the Mid-Life Update programme, and re-entered service with 2 Wing in its new (Block 20 MLU) configuration in early 2001.

Cyprus

Cyprus National Guard Air Wing

Provided with a small air wing, the Cyprus National Guard was reformed as a Greek-Cypriot force in 1982, and in recent years has introduced a combat capacity with the Mi-35 helicopter.

Originally established in 1960, the air wing of the Cyprus National Guard was disbanded following the Turkish invasion of Cyprus in 1974.

When re-established in 1982, the air wing was initially equipped with a single Islander utility transport, and this remains in use. Armed Gazelle utility helicopters were received in the late 1980s and all four examples remain active. More potent fixed-wing equipment then arrived in the form of the PC-9 turboprop trainer, which can also be used for light attack and counter insurgency. One example remains in use. A true combat capability is represented by 11 Mi-35P assault helicopters. Two Bell 206L utility helicopters are also in use, with three AW139 helicopters on order. The air wing operates from bases at Lakatamia and Paphos.

Cyprus also hosts an important RAF presence at Akrotiri, as well as a Turkish-Cypriot Security Force that has helicopters stationed in the northern (Turkish) part of the island.

Denmark

FLYVEVÅBEN

Responsible for a large area that also includes the Faeroe Islands and Greenland, the Danish air arm is part of a unified military, although it operates as an autonomous command.

THE DANISH AIR arm comprises two operational Commands: Tactical Air Command (Flyvertaktisk Kommando) with its headquarters at Karup, and Air Material Command (Flyvemateriel Kommando) with its HQ at Værløse. In addition, there is a Flying School (Flyveskolen), also at Karup.

The sharp end of the Flyvevåben is provided by two multi-role F-16 squadrons sharing a fleet of 62 aircraft: Esk 727 and Esk 730 at Skrydstrup. Esk 730 is assigned to NATO's Rapid Reaction Force, while Esk 727 is also responsible for conversion training.

Air Material Command includes Esk 721 at Værløse, which operates three examples of the C-130J-30 Hercules. In addition, three CL-604s are used for a range of support duties, including maritime surveillance, fishery protection and VIP transport.

▲ **Westland Lynx Mk90B**

The Navy Helicopter Corps consists of eight Lynx Mk90B helicopters that are based at Karup and which deploy aboard Danish Navy warships. This example is armed with a door gun as used for counter-piracy and asymmetric maritime operations.

Specifications

Crew: 1

Powerplant: either 1 x 105.7kN (23,770lb) Pratt & Whitney F100-PW-200 or 1 x 128.9kN (28,984lb) General Electric F110-GE-100 turbofan

Maximum speed: 2142km/h (1320mph)

Range: 925km (525 miles)

Service ceiling: 15,240m (50,000ft)

Dimensions: span 9.45m (31ft); length 15.09m (49ft 6in); height 5.09m (16ft 8in)

Weight: 16,057kg (35,400lb) loaded

Armament: 1 x General Electric M61A1 20mm (0.78in) multi-barrelled cannon, wingtip missile stations; provision for up to 9276kg (20,450lb) of stores

Rotary-wing reorganization

The helicopter arm is in the middle of modernization, with 14 examples of the EH101 replacing the S-61A in the maritime search and rescue and heavylift transport roles. All helicopters are the responsibility of the Flyvevabnet Kommando (Air Force Command), headquartered at Karup. This base now supports the ex-Army Flying Service AS550 observation helicopters and the eight Lynx Mk90s formerly operated by the Danish navy, and which deploy aboard Danish warships.

Karup is also home to Flyvevåben basic flying training, with the Flying School (Flyveskolen) operating the Saab T-17. Future fighter pilots continue their training under the NATO Flying Training in Canada initiative, flying the CT-156 Harvard II and CT-115 Hawk from CFB Moose Jaw and CFB Cold Lake.

▼ **Fokker F-16A Fighting Falcon, Esk 730, Skrydstrup**

Built in the Netherlands by Fokker, this F-16A Block 15AA has undergone upgrade to Block 20 MLU standard. E-004 is seen armed with a wingtip AIM-120 AMRAAM missile and a GBU-12 laser-guided bomb underwing.

Finland

Ilmavoimat

Charged with the aerial defence of neutral Finland, the Ilmavoimat currently possesses exclusively defensive equipment, as well as its own transport, liaison and training facilities.

The command structure of the Finnish Air Force is based around three air defence commands, each responsible for a front-line wing at a single base. In addition, there are separate training, liaison and test squadrons. Main combat type is the F-18C/D Hornet, in three fighter squadrons. Also in use are C-295 transports, Hawk and Vinka trainers, while the Army operates the NH90 helicopter.

Boeing F-18C Hornet

Finland is planning to introduce an air-to-ground capability to its Hornets, which are currently only equipped for defensive operations (hence the F-18 designation).

France

Armée de l'Air, Aviation Navale and ALAT

Upgrade and restructuring have been the order of the day for the Armée de l'Air, with a major reorganization of the air force having been introduced in the late 1990s.

The most significant recent upgrade for the Armée de l'Air has been the induction of the Rafale omni-role fighter, introduced in 2004. The new fighter has replaced the Jaguar, and the Mirage F1 is to be similarly superseded, with the last two squadrons due to disband in 2010.

The current Armée de l'Air structure is headed by a high command, answering to the chief of the air staff, or Chef d'Etat-Major de l'AA (CEMAA). The latter is responsible for four major commands. Air Combat Command (Commandement de la Force

Specifications

Crew: 1
Powerplant: 1 x 83.36kN (18,839lb) thrust SNECMA M53-2 afterburning turbofan
Maximum speed: 2338km/h (1453mph)
Range: 1480km (920 miles)
Service ceiling: 18,000m (59,055ft)
Dimensions: span 9.13m (29ft 11.5in); length 14.36m (47ft 1.25in); height 5.2m (17ft 0.75in)
Weight: 17,000kg (37,480lb) loaded
Armament: 2 x DEFA 554 cannon; 9 external pylons with provision for up to 6300kg of stores

Dassault Mirage 2000-5F, Escadron de Chasse 1/2 'Cigognes', BA102 Dijon

Until the Rafale is fielded in greater numbers, the upgraded Mirage 2000-5F is the premier Armée de l'Air air defence fighter, with 36 examples in use. EC 1/2 maintains a permanent detachment at Al Dhafra, in Oman.

Aérienne de Combat, CFAC), is primarily tasked with defending French airspace, and controls all tactical combat jets. Air Mobility Command (Commandement de la Force Aérienne de Projection, CFAP), undertakes transport and aerial refuelling missions, using A310s, A340s, C-130s, C-135FRs, CN235s and Transalls, together with a large fleet of helicopters (Caracal, Ecureuil, Fennec, Puma, Super Puma) and assorted liaison, VIP transport (A310, A319, A330 and Falcon series) and light transport types. New transport types on order include the A330 tanker/transport and A400M airlifter. The only flying asset assigned to Air Surveillance, Information and Communication Systems Command (Commandement Air des Systèmes de Surveillance, d'Information et de Communication, CASSIC) is the E-3F AWACS. Air Force Education and Training Command (Commandement des Ecoles de l'AA, CEAA) is responsible for tri-service aircrew training, and its fleet includes Alpha Jet Es, Tucanos and Epsilons. There are also two organic commands: Strategic Air Command (Commandement des Forces

Specifications

Crew: 2
Powerplant: 2 x 73kN (16,424lb) SNECMA M88-2 turbofans
Maximum speed: 2130km/h (1324mph)
Range: 1854km (1152 miles)
Service ceiling: classified
Dimensions: span 10.9m (35ft 9in); length 15.3m (50ft 2in); height 5.34m (17ft 6in)
Weight: 19,500kg (42,990lb) loaded
Armament: 1 x 30mm (1.18in) DEFA 791B cannon, up to 6000kg (13,228lb) of external stores

Dassault Rafale M, Flotille 12F, *Charles de Gaulle*

This Rafale M carrier fighter displays a radar-guided Mica air-to-air missile on the wingtip and carries a GBU-12 laser-guided bomb underwing – the latter has been used in action by the Rafale M over Afghanistan.

ARMÉE DE L'AIR – COMMANDEMENT DE LA FORCE AÉRIENNE DE COMBAT (CFAC)

Escadron de Chasse 1/2 'Cigognes'	Mirage 2000-5F	BA102 Dijon
Escadron d'Entrainement 2/2 'Cote d'Or'	Alpha Jet E	BA102 Dijon*
*EC 1/2 and EE 2/2 to move to Luxeuil in 2011. EC 1/2 maintains permanent detachment at Al; Dhafra AB, UAE.		
Escadron de Chasse 1/3 'Navarre'	Mirage 2000D	BA133 Nancy
Escadron de Chasse 2/3 'Champagne'	Mirage 2000D	BA133 Nancy
Escadron de Chasse 3/3 'Ardennes'	Mirage 2000D	BA133 Nancy
Escadron de Chasse 1/4 'Dauphiné'	Mirage 2000N	BA116 Luxeuil*
* scheduled to disband in 2010		
Escadron de Chasse 2/4 'La Fayette'	Mirage 2000N	BA116 Luxeuil
Escadron de Chasse 2/5 'Ile de France'	Mirage 2000C/B	BA115 Orange
Escadron de Chasse 3/4 'Limousin'	Mirage 2000N	BA125 Istres
Escadron de Chasse 1/7 'Provence'	Rafale C/B	BA113 Saint-Dizier
Escadron de Chasse 3/11 'Corse'	Mirage 2000C/D	BA188 Djibouti
Escadron de Chasse 1/12 'Cambresis'	Mirage 2000C	BA103 Cambrai*
* scheduled to disband in 2011		
Escadron de Chasse 1/91 'Gascogne'	Rafale C/B	BA113 Saint-Dizier

ARMÉE DE L'AIR RECONNAISSANCE UNITS

Escadron de Reconnaissance 1/33 'Belfort'	Mirage F1CR	BA112 Reims
Escadron de Reconnaissance 2/33 'Savoie'	Mirage F1CR/CT/B	BA112 Reims

Note: both units scheduled to disband in 2010

OTHER ARMÉE DE L'AIR FIXED-WING UNITS

Escadron de Détection et de Commandement Aéroporté 0/36 'Berry'	E-3F	BA702 Avord
Groupe de Ravitaillement en Vol 2/91 'Bretagne'	C-135FR	BA125 Istres
Escadron de Transport, d'Entraînement et de Calibration 0/65	Falcon 50/7X, TBM 700, A319, AS332	BA107 Villacoublay-Velizy
Groupe Aérien Mixte 0/56 'Vaucluse'	DHC-6, AS532, Transall	IBA105 Evreux

AÉRONAUTIQUE NAVALE – FLOTILLES

Flotille 4F	E-2C	Lorient
Flotille 11F	Super Etendard	Landivisiau
Flotille 12F	Rafale M	Landivisiau
Flotille 17F	Super Etendard	Landivisiau
Flotille 21F	Atlantique NG	Nîmes-Garons
Flotille 23F	Atlantique NG	Lorient
Flotille 24F	Falcon 50, EMB-121	Lorient
Flotille 25F	Falcon 200 Guardian	Faaa, Tahiti*
* detachment at Tontouta, New Caledonia		
Flotille 28F	EMB-121	Nîmes-Garons
Flotille 31F	Lynx HAS2/2(FN)	Hyères
Flotille 32F	SA321G	Lanvéoc-Poulmic*
* Super Frelon scheduled to retire in 2010		
Flotille 34F	Lynx HAS2/2(FN)	Lanvéoc-Poulmic
Flotille 35F	SA365, Alouette III	Hyères*
* SA365 detachments at Cherbourg, La Rochelle and La Touquet.		
Flotille 36F	AS565	Hyères

Note: Nîmes-Garons is scheduled to close down in 2011

Aériennes, CFAS), and Air Defence and Air Operations Command (Commandement de la Défense Aérienne et des Opérations Aériennes, CDAOA). CFAS is responsible for nuclear-tasked assets (Mirage 2000N), while CDAOA is responsible for mission planning and deployment.

Aviation Navale

Part of the Marine Nationale, Aviation Navale includes the air wing for the carrier *Charles de Gaulle*, which comprises Rafale M and upgraded Super Etendard fighters, E-2C airborne early warning aircraft and a detachment of plane-guard helicopters. Land-based aircraft include Atlantique NG maritime patrol aircraft, Falcon 50 and Gardian surveillance aircraft, while Lynx and Panther helicopters detachments are provided for Navy warships.

Army aviation is the responsibility of the Aviation Légère de l'Armée de Terre (ALAT). Combat units are organized under the 4 Brigade Aéromobile, which

Specifications

Crew: 2
Powerplant: 1 x 134kW (180hp) Lycoming AEIO-360-B2F 4-cylinder air-cooled, horizontally opposed, fuel injected piston engine
Maximum speed: 270km/h (168mph)
Range: 1200km (745 miles)
Service ceiling: 5000m (16,400ft)
Dimensions: span 8.06m (26ft 5.25in); length 7.16m (23ft 6in); height 2.55m (8ft 5.4in)
Weight: 830kg (1829lb) loaded

CAP 10B, Ecole de Pilotage Élémentaire de l'Armée de l'Air 05/315, Cognac BA709

The Armée de l'Air no longer operates the CAP 10B in the basic training role, although examples are still flown by the Aviation Navale and by the CEV, the French Air Force test unit. Cognac remains the centre of basic training and operates the Epsilon and Grob 120.

ARMÉE DE L'AIR TRANSPORT UNITS		
Escadron de Transport 1/61 'Touraine'	Transall	BA123 Orléans
Escadron de Transport 1/62 'Vercors'	CN235	BA110 Creil
Escadron de Transport 1/64 'Béarn'	Transall	BA105 Evreux
Escadron de Transport 2/61 'Franche-Comte'	C-130H	BA123 Orléans
Escadron de Transport 2/64 'Anjou'	Transall	BA105 Evreux
Escadron de Transport 3/60 'Esterel'	A310, A340	Paris-Roissy
Escadron de Transport 3/61 'Poitou'	Transall	BA123 Orléans
Escadron de Transport 3/62 'Ventoux'	DHC-6, CN235	BA118 Mont-de-Marsan

includes three combat helicopter regiments (1 Régiment d'Hélicoptères de Combat at Phalsbourg, 3 RHC at Etain and 5 RHC at Pau). ALAT regiments consist of flights, each of which undertakes a specific role. Main reconnaissance type is the Gazelle, while the Tigre is entering service to supplant Gazelles used in the attack, fire support and anti-helicopter roles. Transport types include the Puma, due to be replaced by the NH90, and the Cougar for combat search and rescue. ALAT also maintains training centres at Dax and Le Luc, and a special operations unit 4e Régiment d'Hélicoptères des Forces Spéciales at Pau.

Dassault Mirage 2000D

A Mirage 2000D refuels from a USAF KC-135R over the Adriatic while conducting missions over the Balkans. The Mirage 2000D is a conventional strike specialist, with a range of precision weapons.

Germany

Luftwaffe, Marineflieger and Heeresflieger

Vastly reduced in size since its Cold war heyday, the Luftwaffe is now making the transition to a leaner, more flexible force, with an increasing emphasis on overseas operations.

The modern Luftwaffe is based on three divisional commands (Kommando Luftwaffendivision), respondible for combat assets, together with the Lufttransportkommado responsible for transport and liaison. Divisional commands have command units and surface-to-air missile wings. Aircraft are operated by wings (Geschwader) each with two squadrons (Staffeln), though aircraft are pooled across the wing, with only aircrew being assigned to different squadrons.

Kommando 1. Luftwaffendivision includes Jagdbombergeschwader 32 and Jagdgeschwader 74 and is also responsible for a tactical training detachment at Decimomannu in Italy, and contributes to the NATO E-3 AWACS force. Kommando 2. Luftwaffendivision includes two fighter-bomber wings, JBG 31 and 33, plus JG 73. Kommando 4. Luftwaffendivision includes JG 71, and Aufklärungsgeschwader 51.

The EF2000 will eventually take the place of the Tornado in all fighter-bomber wings with the exception of JBG 32, which is a specialist defence-suppression unit with the Tornado ECR version. The

LUFTWAFFE WINGS		
Reconnaissance Wings		
AG 51 'Immelmann'	Tornado Recce, Heron 1	Schleswig-Jagel
Fighter-Bomber Wings		
JBG 31 'Boelcke'	EF2000, Tornado IDS	Nörvenich
JBG 32	Tornado ECR	Lechfeld
JBG 33	Tornado IDS	Büchel
Fighter Wings		
JG 71 'Richthofen'	F-4F	Wittmund
JG 73 'Steinhoff'	EF2000	Laage
JG 74	EF2000	Neuburg an der Donau
Transport Wings		
LTG 61	Transall, UH-1D	Penzing
LTG 62	Transall UH-1D	Wunsdorf Holzdorf
LTG 63	Transall	Hohn
Flugbereitschaft BMVg	A310, Challenger 601, AS532 Cougar	Köln/Bonn, Berlin-Tegel

EF2000 will also re-equip the final F-4F wing, with the Phantom II due to retire in 2013. Other new equipment includes the Heron 1 UAV, which is due to be joined within AG 51 by the Euro Hawk UAV, this carrying an electronic intelligence payload as a replacement for the Navy's last SIGINT-configured Atlantic. The Flugbereitschaft BMVg is receiving new equipment in the form of the A319, A340 and

Specifications

Crew: 1
Powerplant: 2 x 90kN (20,250lbf) Eurojet EJ200 afterburning turbofans
Maximum speed: Mach 2 (2495km/h; 1550mph)
Range: 2900km (1840 miles)
Service ceiling: 19,810m (65,000ft)
Dimensions: span 10.95m (35ft 11in); length 15.96m (52ft 5in); height 5.28m (17ft 4in)
Weight: 16,000kg (35,300lb) loaded
Armament: 1 x 27mm (1.06in) Mauser BK-27 cannon; 13 hardpoints holding up to 7500kg (16,500lb) of payload

Eurofighter EF2000, Jagdbombergeschwader 31 'Boelcke', Nörvenich

JBG 31 became the first Luftwaffe fighter-bomber wing to receive the EF2000, with initial deliveries in 2009. Currently primarily operating the Tornado IDS, 'Boelcke' is the Luftwaffe's specialist precision-strike unit, for which it is equipped with laser-guided bombs.

Specifications

Crew: 2
Powerplant: 2 x 79.6kN (17,900lb) General Electric J79-GE-17 turbojets
Maximum speed: 2390km/h (1485mph)
Range: 817km (1750 miles)
Service ceiling: 19,685m (60,000ft)
Dimensions: span 11.7m (38ft 5in); length 17.76m (58ft 3in); height 4.96m (16ft 3in)
Weight: 26,308kg (58,000lb) loaded
Armament: 1 x 20mm (0.78in) M61A1 Vulcan cannon and four AIM-7 Sparrow recessed under fuselage or other weapons up to 1370kg (3020lb) on centreline pylon; four wing pylons for two AIM-7, or four AIM-9

McDonnell Douglas F-4F Phantom II, Jagdgeschwader 71 'Richthofen', Wittmund

Germany's final Phantom operator is the 'Richthofen' wing, responsible for maintaining air defence commitments in the north of the country. JG 71 has also undertaken the NATO Baltic Air Policing mission.

Tornado ECR

Operated by a single Luftwaffe fighter-bomber wing, JBG 32 at Lechfeld, the Tornado ECR is a specialist defence-suppression aircraft, and saw active service over the Balkans during the 1990s. Key features of the ECR variant are an emitter-locator system (ELS) to locate enemy radar sites, which are then attacked with the AGM-88 High-speed Anti-Radiation Missile (HARM).

Global 5000 for VIP transport, while one Lufttransportgeschwader will be axed, and the remaining two will receive the A400M as replacements for the Transall. NH90s will supersede UH-1Ds used for combat search and rescue.

Marineflieger assets are divided between two bases, with Marinefliegergeschwader 3 operating the final Atlantic, plus Do 228s and Lynx from Nordholz, and MFG 5 operating Sea Kings from Kiel. The Heeresflieger is upgrading its CH-53 transport helicopters and introducing the Tiger attack helicopter, and NH90s will replace the UH-1D fleet. Heeresflieger helicopter regiments comprise two for medium transport (CH-53), two for transport (UH-1), and two for combat (BO105P and Tiger).

Specifications

Crew: 2
Powerplant: 2 x 2927kW (3925shp) General Electric T64-GE-413 turboshafts
Maximum speed: 315km/h (196mph)
Range: 1000km (540 nautical miles)
Service ceiling: 5106m (16,750ft)
Dimensions: span 22.01m (72ft 2.7in); length 26.97m (88ft 6in); height 7.6m (24ft 11in)
Weight: 15,227kg (33,500lb) loaded
Armament: 2 x 7.62mm (0.3in) MG3 machine guns in the side doors

Sikorsky CH-53GS, Einsatzgeschwader Termez

This is an example of the upgraded CH-53GS, with improved defensive equipment for operations in high-threat environments. The helicopter wears markings associated with its support of the ISAF mission in Afghanistan, for which it was based at Termez, Uzbekistan.

Specifications

Crew: 11
Powerplant: 4 x 3700kW (4600shp) Allison T56-A-14
Maximum speed: 750km/h (466mph)
Range: 8944km (5557.5 miles)
Service ceiling: 10,400m (28,300ft)
Dimensions: span 30.4m (99ft 8in); length 35.61m (116ft 10in); height 10.29m (33ft 9in)
Weight: 64,400kg (142,000lb) loaded
Armament: Bombload of 9000kg (20,000lb), missiles, torpedoes, mines and depth charges

Lockheed P-3C Orion, Marinefliegergeschwader 3 'Graf Zeppelin', Nordholz

To replace its Atlantic maritime patrol aircraft, Germany acquired eight P-3Cs formerly operated by the Netherlands Naval Aviation Service. The aircraft have been deployed to Djibouti to support the anti-terror mission in the Horn of Africa.

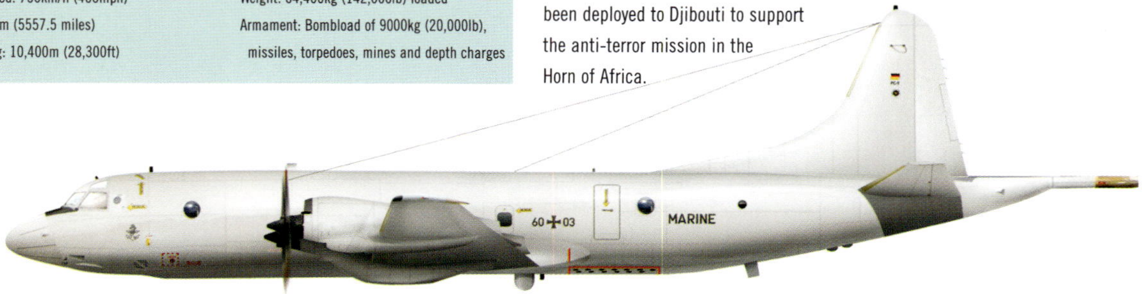

Greece

Hellenic Air Force, Army Aviation and Naval Aviation

The Hellenic Air Force (Elliniki Polemiki Aeroporia) operates a powerful and varied combat fleet, and also possesses transport, liaison, search and rescue, training and firefighting assets.

THE PRIMARY COMBAT types deployed by the Hellenic Air Force are the multi-role F-16C/D, the Mirage 2000 used for naval strike and air defence, upgraded F-4Es for air defence, A-7Es used for ground attack and maritime strike, and RF-4Es for reconnaissance. ERJ-145s are used for airborne early warning, while the primary transports are the C-27J and C-130. Major Hellenic Army types include the AB205 utility helicopter, AH-64A/DHA attack helicopter and CH-47DG/SD transport helicopter. The Hellenic Navy operates the AB212 and S-70B Aegean Hawk for anti-submarine warfare.

Specifications

Crew: 1
Powerplant: 1 x 97kN (21,834lb) SNECMA M53-P2 turbofan
Maximum speed: 2338km/h (1453mph)
Range: 1480km (920 miles)
Service ceiling: 18,000m (59,055ft)
Dimensions: span 9.13m (29ft 11.5in); length 14.36m (47ft 1.25in); height 5.2m (17ft 0.75in)
Weight: 17,000kg (37,480lb) loaded
Armament: 2 x DEFA 554 cannon; nine external pylons with provision for up to 6300kg (13,889lb) of stores, including air-to-air missiles, rocket launcher pods, and various attack loads, including 454kg (1000lb) bombs

Dassault Mirage 2000EGM, 114 PM, Tanagra

Operated by 114 PM 'Antaios', from Tanagra, this Mirage apparently wears a 'kill' marking, representing a Turkish F-16D shot down in 1996. The aircraft is armed with a heat-seeking Magic 2 air-to-air missile.

HELLENIC AIR FORCE COMBAT WINGS

Hellenic Tactical Air Force

110 PM Larissa*		
337 Mira	F-16C/D	Larissa
346 Mira	F-16C/D	Larissa
348 Mira	RF-4E	Larissa
* maintains detachments at Limnos		
111 PM Nea Anchialos*		
330 Mira	F-16C/D	Nea Anchialos
341 Mira	F-16C/D	Nea Anchialos
347 Mira	F-16C/D	Nea Anchialos
* maintains F-16C/D detachments at Kasteli and Limnos		
114 PM Tanagra		
331 Mira	Mirage 2000-5EG/BG	Tanagra
332 Mira	Mirage 2000EG/BG	Tanagra
115 PM Souda		
340 Mira	F-16C/D	Souda
343 Mira	F-16C/D	Souda
116 PM Araxos		
335 Mira	F-16C/D	Araxos
336 Mira	A-7E, TA-7H	Araxos
117 PM Andravida*		
338 Mira	F-4E	Andravida
339 Mira	F-4E	Andravida
* maintains F-4E detachment at Santorini		

AIR FORCE SUPPORT COMMAND		
112 PM Elefsis		
352 Mira	ERJ-135, Gulfstream V	Elefsis
353 Mira	P-3B	Elefsis
354 Mira	C-27J	Elefsis
355 Mira	CL-215, Do 28D	Elefsis
356 Mira	C-130B/H	Elefsis
358 Mira	AB205A, Bell 212	Elefsis
380 Mira	EMB-145 AEW&C	Elefsis*
384 Mira	AS332	Elefsis
Medical Emergency Helicopter Squadron	A109E	Elefsis
** independent unit, based at Elefsis*		
113 PM		Thessaloniki
383 Mira	CL-415	Thessaloniki

▲ F-4E Phantom II
Surviving Hellenic Air Force Phantoms have undergone the Avionics Upgrade Programme and serve with two squadrons of 117 PM at Andravida. The same base also houses F-4Es assigned to the Tactical Weapons School, while 117 PM maintains a detachment on the island of Santorini.

Ireland

Irish Air Corps

One of Western Europe's smallest air arms, the Irish Air Corps (Aer Chór na h-Éireann) operates a fleet of maritime patrol aircraft and VIP transports, as well as liaison and training assets.

OPERATING AS A component of the Irish Army, the Air Corps consists of two Operations Wings and an Air Corps College, with all units based at Baldonnel-Casement. 1 Operations Wing includes 101 (Maritime) Squadron with a pair of CN235 patrol aircraft, 102 (Ministerial Air Transport) Squadron with Beech 200, Gulfstream IV and Learjet 45 aircraft, and 104 (Army Co-operation) Squadron with five Cessna FR172s. 3 Operations Wing includes 301 (Search and Rescue) Squadron with six AW139s, 302 (Army Support) with EC135s. The Air Corps College flies eight PC-9 trainers.

Specifications
Crew: 1–2
Powerplant: 1 x Pratt & Whitney Canada PT6A-62 turboprop, 857kW (1149hp)
Maximum speed: 593km/h (368mph)
Range: 1593km (990 miles)
Service ceiling: 11,580m (37,992ft)
Dimensions: span 10.11m (33ft 2in); length 10.69m (35ft 1in); height 3.26m (10ft 8in)
Weight: 3200kg (7055lb) loaded

▼ Pilatus PC-9M, Flying Training School, Baldonnel-Casement
Irish Air Corps pilots are trained on the PC-9M fleet operated by the Flying Training School, part of the Air Corps College at Baldonnel-Casement. The PC-9M replaced SF260Ws previously in use with the unit.

Italy

Aeronautica Militare, Marina Militare and Aviazione dell' Esèrcito

The Italian Air Force is divided into three geographic regions, or Regioni Aeree, reporting directly to the head of the air force at AMI headquarters in Rome.

Flying units of the AMI are based around the wing (Stormo), which in turn includes a number of air groups (Gruppi). There are also two larger formations organized as air brigades (Brigate Aeree), which include wings and/or groups.

Air defence is the responsibility of manned fighters and surface-to-air missiles, with the EF2000 now entering service to supplant the F-16. The primary offensive assets are the Tornado IDS strike aircraft, flown by a single wing, together with the AMX ground-attack aircraft, the latter equipping two wings. A single wing operates a Gruppo of Tornado IT-ECRs in the defence-suppression role. For reconnaissance, increasing use is being made of UAVs, with five examples of the RQ-1B in service.

Transport aircraft comprise the C-27J and C-130J, with four Boeing 767 tanker/transports due to be delivered in 2010. The last of the G222s are used in the radio calibration role. Initial training is undertaken using the SF260, with fighter pilots

Specifications

Crew: 1

Powerplant: 2 x 90kN (20,250lbf) Eurojet EJ200 afterburning turbofans

Maximum speed: Mach 2 (2495km/h; 1550mph)

Range: 2900km (1840 miles)

Service ceiling: 19,810m (65,000ft)

Dimensions: span 10.95m (35ft 11in); length 15.96m (52ft 5in); height 5.28m (17ft 4in)

Weight: 16,000kg (35,300lb) loaded

Armament: 1 x 27mm (1.06in) Mauser BK-27 cannon; 13 hardpoints holding up to 7500kg (16,500lb) of payload

Eurofighter EF2000, 12° Gruppo, 36° Stormo, Gioia del Colle

Seen in a typical air defence configuration with AIM-120 AMRAAM and IRIS-T air-to-air missiles, this single-seat EF2000 is one of an expected 96 likely to be ordered for the Italian Air Force.

Specifications

Crew: 1

Powerplant: 1 x 49kN (11,000lbf) Rolls-Royce Spey 807 turbofan

Maximum speed: 1160km/h (721mph)

Range: 3330km (2070 miles)

Service ceiling: 13,000m (43,000ft)

Dimensions: span 8.87m (29ft 1in); length 13.23m (43ft 5in); height 4.55m (14ft 11in)

Weight: 10,750kg (23,700lb) loaded

Armament: 1 x 20mm (0.787in) M61 Vulcan rotary cannon; 2 x AIM-9 Sidewinder missiles or MAA-1 Piranha carried on wingtip rails; 3800kg (8380lb) bombload on 5 external hardpoints

AMX-International AMX, 14° Gruppo, 2° Stormo, Rivolto

Known as the Ghibli in Italian service, this AMX served with the now-disbanded 14° Gruppo during NATO's Allied Force campaign over Serbia in 1999, and is armed with laser-guided and retarded free-fall 'dumb' bombs and Sidewinder missile. This jet has since been transferred to 132° Gruppo at Istrana.

progressing to the MB339. The latter is also used by the Frecce Tricolori aerobatic team, the 313° Gruppo at Rivolto. An initial order has been placed for the M-346 advanced trainer, with further examples likely to supplant the MB339. SAR and CSAR are conducted by AB212 and HH-3H helicopters.

The Marine Militare Italiana jointly operates Atlantic maritime patrol aircraft with the AMI, and is otherwise responsible for providing aircraft for embarkation on Italian Navy ships. Key aircraft in use are the AV-8B+/TAV-8B strike fighter and AB212, AW101, NH90 and SH-3D helicopters.

The Aviazione dell' Esèrcito is spearheaded by A109, AB205, AB206, AB212 and AB412 utility helicopters, A129 Mangusta attack helicopters, and CH-47 heavy-lift transport helicopters.

AERONAUTICA MILITARE COMBAT AND TRANSPORT UNITS

Combat Forces Command

2° Stormo Rivolto		
313° Gruppo Addestramento Acrobatico	MB339	Rivolto
4° Stormo Grosetto		
9° Gruppo	EF2000	Grosetto
20° Gruppo	EF2000	Grosetto
5° Stormo Cervia		
23° Gruppo	F-16A/B	Cervia
6° Stormo	**Ghedi**	
102° Gruppo	Tornado IDS	Ghedi
154° Gruppo	Tornado IDS	Ghedi
156° Gruppo	Tornado IDS	Ghedi
32° Stormo	**Amendola**	
13° Gruppo	AMX	Amendola
28° Gruppo	RQ-1B	Amendola
101° Gruppo	AMX	Amendola
36° Stormo	**Gioia del Colle**	
12° Gruppo	EF2000	Gioia del Colle
37° Stormo	**Trapani**	
10° Gruppo	F-16A/B	Trapani
18° Gruppo	F-16A/B	Trapani
50° Stormo	**Piacenza**	
155° Gruppo	Tornado IT-ECR	Piacenza
51° Stormo	**Istrana**	
103° Gruppo	AMX	Istrana
132° Gruppo	AMX	Istrana

1a Brigata Aerea Operazioni Speciali		**Padua**
9° Stormo	**Grazzanise**	
21° Gruppo	AB212	Grazzanise
46a Brigata Aerea	**Pisa**	
2° Gruppo	C-130J	Pisa
50° Gruppo	C-130J	Pisa
98° Gruppo	C-27J	Pisa
14° Stormo	**Pratica di Mare**	
8° Gruppo	Boeing 767TCA, G222RM/VS	Pratica di Mare
71° Gruppo	P-180 Avanti, P-166, MB339	Pratica di Mare
15° Stormo	**Practica di Mare**	
81° Centro SAR	AB212	Practica di Mare
82° Centro CSAR	HH-3F	Trapani
83° Centro CSAR	HH-3F	Rimini
84° Centro CSAR	HH-3F	Brindisi
85° Centro CSAR	HH-3F	Practica di Mare
31° Stormo	**Ciampino**	
93° Gruppo	Falcon 900, SH-3D	Ciampino
306° Gruppo	A319CJ, Falcon 50	Ciampino
41° Stormo	**Sigonella**	
88° Gruppo	Atlantic	Sigonella

Note: Most Stormi (wings) within the AM also maintain a Squadriglia Collegamenti (liaison flight), normally with S-208M aircraft, MB339s in fast-jet units, and AB212AM SAR helicopters. 15° Stormo communication flight operates NH500s.

Specifications

Crew: 1
Powerplant: 1 x 105.8kN (23,800lb) Rolls-Royce Pegasus vectored thrust turbofan
Maximum speed: 1065km/h (661mph)
Combat radius: 277km (172 miles)
Service ceiling: more than 15,240m (50,000ft)
Dimensions: span 9.25m (30ft 4in); length 14.12m (46ft 4in); height 3.55m (11ft 7.75in)
Weight: 14,061kg (31,000lb) loaded
Armament: 1 x 25mm (1in) GAU-12U cannon, six external hardpoints with provision for up to 7711kg (17,000lb) (Short take-off) or 3175kg (7000lb) (Vertical take-off) of stores

▼ Boeing (McDonnell Douglas) AV-8B+ Harrier II, 6° Reparto Aeromobili, 1° GRUPAER, Marine Militare Italiana, *Giuseppe Garibaldi*

Carrying a mixed load of laser-guided bombs and Sidewinder missiles, when not flying from the carriers *Cavour* or *Giuseppe Garibaldi*, this AV-8B+ is one of 15 examples (plus two two-seat TAV-8Bs) that are otherwise home-based at Grottaglie-Taranto.

Specifications

Crew: 1–2
Powerplant: 2 x 634kW (850shp) thrust Pratt & Whitney Canada PT6A-66B turboprop
Maximum speed: 732km/h (455mph)
Service ceiling: 12,500m (41,010ft)
Range: 2592km (1612 miles)
Dimensions: span 14.03m (46ft 0.5in); length 14.41m (47ft 31/2in); height 3.98m (13ft 0.75in)
Weight: 5239kg (11,550lb) loaded

▼ Piaggio P-180AM Avanti, 636a Squadriglia Collegamento, 36° Stormo, Gioia del Colle

This Avanti twin-turboprop executive transport was most recently operated by 71° Gruppo. Versions of the P-180 are also in service with the Air Section of the Marina Militare, the AMI's Aerial Weapons Training Establishment, and with the Army.

Luxembourg

NATO Airborne Early Warning & Control Force

Although Luxembourg has a single A400M airlifter on order, its primary military air assets are the locally registered E-3 AWACS of the NATO Airborne Early Warning & Control Force.

Creation of the NAEW&CF was authorized in 1978 by the NATO Defence Planning Committee. In terms of budget, the multi-national NAEW&CF is the single most important NATO project, and serves to provide Alliance members with air surveillance, airborne early warning and command and control capabilities.

The NATO-owned E-3A Sentry fleet has its main operating base at Geilenkirchen, in Germany, but its aircraft are registered in Luxembourg. Forward Operating Bases (FOB) are at Aktion in Greece, Trapani in Italy, Konya in Turkey, and Ørland in Norway. The fleet comprises 17 E-3A aircraft, one having been lost in an accident. Aircrew training and transport missions are conducted using three examples of the CT-49A Trainer Cargo Aircraft (TCA), these being based on modified Boeing 707-320C airframes.

Netherlands

Royal Netherlands Air Force and Marine Luchtvaartdienst

The Royal Netherlands Air Force (Koninklijke Luchtmacht) is an active participant in NATO missions, with a force based around upgraded F-16 fighters, transports and helicopters.

THE STRUCTURE OF the RNLAF has changed following the end of the Cold War, with a reduced number of front-line F-16 units and a greater emphasis on airlift and overseas operations. Units come under the authority of the Commando Luchtstrijdkrachten (Air Force Command). The combat fleet comprises six squadrons of F-16s based at Leeuwarden, Volkel and Springfield, Ohio.

Main helicopter base is Gilze-Rijen, home of the Defensie Helikopter Commando (Defence Helicopter Commando), with CH-47Ds (with CH-47Fs on order), Cougars and AH-64Ds. Transport aircraft are based at Eindhoven in two squadrons, operating C-130Hs, one DC-10-30, two KDC-10s, Fokker 50s and a Gulfstream IV.

The Marine Luchtvaartdienst is due to receive 20 NH90s, replacing the SH-14D Lynx helicopters in service with two squadrons at De Kooy, as well as the AB412s currently used by a single reduced-size squadron for SAR duties from Leeuwarden.

Specifications

Crew: 2
Powerplant: 2 x 1599.5kW (2145hp) Rolls-Royce/Turbomeca/MTU RTM 322-01/9 turboshaft engines
Maximum speed: 295km/h (183mph)
Combat radius: 1110km (688 miles)
Hovering ceiling: 3500m (3500ft)
Dimensions: rotor diameter 16.3m (53ft 5in); length 16.81m (55ft 2in); height 5.42m (17ft 9in)
Weight: 9100kg (20,020lb) loaded

NH Industries NH90 NFH, Marine Luchtvaartdienst

The Netherlands ordered 20 examples of the NH90 NATO Frigate Helicopter in order to replace the Lynx and AB412 in the anti-submarine warfare and search and rescue roles. NH90s will be stationed at Gilze-Rijen and De Kooy.

Specifications

Crew: 1
Powerplant: either 1 x 105.7kN (23,770lb) Pratt & Whitney F100-PW-200
Maximum speed: 2142km/h (1320mph)
Range: 925km (525 miles)
Service ceiling: 15,240m (50,000ft)
Dimensions: span 9.45m (31ft); length 15.09m (49ft 6in); height 5.09m (16ft 8in)
Weight: 16,057kg (35,400lb) loaded
Armament: 1 x General Electric M61A1 20mm (0.79in) multi-barrelled cannon, wingtip missile stations; provision for up to 9276kg (20,450lb) of stores

Fokker F-16A Fighting Falcon, 322 Squadron, Leeuwarden

Fokker-built F-16A Block 15AC J-063 underwent the MLU upgrade, to become a Block 20-standard 'F-16AM'. J-063 was serving with 322 Squadron during Operation Allied Force in 1999, when it destroyed a Serbian MiG-29 using an AIM-120 missile. Since 2007 the aircraft has been flown by 306 Squadron.

Norway

Royal Norwegian Air Force

A valued NATO member, Norway's armed forces include the Luftforsvaret, or Royal Norwegian Air Force, responsible for all the country's military aviation, and divided into two commands.

THE TWO COMMANDS of the Royal Norwegian Air Force are Luftkommando Nord-Norge and Luftkommando Sør-Norge, with division of forces on a regional basis. Each air command is responsible for a number of squadrons (Skvadron).

Major combat type is the F-16, operated by three squadrons based at Bodø (two squadrons) and Ørland (one squadron). Smaller air stations comprise Andøya, Bardufoss, Sola, Rygge and Gardermoen. The air stations are provided with numbered Air Wings (Luftving), responsible for the various units at each base.

Maritime and transport assets

For maritime patrol, a single squadron of P-3C/Ns is based at Andøya, while Royal Norwegian Air Force transport capability is provided by a squadron of C-130Js based at Oslo. Two Falcon 20s are used in the electronic intelligence role from Rygge , where they serve alongside a single VIP-configured Falcon.

Bardufoss is the major helicopter base, with single squadrons of Lynx and Bell 412s. A total of 14 NH90s will eventually equip both these types, replacing the Lynx Mk86 as the Norwegian Navy's standard ship-based helicopter and superseding the Bell 412 in the special forces role. Bell 412 and SAR-configured Sea King detachments are maintained at Bodø, Floro, Lakselv, Rygge and Ørland. The Sea Kings are home-based at Stavanger.

After initial flying training on the MFI-15 at Bardufoss, subsequent Royal Norwegian Air Force pilot training is conducted in the USA under the Euro-NATO Joint Jet Pilot Training Program.

▲ **Bell 412SP**

Norway maintains a fleet of 15 Bell 412SP helicopters, some of which were assembled locally. These serve with 339 Skvadron at Bardufoss and with 720 Skvadron at Rygge, the latter with a special forces support role.

Specifications

Crew: 1
Powerplant: either 1 x 105.7kN (23,770lb) Pratt & Whitney F100-PW-200
Maximum speed: 2142km/h (1320mph)
Range: 925km (525 miles)
Service ceiling: 15,240m (50,000ft)
Dimensions: span 9.45m (31ft); length 15.09m (49ft 6in); height 5.09m (16ft 8in)
Weight: 16,057kg (35,400lb) loaded
Armament: 1 x General Electric M61A1 20mm (0.79in) multi-barrelled cannon, wingtip missile stations; provision for up to 9276kg (20,450lb) of stores

▼ **Fokker F-16A Fighting Falcon, 331 Skvadron, Bodø**

This Fokker-built, MLU-upgraded F-16A was operated by 331 Skvadron until 2005, when changes within the Royal Norwegian Air Force saw it pooled within the NDLO (Norwegian Defence Logistics Organization), otherwise known as FLO (Forsvarets Logistikk Organisasjon).

Portugal

Forca Aerea Portuguesa

The Portuguese Air Force (Força Aerea Portuguesa, FAP) is organized around numbered bases (Bases Aéreas, BA), each of which maintains operational, material and support groups.

THE ASSETS OF the FAP are divided among three major commands: Operational Command; Logistic and Administrative Command; and Personnel Command. The combat fleet is based on the F-16A/B, serving with two units at BA5 Monte Real. Overall air defence responsibility lies with the Portuguese Air Command and Control System.

The FAP transport fleet is centred at BA6 Montijo, with four squadrons under the command of Grupo Operativo 61. Three fixed-wing squadrons at BA6 operate the C-130H, C-212 and C-295, respectively. In addition to transport, the C-295 can also be configured for maritime patrol duties. The final units at BA6 are a SAR squadron with Pumas, and a squadron of Lynx Mk95 operated by the Navy (Marinha). Three Falcon 50s are permanently detached from Montijo to Lisbon for VIP duties.

▲ **Aérospatiale SA330S1 Puma**

Although mainly replaced in the SAR role by the EH101, the FAP maintains a few Pumas. After being retired in 2006, five SA330s were reactivated in 2007 to provide island SAR cover for the Azores and Madeira.

Specifications

Crew: 1
Powerplant: either 1 x 105.7kN (23,770lb) Pratt & Whitney F100-PW-200
Maximum speed: 2142km/h (1320mph)
Range: 925km (525 miles)
Service ceiling: 15,240m (50,000ft)
Dimensions: span 9.45m (31ft); length 15.09m (49ft 6in); height 5.09m (16ft 8in)
Weight: 16,057kg (35,400lb) loaded
Armament: 1 x General Electric M61A1 20mm (0.79in) multi-barrelled cannon, wingtip missile stations; provision for up to 9276kg (20,450lb) of stores

FAP training fleet

Grupo Operativo 11 at BA11 Beja is home to the training effort, with three squadrons equipped with the Alouette III helicopter, Alpha Jet A advanced jet trainer and Epsilon basic trainer, respectively. Some pilots train in the USA under the Euro-NATO Joint Jet Pilot Training Program. Maritime patrol is the responsibility of the P-3P/C, which are also assigned to a single squadron at BA11.

Grupo Operativo 1 is at BA1 Sintra, and includes the Air Force Academy, equipped with gliders.

BA4 Lajes is home to Grupo Operativo 41, which maintains detachments of C-212s used for photo-survey and maritime patrol, and EH101s for SAR. A single SAR squadron with Pumas remains active at Lajes, until the EH101 attains full operational capability.

▼ **General Dynamics F-16A Fighting Falcon, Esquadra 301 'Jaguares', BA5 Monte Real**

F-16A Block 15J 82-0918 has been upgraded to F-16A Block 20 MLU standard. Monte Real is home to two F-16 units: Esquadra 201 'Falcões' and Esquadra 201 'Jaguares'.

Spain

Ejército del Aire, Armada and Army Aviation

The Spanish Air Force maintains a varied and powerful fleet, while the Armada possesses a carrier air wing and other ship-based assets, and Army Aviation has a large helicopter force.

Spain's air arm is organized on a regional basis, with three separate air commands: Mando Aéreo del Centro (MACEN, headquartered in Madrid); Mando Aéreo del Estrecho (MAEST, headquartered in Seville); and Mando Aéreo de Levante (MALEV, with its headquarters in Zaragoza).

Combat and transport assets of MACEN include and F/A-18A+/B+ wing at Torrejón and a transport wing with CN235s and C-295s at Getafe. A C-212 wing is based at Valladolid, while Cuatro Vientos has a mixed wing of AS332, AS532 C-212 and CN235 aircraft. Torrejón also supports a wing of CL-215T and CL-415 firefighters, a VIP squadron with A310 and Falcon 900 aircraft, a mixed group of Boeing 707, C-212 and Falcon 20 aircraft and a single squadron of C-212s and C-101 jet trainers.

MAEST combat types comprise an EF2000 fighter wing at Morón, and a Mirage F1M/BM fighter wing at Albacete. A wing of modernized F-5Ms operates from Badajoz. Also at Morón is a maritime patrol squadron with P-3A/B/M aircraft.

Specifications

Crew: 1
Powerplant: 1 x 105.8kN (23,800lb) Rolls-Royce Pegasus vectored thrust turbofan
Maximum speed: 1065km/h (661mph)
Combat radius: 277km (172 miles)
Service ceiling: more than 15,240m (50,000ft)
Dimensions: span 9.25m (30ft 4in); length 14.12m (46ft 4in); height 3.55m (11ft 7.75in)
Weight: 14,061kg (31,000lb) loaded
Armament: 1 x 25mm (1in) GAU-12U cannon, six external hardpoints with provision for up to 7711kg (17,000lb) (Short take-off) or 3175kg (7000lb) (Vertical take-off) of stores

Boeing (McDonnell Douglas) EAV-8B+ Harrier II, 9a Escuadrilla, Flotilla de Aeronaves de la Armada, *Príncipe de Asturias*

Known as the VA.1 Matador II in Armada service, Spain operates 12 single-seat AV-8B+ fighters and a single TAV-8B trainer. When not assigned to the carrier *Príncipe de Asturias*, the Harriers operate from Rota.

Specifications

Crew: 1
Powerplant: 2 x 90kN (20,250lbf) Eurojet EJ200 afterburning turbofans
Maximum speed: Mach 2 (2495km/h; 1550mph)
Range: 2900km (1840 miles)
Service ceiling: 19,810m (65,000ft)
Dimensions: span 10.95m (35ft 11in); length 15.96m (52ft 5in); height 5.28m (17ft 4in)
Weight: 16,000kg (35,300lb) loaded
Armament: 1 x 27mm (1.06in) Mauser BK-27 cannon; 13 hardpoints holding up to 7500kg (16,500lb) of payload

Eurofighter EF2000, 111 Escuadrón, Ala 11, Morón

Armed with AIM-120 AMRAAM and AIM-9L/M air-to-air missiles, this EF2000 is operated by the lead Spanish wing, Ala 11, based at Morón air base, near Seville. The fighter has the local designation C.16, while the two-seat version is the CE.16.

Combat units within MALEV consist of a Zaragoza-based wing with three squadrons of F/A-18A+/B+ Hornets, and a wing of KC/C-130H tanker/transport aircraft at the same base.

Mando Aéreo de Canarias (MACAN) provides airpower for the Canary Islands, and consists of a single squadron of F/A-18As together with a mixed squadron of F27 maritime patrol aircraft and AS332 SAR helicopters, based at Las Palmas.

Combat assets of the Armada comprise AB212 and SH-60B anti-submarine and utility helicopters, EAV-8B and EAV-8B+ carrier strike fighters, and SH-3s used for airborne early warning and transport.

The BO105 is the most numerous Army Aviation type, but a replacement is now required. A total of 45 NH90s are on order, while other current Army types include the AB212, AS332, AS532, CH-47D, EC135, Tiger HAD attack helicopter and the UH-1H.

▲ McDonnell Douglas F/A-18A+ Hornet

An Ala 12 Hornet armed with 228kg (500lb) laser-guided bombs and wingtip Sidewinders during Operation Allied Force. The Hornet fleet comprises 55 upgraded F/A-18A+ and 11 F/A-18B+ aircraft built for Spain under the manufacturer's EF-18 designation, together with 22 ex-U.S. Navy F/A-18As.

Specifications

Crew: 1
Powerplant: 2 x 79.2kN (17,750lb) thrust General Electric F404-GE-402 afterburning turbofan engines
Maximum speed: 1915km/h (1190mph)
Range: 3330km (2070 miles)
Service ceiling: 15,000m (50,000ft)
Dimensions: span 12.3m (40ft); length 17.1m (56ft); height 4.7m (15ft 4in)
Weight: 16,850kg (37,150lb) loaded
Armament: 1 x 20mm (0.787in) M61A1 Vulcan nose-mounted gatling gun; 9 external hardpoints for up to 6215kg (13,700lb) of stores

▼ McDonnell Douglas F/A-18A+ Hornet, 462 Escuadrón 'Halcones', Ala 66, Gran Canaria

In Spain, Hornets received the local designation C.15. This example is former U.S. Navy BuNo 161939, now in service at Gran Canaria to provide defence for the Canary Islands. The F/A-18A+/B+ upgrades brings the aircraft to near-F/A-18C/D standard.

Specifications

Crew: 2
Powerplant: 2 x 79.6kN (17900lb) thrust General Electric J79-GE-17 afterburning turbojet engines
Maximum speed: 2390km/h (1485mph)
Range: 800km (500 miles)
Service ceiling: 18,900m (62,000ft)
Dimensions: span 11.7m (38ft 5in); length 18m (59ft); height 4.96m (16ft 3in)
Weight: 24,766kg (54,600lb) loaded

▼ McDonnell Douglas RF-4C Phantom II, 123 Escuadrón, Ala 12, Torrejón

Spain's RF-4Cs received upgrades including AN/APQ-172 radar, updated avionics, digital radios, revised countermeasures, an Israeli refuelling probe and provision for AIM-9L Sidewinder missiles, allowing them to serve until 2002.

Sweden

Flygvapnet

Neutral, but with a strong tradition of military self-sufficiency, Sweden's Flygvapnet is a modern and well-equipped force, although in recent years a number of units have been deactivated.

The various units of the Flygvapnet are part of the Försvarsmakten (Swedish Armed Forces). Previously organized on the basis of three independent regional Air Commands (South, Central and North), the Flygvapnet's units are now headed by a single unified command, the FlygTaktiska Kommando (FTK), with headquarters at Uppsala. Today, the military districts comprise the Northern Military District (HQ at Boden), Central Military District (HQ at Strängnäs), the Southern Military District (HQ at Gothenburg) and the Gotlands Military District (HQ at Visby).

The Flygvapnet's wings (Flygflottiljen) and helicopter battalions (Helikopterbataljonen) report to the four military districts. The fighter wings are equipped with the multi-role Gripen, with the original JAS 39A/B variants now undergoing upgrade to JAS 39C/D standard, which includes in-flight refuelling capability, large screen, full-colour cockpit displays, and a strengthened wing structure that allows new pylons to be fitted. Fighter pilots train on the Sk 60 jet trainer with the air combat school (Luftstridsskolan), and these aircraft are assigned to each of the three fighter wings, alongside two Gripen units. A final operator of the Sk 60 is the Flygvapnet aerobatic display team, or TEAM 60.

Helicopter structure

The helicopter units have been integrated within a common structure as the Försvarsmaktens Helikopterflottilj Swedish Armed Forces Helicopter Wing, which is now equipped with four helicopter squadrons and a single independent direct-reporting unit. The Helikopterflottilj is in the process of modernization, for which it is receiving Hkp 15 (A109) and Hkp 14 (NH90) helicopters. The NH90 will be used for anti-submarine warfare and search and rescue (SAR), while the Hkp 15 will be used for utility and SAR and deploys on board Swedish Navy warships. Other helicopters currently in use are the Hkp 9 (B0105) for anti-armour and observation, and the Hkp 10 (Super Puma) for SAR.

Largest of the military districts are the Northern and Southern, each of which are provided with two fighter wings and five transport/communications

Specifications

Crew: 1
Powerplant: 1 x 80.5kN (18,100lb. thrust) Volvo Flygmotor RM12 turbofan
Maximum speed: 2126km/h (1321mph)
Range: 3250km (2020 miles)
Dimensions: span 8m (26ft 3in); length 14.10m (46ft 3in); height 4.70m (15ft 5in)
Weight: 12,473kg (27,500lb) loaded
Armament: 1 x 27mm (1.06in) Mauser BK27 cannon; 6 external hardpoints with provision for Rb71 Sky Flash and Rb24 Sidewinder air-to-air missiles, Maverick air-to-surface missiles and other stores

SAAB JAS 39A Gripen, F7, Såtenäs

The Gripen spearheads the Swedish Air Force and is equipped for air defence, attack, anti-shipping and reconnaissance missions. JAS 39A/Bs are being upgraded to C/D standard, with a refuelling probe, NATO-compatible avionics and other improvements.

FLYGVAPNET

F7 – Skaraborgs flygflottilj Såtenäs

1. Division	JAS 39A/B	Såtenäs
2. Division	JAS 39A/B	Såtenäs
Sambandsflygrupp	Sk 60	
TSFE Såtenäs	TP 84	Såtenäs
TSFE	S 100B, S 102B	Linköping
TSFE (Det) Bromma	OS 100, TP 102	Stockholm-Bromma

F17 – Blekinge flygflottilj Ronneby

1. Division	JAS 39C/D	Ronneby
2. Division	JAS 39C/D	Ronneby
Sambandsflygrupp	Sk 60	
TSFE (Det)	TP 100*	Ronneby

* TP 100 fleet is part of F7.

F21 – Norbottens flygflottilj Luleå

1. Division	JAS 39C/D	Luleå
2. Division	JAS 39C/D	Luleå
Sambandsflygrupp	Sk 60	
TSFE (Det)	TP 100*	Kallax

* TP 100 fleet is part of F7.

Hkpflj – Helicopterflottiljen

1.Hkpskv	Hkp 10	Luleå
2.Hkpskv	Hkp 9, Hkp 14, Hkp 15	Linköping
3.Hkpskv	Hkp 9, Hkp 10, Hkp 14, Hkp 15	Ronneby
3.Hkps Såtenäs	Hkp 10	Såtenäs

LSS – Luftstridsskolan

FlygS	Sk 60A/B/C	Linköping
TEAM 60	Sk 60A	Linköping

squadrons, the latter operating fixed-wing TP 84 Hercules, TP 100 Argus (Saab 340) and TP 102 (Gulfstream IV) VIP transports.

Other units include separate airborne early warning and signals intelligence units at Linköping, as part of the TSFE, with two S 102B (Gulfstream IV) aircraft equipped for SIGINT and six S 100 Argus (Saab 340) AEW platforms. A single OS 100 is equipped for Open Skies surveillance missions and serves at Stockholm-Bromma.

Miscellaneous units comprise a communications flight (Sambandsflygrupp), a basic flying training unit (Grundläggande Flygutbildning), a basic tactical training unit (Grundläggande Taktisk Utbildning) and a test centre (Försökscentralen).

▼ NH Industries NH90, 2.Hkpskv, Försvarsmaktens Helikopterflottilj, Linköping

Known as the Hkp 14 in local service, Sweden placed orders for 13 Tactical Troop Transport (TTT) versions of the NH90 that will also be used for SAR, plus five that will be dedicated to anti-submarine warfare. Sweden was launch customer for the High Cabin Version of the NH90.

Specifications

Crew: 2
Powerplant: 2 x 1599.5kW (2145hp) Rolls-Royce/Turbomeca/MTU RTM 322-01/9 turboshaft engines
Maximum speed: 295km/h (183mph)
Combat radius: 1110km (688 miles)
Hovering ceiling: 3500m (3500ft)
Dimensions: rotor diameter 16.3m (53ft 5in); length 16.81m (55ft 2in); height 5.42m (17ft 9in)
Weight: 9100kg (20,020lb) loaded

Agusta-Bell AB412SP, Helicopterflottiljen, Linkoping

Receiving the local designation Hkp 11, five examples of the AB412 were operated in the SAR and medical evacuation roles from 1994, although the type was retired from service in the mid-2000s and has been superseded by the NH90.

Specifications

Crew: 3
Powerplant: 2 x 671 kW (900hp) Pratt & Whitney Canada PT6T-3D turboshafts
Maximum speed: 260km/h (160mph)
Range: 656km (405 miles)
Capacity: 10 troops or 6 stretchers
Dimensions: rotor diameter 14m (45ft 11in); length 17.1m (56ft 1in); height 4.6m (15ft 1in)
Weight: 5355kg (11,900lb)
Armament: 1 x 7.62mm (0.29in) C6 GPMG; 1 x 7.62mm (0.29in) Dillon Aero M134D 'Minigun'

Switzerland

Schweizer Luftwaffe

Highly trained and thoroughly equipped, the Swiss Air Force is tasked with preserving Swiss sovereignty, if threatened, and makes considerable use of reservists and reserve bases.

THE COMBAT EQUIPMENT of the Swiss Air Force is led by the multi-role F/A-18C/D, supplemented in the air defence role by the F-5E/F, for which a replacement is now sought. Helicopter transport is provided by the AS332 and AS532, supported by EC635 utility helicopters. Training is conducted on the PC-7 and the advanced PC-21, while PC-9s are in use for electronic warfare training and target towing. VIP transport is the primary role of single examples of the Cessna 560 Citation and Falcon 50. Light fixed-wing transport capacity is provided by the PC-6, also used for parachute training, and the PC-12. Mountain rescue and SAR are of particular importance to the Swiss Air Force, for which it relies on a large fleet of SA316 helicopters.

Restructuring had been pursued under the Armée XXI programme. The Überwachungsgeschwader 85, (surveillance wing) is now responsible for operational and training activities, via the Kommando Piloten Schule Luftwaffe 85, Kommando Lufttransporte and the Kommando Luftverteidigung 85, the latter commanding the Flieger Geschwader (air wings).

Specifications

Crew: 1
Powerplant: 2 x 79.2kN (17,750lb) thrust General Electric F404-GE-402 afterburning turbofan engines
Maximum speed: 1915km/h (1190mph)
Range: 3330km (2070 miles)
Service ceiling: 15,000m (50,000ft)
Dimensions: span 12.3m (40ft); length 17.1m (56ft); height 4.7m (15ft 4in)
Weight: 16,850kg (37,150lb) loaded
Armament: 1 x 20mm (0.78in) M61A1 Vulcan nose mounted gatling gun; 9 external hardpoints for up to 6215kg (13,700lb) of stores

Boeing F/A-18C Hornet, Fliegerstaffel 11, Fliegergeschwader 13, Meiringen

J-5014 has been operated by Fliegerstaffel 11 since 1999. The Swiss Hornet has been upgraded locally by RUAG, adding a helmet-mounted sight, AIM-9X Sidewinder missiles and Link 16 datalink, among others.

Turkey

Türk Hava Kuvvetleri

The Turkish Air Force (Türk Hava Kuvvetleri) is divided into two Air Force Commands (Hava Kuvvet Komutanligi): 1nci HKK in the west of the country, and 2nci HKK in the east.

THE LARGER OF the two commands, 1nci HKK is headquartered in Eskisehir and includes five air wings (or Ana Jet Üs, or AJÜ). In addition to its major operating bases, 1nci HKK also makes use of a number of secondary air bases (Hava Meydani), to which it regularly deploys its aircraft. With headquarters at Diyarbakir, the smaller 2nci HKK operates four air wings from a similar number of bases, and also from secondary air bases in the eastern part of the country.

The Turkish Air Force maintains an Air Logistics Command, responsible for military and VIP transport as well as maintenance. The final flying command is Air Training Command, with its headquarters in Izmir.

At the forefront of the Turkish Air Force is the F-16C/D, which is also assembled locally by Turkish Aerospace Industries (TAI). The upgraded F-4E remains an important fighter, while the RF-4E serves in the reconnaissance role. Surviving F-5s provide

Specifications

Crew: 2
Powerplant: 2 x 79.6kN (17,900lb) General Electric J79-GE-17C or 17E turbojets
Maximum speed: 2390km/h (1485mph)
Range: 817km (1750 miles)
Service ceiling: 19,685m (60,000ft)
Dimensions: span 11.7m (38ft 5in); length 17.76m (58ft 3in); height 4.96m (16ft 3in)
Weight: 25,558kg (56,346lb) loaded
Armament: 1 x 20mm (0.79in) M61A1 Vulcan cannon, capability to launch AGM-65D/G Maverick, AGM-88 HARM, GBU-8 HOBOS, GBU-10/12 Paveway II LGBs, general purpose and cluster bombs for air-to-ground missions

McDonnell Douglas F-4E Phantom II, 171 Filo, Malatya

Turkey upgraded 54 of its Phantoms to F-4E-2020 Terminator standard with Israeli assistance, this consisting of structural and avionics improvements, including new strakes above the air intakes, multi-function cockpit displays, multi-mode fire-control radar and Litening II targeting pod for use with a range of precision weapons.

Specifications

Crew: 1
Powerplant: 1 x 126.7kN (28,500lb) thrust Pratt & Whitney F100-PW-229 afterburning turbofan
Maximum speed: 2177km/h (1353mph)
Range: 3862km (2400 miles)
Service ceiling: 15,240m (49,000ft)
Dimensions: span 9.45m (31ft); length 15.09m (49ft 6in); height 5.09m (16ft 8in)
Weight: 19,187kg (42,300lb) loaded
Armament: 1 x General Electric M61A1 20mm (0.79in) multi-barrelled cannon, wingtip missile stations; 7 external hardpoints with provision for up to 9276kg (20,450lb) of stores

General Dynamics F-16C Fighting Falcon, 162 Filo, Bandirma

Turkey received 240 F-16C/D aircraft from the Block 30/40/50 production standards. 92-0003 is a Block 40L jet delivered in 1993, and it entered service with 162 Filo in 2001.

TURKISH AF COMBAT AND TRANSPORT UNITS

1nci HKK – 1st Air Force Command HQ Eskisehir

1nci AJÜ	**Eskisehir**	
111 Filo	F-4E	Eskisehir
112 Filo	F-4E	Eskisehir
113 Filo	RF-4E	Eskisehir
201 Filo	CN235, AS532	Eskisehir

3ncu AJÜ	**Konya**	
131 Filo	Boeing 737AEW&C	Konya
132 Filo	F-4E, F-16C/D	Konya
133 Filo	(N)F-5A/B	Konya
134 Filo Turkish Stars	NF-5A/B	Konya

4ncu AJÜ	**Ankara/Akinci**	
141 Filo	F-16C/D	
142 Filo	F-16C/D	
143 Filo	F-16C/D	

6nci AJÜ	**Bandirma**	
161 Filo	F-16C/D	Bandirma
162 Filo	F-16C/D	Bandirma

9nci AJÜ	**Balikesir**	
191 Filo	F-16C/D	Balikesir
192 Filo	F-16C/D	Balikesir

Hava Meydani (secondary air bases)
Izmir-Adnan Menderes
Çorlu
Afyon
Akhisar
Sivrihisar
Istanbul Atatürk International Airport

2nci HKK – 2nd Air Force Command HQ Diyarbakir

5nci AJÜ	**Merzifon**	
151 Filo	F-16C/D	Merzifon
152 Filo	F-16C/D	Merzifon

7nci AJÜ	**Malatya**	
171 Filo	F-4E	Malatya
173 Filo	F-4E, RF-4E	Malatya

8nci AJÜ	**Diyarbakir**	
181 Filo	F-16C/D	Diyarbakir
182 Filo	F-16C/D	Diyarbakir
202 Filo	CN235, AS532	

10nci TUK	**Incirlik**	
101 Filo	KC-135R	Incirlik

Hava Meydani (secondary air bases)
Batman
Erzurum
Mus
Sivas
Note: Most bases support a liaison and SAR flight (AJÜ A&KK) equipped with AS532 helicopters.

Hava Lojistik Komutanligi – Air Logistics Command HQ Etimesgut/Ankara

11nci HUAÜK	**Etimesgut/Ankara**	
211 Filo	CN235	Etimesgut/Ankara
212 Filo	CN235, Cessna 550/650, Gulfstream IV/550, UH-1H	Etimesgut/Ankara

12nci HUAU	**Kayseri**	
221 Filo	Transall	Kayseri
222 Filo	C-130B/E	Kayseri
223 Filo	CN235	Kayseri

lead-in fighter training and also equip the aerobatic demonstration team, the Turkish Stars. Training is also carried out on the T-37B/C and T-38A jet trainers, and the SF260 and T-41D primary trainer, although KT-1 Ungbis are on order to replace the latter types. Due to be delivered in 2010 were four Boeing 737 airborne early warning and control aircraft, together with additional Block 50 F-16C/Ds. The Turkish Army relies on a large fleet of helicopters to support its operations, the major front-line types being the AB204, AB205 and UH-H utility types, AH-1 attack helicopters, AS532s for combat search and rescue and S-70As for transport.

Front-line Naval Aviation aircraft are the AB212 and S-70B for anti-submarine warfare, with CN-235s used for maritime patrol. ATR-72s are on order.

United Kingdom

Royal Air Force, Fleet Air Arm and Army Air Corps

In common with many Western European air arms, the RAF has undergone drastic cuts in recent years, while at the same time facing increasing operational demands.

As a result of cuts, the strength of the RAF has been reduced to 44,000 personnel, with front-line assets divided among nine Expeditionary Air Wings, which fall under the Air Command with its HQ at High Wycombe. Air Command is divided into Nos 1, 2 and 22 Groups, respectively responsible for fast jet, transport/refuelling and ISTAR, and training. Support helicopters are operated by Joint Helicopter Command (JHC), a tri-service organization. Another joint operation is the Harrier GR9 force, in which RAF Harriers operate alongside those of the Fleet Air Arm's Naval Strike Wing within Joint Force Harrier. The Harrier is ultimately to be replaced by the F-35 Joint Combat Aircraft. Eventually, the RAF hopes to field a 12-squadron front-line force, with seven Typhoon units, at least three F-35 units, and Unmanned Combat Aerial Vehicles (UCAVs).

Maritime patrol is handled by the Nimrod MR2, which is due to be replaced by the entirely rebuilt Nimrod MRA4. Three Nimrod R1s used for intelligence gathering will be replaced by RC-135V/W Rivet Joints. Battlefield ISTAR requirements are met by the Sentinel R1 ASTOR (Airborne STand-Off Radar), based on the Bombardier Global Express airframe. These latter serve alongside the Sentry AEW1 at Waddington.

Operational support

Transport and tanking capability is due to be overhauled by the A400M airlifter and A330 tanker transports. Currently the C-17 Globemaster III

RAF FLYING SQUADRONS

Offensive Support

No 1(F) Squadron	Harrier GR9/9A	Cottesmore
No 2(AC) Squadron	Tornado GR4/4A	Marham
No 4(AC) Squadron	Harrier GR9/9A	Cottesmore
No 9(B) Squadron	Tornado GR4	Marham
No 12(B) Squadron	Tornado GR4	Lossiemouth
No 13 Squadron	Tornado GR4/4A	Marham
No 14 Squadron	Tornado GR4	Lossiemouth
No 31 Squadron	Tornado GR4	Marham
No 617 Squadron	Tornado GR4	Lossiemouth

Specifications

Crew: 1
Powerplant: 2 x 88.9kW (20,000lbs) thrust Eurojet EJ200 turbojets
Max speed: Mach 2 (2495km/h; 1550mph)
Range: 2900km (1840 miles)
Service ceiling: 19,812m (65,000ft)
Dimensions: span 11.09m (36ft 4.8in); length 15.96m (52ft 4in); height 5.28m (17ft 4in)
Weight: 16,000kg (35,300lb) loaded
Armament: 1 x 27mm (1.06in) Mauser BK-27 cannon; 13 hardpoints with provision for AMRAAM, ASRAAM air-to-air missiles; Storm shadow and Brimstone air-to-surface missiles, Enhanced Paveway laser-guided bombs

Eurofighter Typhoon F2, No 3(F) Squadron, Coningsby

No 3(F) Squadron's Typhoons share the Quick Reaction Alert air defence mission with Tornado F3s based at Leuchars. No 3(F) Squadron stood up as the RAF's first operational front-line Typhoon squadron in 2006.

Specifications

Crew: 2

Powerplant: 1 x 23.1kN (5200lb) Rolls Royce/Turbomeca Adour Mk 151 turbofan

Maximum speed: 1038km/h (645mph)

Endurance: 4 hours

Service ceiling: 15,240m (50,000ft)

Dimensions: span 9.39m (30ft 9.75in); length 11.17m (36ft 7.75in); height 3.99m (13ft 1.75in)

Weight: 7750kg (17,085lb) loaded

BAe Hawk T1, No 208(R) Squadron, Valley

Valley is home to RAF fast-jet training. Prospective fighter pilots complete Basic Fast Jet Training, beginning on the Tucano before moving to Valley and No 208(R) Squadron (conversion and advanced flying training) and No 19(R) Squadron (tactical weapons training).

Specifications

Crew: 2

Powerplant: 2 x 73.5kN (16,520lb) Turbo-Union RB.199-34R Mk 104 turbofans

Maximum speed: 2337km/h (1452mph)

Intercept radius: more than 1853km (1150 miles)

Service ceiling: 21,335m (70,000ft)

Dimensions: span 13.91m (45ft 7.75in) spread and 8.6m (28ft 2.5in) swept; length 18.68m (61ft 3in); height 5.95m (19ft 6.25in)

Weight: 27,987kg (61,700lb) loaded

Armament: 2 x 27mm (1.06in) IWKA-Mauser cannon, 6 external hardpoints with provision for up to 5806kg (12,800lb) of stores

Panavia Tornado F3, No 111(F) Squadron, Leuchars

Based at Leuchars in Scotland, No 111(F) Squadron is the final RAF operator of the Tornado F3 interceptor. The RAF maintains two pairs of Quick Reaction Alert aircraft on round-the-clock alert at Leuchars (Northern QRA) and Coningsby (Southern QRA, with Typhoons).

Air Defence and Airborne Early Warning

No 3(F) Squadron	Typhoon F2	Coningsby
No 8 Squadron	Sentry AEW1	Waddington
No 11(F) Squadron	Typhoon FGR4	Coningsby
No 23 Squadron	Sentry AEW1	Waddington
No 43(F) Squadron	Tornado F3	Leuchars
No 111(F) Squadron	Tornado F3	Leuchars

Reconnaissance

No 5(AC) Squadron	Sentinel R1	Waddington
No 51 Squadron	Nimrod R1	Waddington

Flying Training

No 19(R) Squadron	Hawk T1A	Valley
No 45(R) Squadron	King Air 200	Cranwell
No 55(R) Squadron	Dominie T1	Cranwell
No 60(R) Squadron	Griffin HT1	Shawbury
No 72(R) Squadron	Tucano T1	Linton-on-Ouse
No 100 Squadron	Hawk T1A	Leeming
No 207(R) Squadron	Tucano T1	Linton-on-Ouse
No 208(R) Squadron	Hawk T1	Valley

Operational Conversion Units

No 15(R) Squadron	Tornado GR4	Lossiemouth
No 17(R) Squadron	Typhoon F2/FGR4	Coningsby
No 20(R) Squadron	Harrier GR9/T12	Wittering
No 29(R) Squadron	Typhoon T1/F2	Coningsby
No 41(R) Squadron	Harrier GR9, Tornado GR4	Coningsby
No 56(R) Squadron	Nimrod MR2/MRA4/R1, Sentinel R1, Sentry AEW1	
No 203(R) Squadron	Sea King HAR3	Valley

Air Transport and Air-to-Air Refuelling

No 24 Squadron	Hercules C4/5	Lyneham
No 30 Squadron	Hercules C4/5	Lyneham
No 32 (The Royal) Squadron	BAe 125 CC3, BAe 146 CC2, A109E	Northolt
No 47 Squadron	Hercules C1/C3/C3A	Lyneham
No 70 Squadron	Hercules C3	Lyneham
No 99 Squadron	C-17A	Brize Norton
No 101 Squadron	VC10 C1K/K3/K4	Brize Norton
No 216 Squadron	TriStar C2/C2A/K1/KC1	Brize Norton

Support Helicopter

No 7 Squadron	Chinook HC2/2A	Odiham
No 18 Squadron	Chinook HC2/2A	Odiham
No 27 Squadron	Chinook HC2/2A	Odiham
No 28(AC) Squadron	Merlin HC3	Benson
No 33 Squadron	Puma HC1	Benson
No 78 Squadron	Merlin HC3A	Benson
No 230 Squadron	Puma HC1	Benson

Maritime Patrol and Search and Rescue

No 22 Squadron	Sea King HAR3/3A	A Flight Chivenor, B Flight Wattisham C Flight Valley
No 42(R) Squadron	Nimrod MR2	Kinloss
No 84 Squadron	Griffin HT1	Akrotiri
No 120 Squadron	Nimrod MR2	Kinloss
No 201 Squadron	Nimrod MR2	Kinloss
No 202 Squadron	Sea King HAR3/3A	A Flight Boulmer, D Flight Lossiemouth, E Flight Leconfield

Unmanned Aerial Vehicle

No 39 Squadron	MQ-9	Creech AFB

Specifications

Crew: 2
Powerplant: 2 x 76.8kN (17,270lbf) Turbo-Union RB199-34R Mk 103 afterburning turbofans
Maximum speed: Mach 2.34 (2417.6km/h; 1511mph)
Combat radius: 1390km (870 miles)
Service ceiling: 15,240m (50,000ft)
Dimensions: span 13.91m (45.6ft) unswept, 8.60m (28.2ft) swept; length 16.72m (54ft 10in); height 5.95m (19.5ft)
Weight: 28,000kg (61,700lb) loaded
Armament: 2 x 27mm (1.06in) Mauser BK-27 cannon, 4 x under-fuselage and 4 x swivelling underwing pylon stations holding up to 9000kg (19,800lb) of payload

Panavia Tornado GR4, No 12(B) Squadron, Lossiemouth

The RAF has seven front-line Tornado GR4/4A strike/attack squadrons, divided between Lossiemouth in Scotland and Marham. Tornados have seen combat over Afghanistan and Iraq, and are now equipped with Litening III targeting pods for precision-weapons delivery and ISTAR.

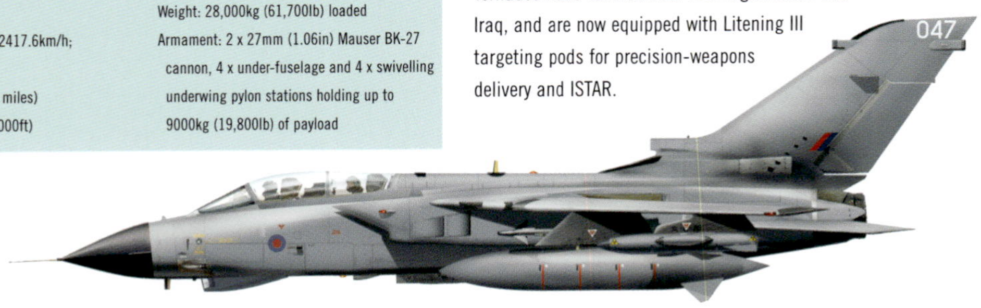

provides the backbone of the RAF's airlift capability, together with the Hercules force. The older Hercules C1/3 models will be replaced by 25 A400Ms.

The Royal Navy's Fleet Air Arm is responsible for providing airpower to be deployed aboard its warships, and the primary aviation assets are the Lynx shipborne anti-submarine helicopter, due to be replaced by the new Lynx Wildcat from 2011. Other front-line helicopters are the Merlin for anti-submarine warfare and the Sea King, used for airborne early warning, special operations and SAR.

The Army Air Corps inventory includes Apache attack helicopters, Lynx battlefield mobility helicopters (to be replaced by Lynx Wildcats from 2011), and Gazelle utility helicopters. 7 Regiment AAC is responsible for training. The AAC maintains a number of independent flights, including flights stationed in Belize, Brunei and Canada.

Specifications

Crew: 4
Powerplant: 3 x 1688kW (2263shp) Rolls-Royce Turbomeca RTM 322 turbines
Maximum speed: 167 knots (309km/h; 192mph)
Range: 1380km (863 miles)
Service ceiling: 4572m (15,000ft)
Dimensions: span 18.6m (61ft); length 22.8m (74ft 8in); height 6.65m (21ft 10in)
Weight: 15,600kg (32,188lb) loaded
Armament: 5 x general-purpose machine guns; 960kg (2116lb) of anti-ship missiles, homing torpedoes, depth charges and rockets

AgustaWestland Merlin HM1, 829 Naval Air Squadron, Culdrose

Royal Navy Merlins operate within five squadrons, all based at Culdrose when disembarked. With a primary role of anti-submarine warfare, Merlins are flown from the flight decks of warships including aircraft carriers, Auxiliary Oilers (Replenishment), and Type 23 frigates.

FLEET AIR ARM FLYING SQUADRONS

Naval Strike Wing	Harrier GR7/7A/9/9A	Cottesmore	820 Naval Air Squadron	Merlin HM1	Culdrose
702 Naval Air Squadron	Lynx HAS3/HMA8	Yeovilton	824 Naval Air Squadron	Merlin HM1	Culdrose
703 Naval Air Squadron	Firefly T67/Tutor T1	RAF Barkston Heath	829 Naval Air Squadron	Merlin HM1	Culdrose
705 Naval Air Squadron	Squirrel HT1	RAF Shawbury	845 Naval Air Squadron	Sea King HC4/HC6CR	Yeovilton
727 Naval Air Squadron	Tutor T1	Yeovilton	846 Naval Air Squadron	Sea King HC4	Yeovilton
750 Naval Air Squadron	Jetstream T2/3, Super King Air	Culdrose	847 Naval Air Squadron	Lynx AH7	Yeovilton
771 Naval Air Squadron	Sea King HAS5/6	Culdrose	848 Naval Air Squadron	Sea King HC4	Yeovilton
792 Naval Air Squadron	Mirach 100/5	Culdrose	849 Naval Air Squadron	Sea King ASaC7	Culdrose
814 Naval Air Squadron	Merlin HM1	Culdrose	854 Naval Air Squadron	Sea King ASaC7	Culdrose
815 Naval Air Squadron	Lynx HAS3/HMA8	Yeovilton	857 Naval Air Squadron	Sea King ASaC7	Culdrose

RUSSIA
ESTONIA
LATVIA
LITHUANIA
RUSSIAN FED.
RUSSIA
BELARUS
POLAND
UKRAINE
CZECH REPUBLIC
SLOVAKIA
MOLDOVA
HUNGARY
SLOVENIA
ROMANIA
CROATIA
BOSNIA &
HERZEGOVINA
SERBIA
BLACK SEA
BULGARIA
KOSOVO
MONTENEGRO
MACEDONIA
ALBANIA

Chapter 4

Eastern Europe

The air forces of Eastern Europe have changed immeasurably since the fall of the Soviet Bloc. The former Warsaw Pact countries now increasingly look to the West, and a number have now joined NATO, or are hopeful of future membership in the alliance. The disintegration of the USSR also granted independence to former Soviet Republics in the European zone, and these have gone about establishing independent air forces, typically based on equipment inherited from the USSR. The traumatic break-up of the former Yugoslavia has left new entities in its wake, and these all now operate air arms, some of which are also within the NATO alliance. Russia, the dominant power in the region, has seen its air forces contract, and is proceeding to adapt from the previous Cold War structure to a leaner, more flexible air force of a significantly reduced size.

Albania

Albanian Air Brigade

NATO member Albania's air arm, or Forcat Ashtarake Ajore Shgipetare, operates a modest force of mainly helicopters now that its last Chinese-supplied jet types have been withdrawn.

Operating under the Albanian Joint Forces Command, it is organized as a single Air Brigade. In addition to a single A109, three AB205s, seven AB206s and six BO105 helicopters, Albania has four Y-5 transports. Orders have been placed for five AS532s. Major bases are at Kuçova and Tirana.

Specifications

Crew: 1–2

Powerplant: 1 x 820kW (1100shp) Lycoming T53-L-11A turboshaft

Maximum speed: 220km/h (135mph)

Range: 533km (331 miles)

Service ceiling: 5910m (19,390ft)

Dimensions: 14.63m (48ft); length 12.69m (41ft 8in); height 4.5m (14ft 7in)

Weight: 4310kg (9500lb) loaded

Agusta-Bell AB205, Helicopter Regiment 3340, Farke

Albania received seven AB205s donated by the Italian Army in 2004.

Bosnia and Herzegovina

Air Force and Anti-Air Defence Brigade

Headquartered in Sarajevo, the air arm of Bosnia and Herzegovina was created after the end of the Bosnian War in 1995, with the assistance of the U.S. 'Train and Equip' programme.

Strictly controlled by the limits of the Dayton Peace Accords, the air component consists of 14 UH-1Hs, a similar number of Mi-8s, and eight Gazelle utility helicopters, plus a single VIP-configured Mi-17. Primary operating bases are Sarajevo, Banja Luka and Tuzla, with a helicopter squadron deployed at each.

Specifications

Crew: 1–4

Powerplant: 1 x 1044kW (1400hp) Avco Lycoming T53-L-13 turboshaft engine

Maximum speed: 204km/h (127mph)

Range: 511km (317 miles)

Service ceiling: 3840m (12,600ft)

Dimensions: rotor diameter 14.63m (48ft); length 12.77m (41ft 11in); height 4.41m (14ft 5in)

Weight: 4309kg (9500lb) loaded

Bell UH-1H, 1st Helicopter Squadron, Rajlovac/Sarajevo

A total of 15 UH-1Hs were delivered as U.S. Army surplus in the mid-1990s.

Belarus

Belarus Air and Defence Force

The air force of Belarus was merged with the Air Defence Troops in 2001, creating a single Air and Air Defence Force. The structure of the air arm is organized around air bases.

Backbone of the Belarus Air and Air Defence Force, which has its headquarters in Minsk, is the fighter component, consisting of approximately 40 MiG-29s and 20 Su-27s, with a mixed fleet operated by the 61st Fighter Air Base (IAB) at Baranovichi, and a further MiG-29 regiment operating from the 927th IAB at Bereza. Su-24M frontal bombers and Su-24MR reconnaissance aircraft equip the 116th Bomber and Reconnaissance Base (BRAB) at Ross, while Su-25 attack aircraft serve with the 206th Attack Air Base (ShAB) at Lida. The transport force consists of the 50th Transport Aviation Base at Minsk-Machulishche, with two squadrons of Il-76, An-26 and An-12 aircraft, as well as helicopters. It is likely that a single Tu-134 and a Mi-8S are retained by the presidential flight. An army aviation component is integrated within the Air and Air Defence Force, and this operates around 100 Mi-8, 40 Mi-24 and 10 Mi-26 helicopters. Helicopter units include the 181st Helicopter Air Bases (VAB) at Pruzhany and the aforementioned 50th TAB, as well as a training unit with Mi-2s at Minsk. The training fleet, with facilities at Bobruyk, Vitebsk and Vyaz'ma (in Russia) includes L-39s and Yak-52s.

Specifications

Crew: 5
Powerplant: 2 x 2103kW (2820ehp) Progress AI-24VT turboprops (plus 1 x 7.85kN (1795lb st) Tumansky Ru-19-A300 turbojet in right nacelle)
Maximum speed: 440km/h (273mph)
Range: 1100km (683 miles) with max payload
Service ceiling: 7500m (24,600ft)
Dimensions: span 29.2m (95ft 9.5in); length 23.80m (78ft 1in); height 8.58m (28ft 1.5in)
Weight: 24,000kg (52,911lb) loaded

▼ Antonov An-26, Belarus Air and Air Defence Force

This An-26 transport is operated by an unknown unit of the Belarus Air and Air Defence Force, but is likely home-based at Minsk-Machulishche, where the transport fleet is concentrated. As well as 'straight' An-26 transports, Belarus inherited former Soviet An-26RT 'Curl-B' electronic intelligence aircraft.

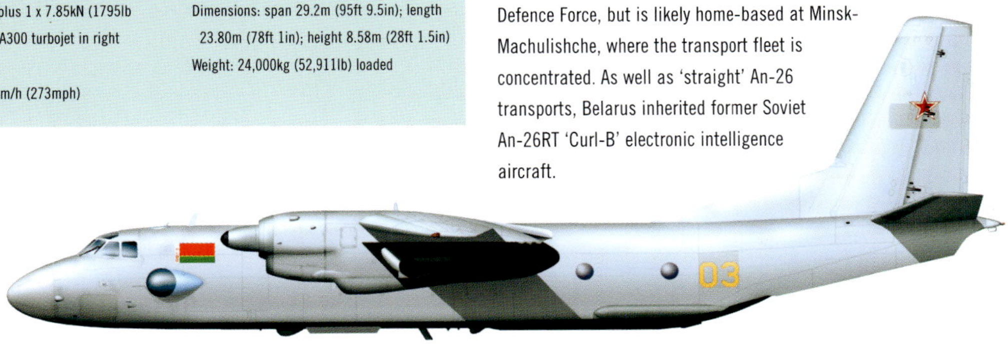

Specifications

Crew: 1
Powerplant: 2 x 122.5kN (27,557lb) Lyul'ka AL-31M turbofans
Maximum speed: 2150km/h (1335mph)
Range: 500km (930 miles)
Service ceiling: 17,500m (57,400ft)
Dimensions: span 14.7m (48ft 2.75in); length 21.94m (71ft 11.5in); height 6.36m (20ft 10.25in)
Weight: 30,000kg (66,138lb) loaded
Armament: 1 x 30mm (1.18in) GSh-3101 cannon with 149 rounds; 10 external hardpoints with provision for 6000kg (13,228lb) of stores

▼ Sukhoi Su-27UB, 2nd Squadron, 61st Fighter Air Base, Baranovichi

Baranovichi is home to the Belarus Su-27 fleet, the 2nd Squadron operating alongside the 1st Squadron that is equipped with MiG-29s.

Bulgaria

Bulgarian Air Force and Naval Aviation

The Bulgarski Voenno Vzdushni Sili (BVVS) has suffered significant cutbacks since the end of the Cold War. Today, its units are controlled by the Air Defence Corps.

THE AIR DEFENCE Corps, or Korpus Protivovazdushna Otbrana is the controlling authority for the Bulgarian Air Force. In the 1990s the BVVS introduced a new organizational structure, using numbered air bases rather than regiments, all bases being commanded by the Korpus Takticheska Aviatsia. The five major bases of the BVVS respectively house air defence (3rd Fighter Base, at Graf Ignatievo, with MiG-21s and MiG-29s of the 1st Fighter Squadron, the MiG-21s due to remain in use until 2011-12), ground attack/reconnaissance (22nd Attack Base, Bezmer, Su-25), transport (16th Transport Base, Vrazhdebna, C-27J, An-24/26/30, L-410, PC-12), helicopter (24th Helicopter Base, Krumovo, AS532, Bell 206, Mi-17, Mi-24) and training (12th Training Air Base, Kamenets, PC-9 and L-39) elements. Bulgaria joined NATO in 2004 and recently received equipment includes AS532 helicopters and C-27J transports. Further new equipment on order includes AS565s for Aviatzia na Balgarski Voenno Morski Flot (Naval Aviation), these latter replacing the Mi-14s in use at Varna.

Specifications

Crew: 2–3
Powerplant: 2 x 1600kW (2200hp) Isotov TV3-117 turbines
Maximum speed: 335km/h (208mph)
Range: 450km (280 miles)
Service ceiling: 4500m (14,750ft)
Dimensions: span 6.5m (21ft 3in); length 17.5m (57ft 4in); height 6.5m (21ft 3in)
Weight: 12,000kg (26,500lb) loaded
Armament: 1 x 12.7mm (0.5in) Yakushev-Borzov gun, 4 x S-8 80mm (3.15in) rocket pods or up to 3460kg (7612lb) of rockets or missiles

▼ Mil Mi-24, 1st Attack Helicopter Squadron, 24th Helicopter Base, Krumovo

The 24th Vertoletna Avio Basa (4th Helicopter Base) hosts a squadron of Mi-24D/V assault helicopters, and a mixed squadron of transport helicopters, with AS532s, Bell 206s and Mi-17s.

Specifications

Crew: 1
Powerplant: 2 x 81.4kN (18,298lb) Sarkisov RD-33 turbofans
Maximum speed: 2443km/h (1518mph)
Range: 1500km (932 miles)
Service ceiling: 17,000m (55,775ft)
Dimensions: span 11.36m (37ft 3.75in); length (including probe) 17.32m (56ft 10in); height 7.78m (25ft 6.25in)
Weight: 18,500kg (40,785lb) loaded
Armament: 1 x 30mm (1.18in) GSh-30 cannon, provision for up to 4500kg (9921lb) of stores

▼ Mikoyan MiG-29, 2nd Fighter Squadron, 3rd Fighter Base, Graf Ignatievo

Bulgaria's 12 single-seat and four two-seat MiG-29s are flown by the 2nd Squadron at Graf Ignatievo, near Plovdiv. Resident MiG-21s and MiG-29s are both technically assigned to the base's line-maintenance unit.

Croatia

Croatian Air Force and Air Defence

Established as a fledgling air arm in the wake of Croatia's declaration of independence in 1991, the Croatian Air Force entered NATO structure in 2009, and activities now focus on two bases.

When first established, the Croatian Air Force relied on mainly impressed civil types and light aircraft, with all combat aircraft from the former Socialist Federal Republic of Yugoslavia being evacuated from Croatia.

After the end of the Bosnian War in 1995, the lifting of the arms embargo allowed the Croatian Air Force to re-equip, acquiring Bell 206 helicopters and PC-9 trainers. In the meantime, MiG-21s had been obtained illicitly, and these, now upgraded, provide the main combat capability. Eight MiG-21bis and four two-seat MiG-21UM jets have been equipped to NATO standards in Romania. They serve at the 91st Air Force Base at Pleso, and are assigned to the 21st Fighter Squadron. The MiGs are also deployed to other bases around the country as required. Pleso is also responsible for the 27th Transport Aircraft Squadron with two An-32s. Pleso, home of the air arm's headquarters, also commands a rotary-wing unit, the 28th Transport Helicopter Squadron with Mi-171s.

Training and fire-fighting

Basic training is carried out on the Zlin 242s at the 93rd Air Force Base at Zadar, also home to PC-9 advanced trainers, Bell 206s (and a smaller number of Mi-8/17s) for training rotary-wing aircrew, and the 885th Firefighting Squadron with CL-215/415 and AT-802 aircraft. The latter unit also operates Mi-8/17s, from the Pleso-based 20th Transport Helicopter Squadron, and fire-fighting aircraft are detached around the country during fire season. Zadar is home to the military display team, Wings of Storm, flying PC-9s.

▲ **An-32s**

An An-32 releases flares. The Croatian Air Force includes two examples of this twin-turboprop transport, which are used for regular supply flight between bases. The aircraft can carry 40 passengers, or alternatively a typical cargo load of 6700 kg (14,700 lb) over 900 km (486 nm).

Specifications

Crew: 1
Powerplant: 1 x 73.5kN (16,535lb) Tumanskii R-25 turbojet
Maximum speed: 2229km/h (1385mph)
Range: 1160km (721 miles)
Service ceiling: 17,500m (57,400ft)
Dimensions: span 7.15m (23ft 5.5in); length (including probe) 15.76m (51ft 8.5in); height 4.1m (13ft 5.5in)
Weight: 10,400kg (22,925lb) loaded
Armament: 1 x 23mm (0.9in) GSh-23 twin-barrel cannon in underbelly pack, provision for about 1500kg (3307kg) of stores

▼ **Mikoyan-Gurevich MiG-21bisD, 21st Fighter Squadron, Pleso**

Based at Pleso, near Zagreb, the Croatian MiG-21 fleet is expected to be retained until 2013, by which time a new multi-role fighter ought to have been selected. This aircraft carries R-60 air-to-air missiles underwing.

Czech Republic

Czech Air Force

Renamed as the Vzdusné Síly Armády Ceské Republiky in 1998, the Czech Air Force is part of NATO and is now organized around four major air bases, with its headquarters in Olomouc.

THE FIVE MAJOR bases currently utilized by the Czech AF (Cáslav, Prague-Kbely, Námest nad Oslavou and Prerov) are responsible for the various flying squadrons. Current unit structure includes the 21st Tactical Air Force Base at Cáslav, responsible for the 211th Tactical Squadron that flies the JAS39 Gripen in the air defence role. Fourteen leased JAS39C/D fighters were delivered in the course of 2005. Cáslav is also home to a unit equipped with around 24 L-159 Advanced Light Combat Aircraft (ALCA), the 212th Tactical Squadron.

The 22nd Air Force Base at Námest nad Oslavou operates the 221st Attack Helicopter Squadron with Mi-24/35s, and the 222nd Tactical Squadron with L-39 jet trainers. Further rotary-wing forces can be found with the 23rd Helicopter Base at Prerov, where the 231st Helicopter Squadron operates Mi-17s, Mi-171s and W-3s. Smaller helicopter detachments are maintained at Plzen and Prerov, with W-3s of the 243rd Helicopter Squadron outfitted for SAR.

Transport fleet

The 24th Air Transportation Base at Prague-Kbely includes the VIP fleet, in which the first of two A319s arrived in 2007 to begin to replace Tu-154s with the 241st Transport Squadron. Other duties of the 24th Air Transportation Base include movements of personnel and material, and the fleet also includes An-26, C-295 and L-410 tactical transport (242nd Transport and Special Squadron), CL-601 and Yak-40 short-range VIP transports (241st Transport Squadron) and Mi-8/17 and W-3 helicopters (243rd Helicopter Squadron).

Basic training is conducted at Pardubice, on civilian-owned Zlin 142s, fast-jet pilots then progressing to 222nd Tactical Squadron L-39s.

▲ Aero L-159 Advanced Light Combat Aircraft

Developed from the L-39 indigenous trainer, the L-159 ALCA provides the Czech Air Force with its air-to-ground capability. The aircraft are based alongside the Gripens at Cáslav, and are complemented by eight two-seat L-159T1 trainers.

Specifications

Crew: 1
Powerplant: 1 x 80.5kN (18,100lb) Volvo Flygmotor RM12 turbofan
Maximum speed: more than Mach 2
Range: 3250km (2020 miles)
Service ceiling: 15,240m (50,000ft)
Dimensions: span 8m (26ft 3in); length 14.1m (46ft 3in); height 4.7m (15ft 5in)
Weight: 12,473kg (27,500lb) loaded
Armament: 1 x 27mm (1.06in) Mauser BK27 cannon, plus rockets, cluster bombs and missiles

▼ SAAB JAS 39C Gripen, 211th Tactical Squadron, 21st Tactical Air Force Base, Cáslav

Selected by the Czech Republic as its new fighter in 2002, the Gripen is operated in JAS39C/D form, acquired under a 10-year lease arrangement.

Hungary

Hungarian Air Force

Hungary joined the NATO alliance in 1999 and its air arm, the Magyar Légierö, is now much depleted compared to its Warsaw Pact days, and is organized as a single air command.

Force reductions mean that the Hungarian Air Force's fixed-wing aircraft now all operate from a single base, Kecskémet, or the 59th Air Wing. The air base supports one (reduced) squadron of five upgraded MiG-29s, and one of Gripens. The first of 14 leased JAS39s (including two twin-seaters) arrived at Kecskémet in March 2006. Transport assets comprise five An-26s of the wing's 3rd Squadron, but these are to be replaced after 2012. Pilot training begins on the Yak-52 at Szolnok's air academy. Fighter pilots finish their training under the NATO Flying Training in Canada (NFTC) programme.

Szolnok, the 86th Helicopter Regiment, is also home to the helicopter arm, with its 1st Squadron consisting of seven Mi-8s and seven Mi-17s, and the 2nd squadron being equipped with seven Mi-24s. Three R22s were purchased in 2010 in order to serve as training helicopters.

The Hungarian Pápa air base is also home to the three C-17A airlifters that are currenlty operated by NATO's Heavy Airlift Wing as part of the multi-national Strategic Airlift Capability initiative. The aircraft are operated in Hungarian Air Force markings.

Specifications

Crew: 2
Powerplant: 1x 16.87kN (3792lbf) Ivchenko AI-25TL turbofan
Maximum speed: 750km/h (466mph)
Range: 1100km (683 miles)
Service ceiling: 11,000m (36,100ft)
Dimensions: span 9.46m (31ft 0.5in); length 12.13m (39ft 9.5in); height 4.77m (15ft 7.75in)
Weight: 3455kg (7617lb) loaded
Armament: External bomb load up to 1150kg (2250lb)

Aero L-39ZO Albatros, 2nd Squadron 'Dongó', 59th Air Wing, Kecskémet

Hungary's ex-East German Air Force L-39s were operated by the 2nd Squadron of the 59th Air Wing alongside that unit's MiG-29s.

Specifications

Crew: 1
Powerplant: 1 x 80.5kN (18,100lb) Volvo Flygmotor RM12 turbofan
Maximum speed: more than Mach 2
Range: 3250km (2020 miles)
Service ceiling: 15,240m (50,000ft)
Dimensions: span 8m (26ft 3in); length 14.1m (46ft 3in); height 4.7m (15ft 5in)
Weight: 12,473kg (27,500lb) loaded
Armament: 1 x 27mm (1.06in) Mauser BK27 cannon, six external hardpoints, provision for missiles, bombs, drop tanks and ECM pods

SAAB JAS39EBS HU Gripen, 1st Squadron 'Puma', 59th Air Wing, Kecskémet

Hungary's Gripens are broadly similar to the JAS39C/D model. They are operated by the 1st Squadron of the 59th Air Wing, from Kecskémet.

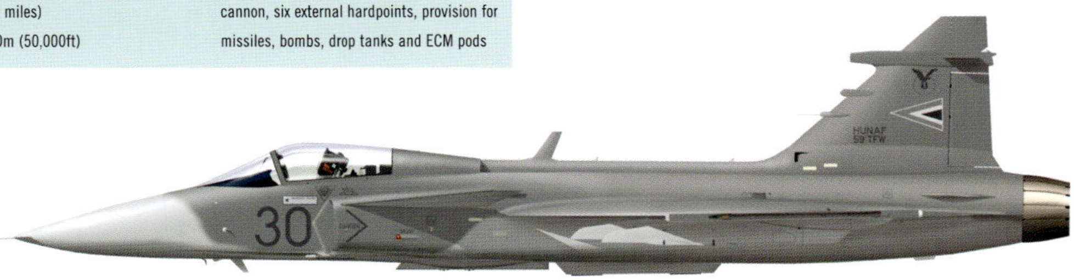

Baltic States

Estonia, Latvia and Lithuania

The air arms of the three Baltic States are among the smallest in Europe, but all have been declared to NATO since 2004. Among them, only Lithuania operates its own jet equipment.

THE SMALLEST OF the Baltic States, Estonia's air arm (Eesti Õhuvägi) is equipped with two An-2 utility transports and two R22 light helicopters. These are based at Ämari.

The Latvijas Gaisa Spéki, or Latvian Air Force, maintains the 1 Aviacijas Eskadrila at Lielvarde. The unit is divided into transport and helicopter squadrons, equipped with An-2, L-410, Mi-2 and Mi-171 aircraft. The Mi-171s are also detached to Riga-Skulte for SAR duties.

Home of the Lithuanian Air Force is Siauliai, which also hosts rotating NATO air defence fighters from various air arms, these being charged with defending Baltic airspace. Lithuanian assets at Siauliai include two L-39s and seven Mi-8s, as well as a transport squadron with C-27J and L-410 aircraft. Mi-8 SAR detachments are maintained at Nemirseta and Kaunas. A single Yak-18T is in use for training.

Specifications

Crew: 3

Powerplant: 2 x 3460kW (4640hp) Rolls-Royce AE2100-D2A turboprops

Maximum speed: 602km/h (374mph)

Range: 11852km (1151 miles) with 10,000kg (22,000lb) payload

Service ceiling: 9144m (30,000ft)

Dimensions: span 28.7m (94ft 2in); length 22.7m (74ft 6in); height 9.64m (31ft 8in)

Weight: 30,500kg (67,241lb) loaded

Alenia C-27J Spartan, Transporto Eskadrile, 1 Aviacijos Baze, Siauliai-Zokniai

Lithuania ordered three C-27Js to replace its An-26 tactical transports.

Macedonia

Macedonian Air Force

Macedonia has emerged from the war against Kosovar extremists that broke out in 2001, and its air arm – with a single air brigade – is now hopeful of securing NATO membership.

ESTABLISHED IN JUNE 1991, the Macedonian Air Force's centre of operations is Pterovec air base. Initially, arms embargoes hindered the establishment of the air arm, but Mi-17s were inducted in 1994, and today three Mi-17s are complemented by two Mi-8s and four upgraded Mi-24s, the latter representing the air force's most capable combat equipment. Units comprise 101 Squadron with a single An-2, 201 Squadron responsible for the Mi-24s, 301 Squadron (Mi-8/17) and 401 Squadron with Zlin 143 and 242 trainers together with a pair of UH-1Hs delivered during the 2001 conflict.

Specifications

Crew: 1
Powerplant: 2 x 44.1kN (9921lb) Tumanskii R-195 turbojets
Maximum speed: 975km/h (606mph)
Range: 750km (466 miles)
Service ceiling: 7000m (22,965ft)
Dimensions: span 14.36m (47ft 1.5in); length 15.53m (50ft 11.5in); height 4.8m (15ft 9in)
Weight: 17,600kg (38,800lb) loaded
Armament: 1 x 30mm (1.18in) GSh-30-2 cannon; eight external pylons with provision for up to 4400kg (9700lb) of stores

Sukhoi Su-25, 101 Squadron, Airborne Brigade, Petrovec

This Su-25 was one of four (including one two-seater) acquired from Ukraine in the run-up to the fighting that broke out in 2001. Operated by 101 Squadron, the Su-25 fleet has now been placed in storage.

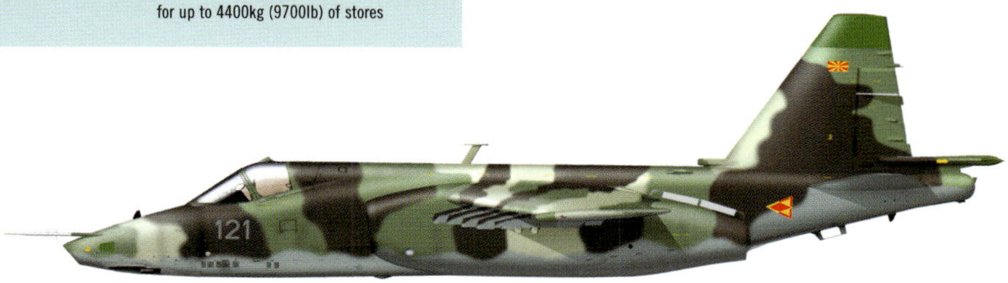

Moldova

Moldovan Air Force

The modestly sized Moldovan Air Force was created following Moldova's independence from the USSR in 1991. Current levels of strength are far below Conventional Forces in Europe limits.

According to the legislation of the CFE Treaty, Moldova is permitted 50 armed helicopters and 50 armed aircraft, but the current fleet consists entirely of unarmed light transports and helicopters. Moldova inherited 34 MiG-29 fighters from the Soviet Navy, but these were sold off by the late 1990s.

The Moldovan Air Force maintains a personnel strength of just over 1000, and assets are organized into one helicopter squadron, and one missile battalion, the air arm being separated into separate air force and air defence organizations, along Soviet lines. Marculesti air base supports eight Mi-8 helicopters (including one in VIP configuration), two An-72 jet transports, two An-2 Colt utility transports, a single An-26 Curl tactical transport, and six PZL-104 Wilga utility transports.

Specifications

Crew: 3
Powerplant: 2 x 1454kW (1950shp) Klimov TV3-117Mt turboshafts
Maximum speed: 260km/h (162mph)
Range: 450km (280 miles)
Service ceiling: 4500m (14,765ft)
Dimensions: rotor diameter 21.29m (69ft 10in); length 18.17m (59ft 7in); height 5.65m (18ft 6in)
Weight: 11,100kg (24,470lb) loaded
Armament: up to 1500kg (3300lb) of disposable stores on six hardpoints, including 57mm (2.24in) S-5 rockets, bombs, or 9M17 Phalanga ATGMs

Mil Mi-8MTV-1, Helicopter Squadron, Marculesti

Moldova's Mi-8 fleet is reported to include just four airworthy examples of the Mi-8MTV-1 and a single Mi-8PS VIP transport. This aircraft took part in the NATO Partnership for Peace exercise Cooperative Key in 1996.

Montenegro

Montenegrin Air Force

The Montenegrin Air Force, or Vazduhoplovstvo i protivvazdusna odbrana (ViPVO) was formed following the disintegration of Serbia and Montenegro in 2006, and operates around 40 aircraft.

After Montenegro broke away from Serbia, the new republic was left with a number of aircraft at Golubovci air base. These included 17 G-4 Super Galebs and three Utva 75 trainers, which will likely be returned to Serbia. Montenegro has meanwhile expressed its intention to operate only helicopters. Headquartered at Podgorica, the air arm operates 15 Gazelles in Gama and Hera configuration, and a single Mi-8T, although the latter was reportedly no longer airworthy as of 2010. These serve with a single helicopter squadron, headquartered at Golubovci, which maintains close air support, transport and utility flights. Three Air Tractor AT-802s have also been purchased for fire-fighting.

Specifications

Crew: 2
Powerplant: 1 x 17.8kN (4000lbf) licence-built Rolls-Royce Viper 632-46
Maximum speed: 910km/h (565mph)
Range: 2500km (1553 miles)
Service ceiling: 12,850m (42,160ft)
Dimensions: span 9.88m (32ft 5in); length 11.35m (37ft 27/8in); height 4.3m (14ft 1.25in)
Weight: 6300kg (13,889lb) loaded
Armament: 1 x 23mm (0.9in) GSh-23L cannon in ventral gun pod; 4 underwing pylons

SOKO G-4 Super Galeb, Montenegrin Air Force, Golubovci

The only G-4 Super Galeb known to have received the markings of the new Montenegrin Air Force. Although still extant, the aircraft is apparently not in service, and the air force intends to operate Gazelle helicopters exclusively.

Poland

Polish Air Force, Army Aviation and Naval Aviation

The Sily Powietrzne, or Polish Air Force, has undergone great changes as it has transitioned from its Cold War structure to join the NATO alliance, to which Poland was admitted in 1999.

Overhauling the Polish Air Force introduced the new F-16 Block 52+ fighter. Structural changes in 2009 saw the air brigades and subordinated units reorganized into air wings. Air Force Command is headquartered in Warsaw.

The 1st Tactical Aviation Wing is responsible for MiG-29 and Su-22 aircraft. The MiG-29 fighter is in use with 41.ELT (Tactical Aviation Squadron) at Malbork, the unit's aircraft comprising 14 ex-German Air Force machines from a total of 22 delivered from 2005. The second MiG-29 unit is 1.ELT at Minsk-Mazowiecki, and both squadrons provide aircraft for the national Quick Reaction Alert air defence mission. 1.ELT aircraft were acquired directly from the USSR and as part of an exchange deal with the Czech Air Force in the mid-1990s. The Su-22M4K attack aircraft (and its two-seat trainer derivative, the Su-22UM3K) is based at Miroslawiec

Specifications

Crew: 2
Powerplant: 1 x 126.7kN (28,500lb) thrust Pratt & Whitney F100-PW-229 afterburning turbofan
Maximum speed: 2177km/h (1353mph)
Range: 3862km (2400 miles)
Service ceiling: 15,240m (49,000ft)
Dimensions: span 9.45m (31ft); length 15.09m (49ft 6in); height 5.09m (16ft 8in)
Weight: 19,187kg (42,300lb) loaded
Armament: 1 x GEc M61A1 20mm (0.79in) multi-barrelled cannon, seven external hardpoints with provision for up to 9276kg (20,450lb) of stores

Lockheed Martin F-16D Fighting Falcon, 31.Baza Lotnictwa Taktycznego (31st Tactical Aviation Base), Poznan-Krzesiny

The 31st Tactical Air Base supports two squadrons of F-16C/Ds, which were acquired under the Peace Sky programme as a replacement for ageing MiG-21 and Su-22 aircraft.

and Swidwin, home to a total of three squadrons. The 2nd Tactical Aviation Wing operates F-16s, and began to receive its 48 Block 52+ F-16C/Ds in 2006. The initial recipient was 3.ELT (3rd Tactical Aviation Squadron), and the type is also in service with 6.ELT and 10.ELT.

The 3rd Aviation Transport Wing operates a variety of transport aircraft, including the latest

SILY POWIETRZNE, POLISH AF COMBAT AND TRANSPORT UNITS

Unit	Base	Aircraft
36.Specialny Pulk Lotnictwa Transportowego	Warsaw-Okecie	Bell 412, M-28, Mi-8, Tu-154M, W-3, Yak-40
Lotniczej Grupy Poszukiwawczo-Ratowniczej	Bydgoszcz* *detachment at Kraków-Balice	W-3, Mi-8
1.Skrzydlo Lotnictwa Taktycznego – 1st Tactical Aviation Wing, HQ Swidwin		
1.Eskadra Lotnictwa Taktycznego	Minsk-Mazowiecki	MiG-29, MiG-29UB, TS-11, Mi-2
41.Eskadra Lotnictwa Taktycznego	Malbork	MiG-29, TS-11
7.Eskadra Lotnictwa Taktycznego	Swidwin	Su-22M4K, Su-22UM3K, TS-11
8.Eskadra Lotnictwa Taktycznego	Miroslawiec	Su-22M4K, Su-22UM3K, TS-11
40.Eskadra Lotnictwa Taktycznego	Swidwin	Su-22M4K, Su-22UM3K, TS-11

Unit	Base	Aircraft
2.Skrzydlo Lotnictwa Taktycznego – 2nd Tactical Aviation Wing, HQ Poznan-Krzesiny		
31.Baza Lotnictwa Taktycznego – 31st Tactical Aviation, Base Poznan-Krzesiny		
3.Eskadra Lotnictwa Tactycznego	Poznan-Krzesiny	F-16C/D
6.Eskadra Lotnictwa Taktycznego	Poznan-Krzesiny	F-16C/D
32.Baza Lotnictwa Taktycznego – 32nd Tactical Aviation, Base Lask		
10.Eskadra Lotnictwa Tactycznego	Lask	F-16C/D
3.Skrzydlo Lotnictwa Transportowego – 3rd Aviation Transport Wing, HQ Powidz		
2.Eskadra Lotnictwa Transportowo-Lacznikowego	Bydgoszcz	An-28, W-3
3.Eskadra Lotnictwa Transportowo-Lacznikowego	Wroclaw	Mi-2, TS-11, W-3
13.Eskadra Lotnictwa Transportowego	Kraków-Balice	M-28, C-295M
14.Eskadra Lotnictwa Transportowego	Powidz	C-130E, M-28

Specifications

Crew: 1
Powerplant: 2 x 81.4kN (18,298lb) Sarkisov RD-33 turbofans
Maximum speed: 2443km/h (1518mph)
Range: 1500km (932 miles)
Service ceiling: 17,000m (55,775ft)
Dimensions: span 11.36m (37ft 3.75in); length (including probe) 17.32m (56ft 10in); height 7.78m (25ft 6.25in)
Weight: 18,500kg (40,785lb) loaded
Armament: 1 x 30mm (1.18in) GSh-30 cannon, provision for up to 4500kg (9921lb) of stores

Mikoyan MiG-29, 1.Eskadra Lotnictwa Taktycznego 'Warszawa', Minsk-Mazowiecki

MiG-29s of 1.ELT comprise aircraft that were received from the USSR in between 1989-90 and 10 surplus Czech Air Force jets received in 1995-96.

Specifications

Crew: 5
Powerplant: 4 x 3021kW (4050hp) Allison T56-A-7A turboprop engines
Maximum speed: 547km/h (340mph)
Range: 3896km (2420 miles)
Service ceiling: 7010m (23,000ft)
Dimensions: span 40.4m (132ft 7in); length 29.8m (97ft 9in); height 11.7m (38ft 6in)
Weight: 79,375kg (175,000lb) loaded

Lockheed C-130E Hercules, 14.Eskadra Lotnictwa Transportowego, Powidz

Formerly operated by the USAF as 70-1262, this is one of two C-130Es loaned to Poland pending the five refurbished examples from the U.S. The type made its combat debut in 2009 in Afghanistan.

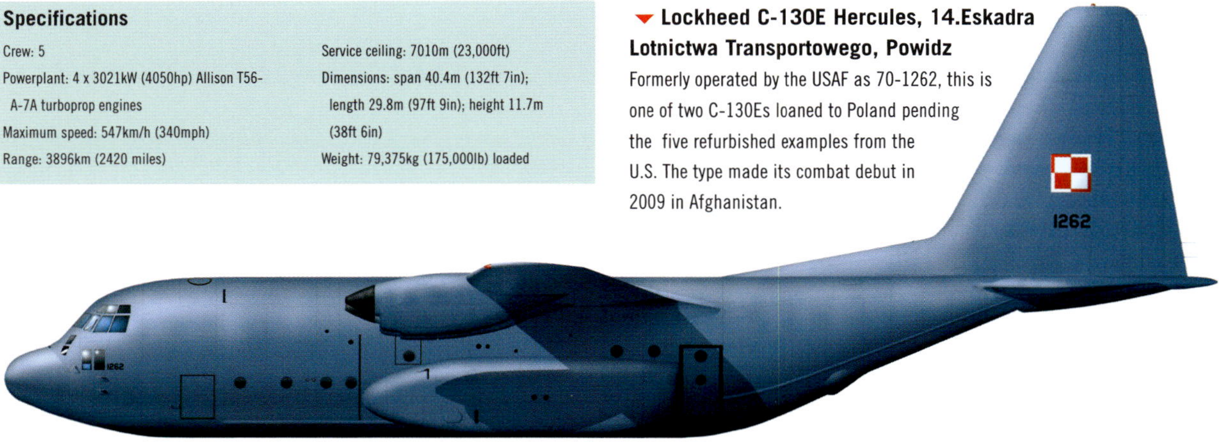

addition, the C-130E, delivered to the 14th ELTR (Transport Aviation Squadron) in 2009. The 13.ELTR at Kraków employs C-295 and M-28 aircraft, while 2.ELTR at Bydgoszcz operates An-28s and W-3s. Wroclaw is home to 3.ELTR with Mi-2, TS-11 and W-3 aircraft.

The 4th Flight Training Wing is responsible for training pilots from the Polish Air Force Academy and operates TS-11 jet trainers, PZL-130 turboprop trainers, and SW-4s, from separate Air Training Centres at Deblin and Radom.

The 36th Special Assignment Regiment at Warsaw transports VIPs, and is equipped with Tu-154, Yak-40 Mi-2, Mi-8, W-3, SW-4 and Bell 412 aircraft.

The Lotnictwo Marynarki Wojennej, or Polish Naval Aviation, is headed by the 'City of Gdynia' Aviation Brigade, responsible for three Eskadra Marinarki Wojennej (Naval Air Squadrons): 28.elMW at Gdynia-Babie Doly (with M-28s, Mi-8/17s, SH-2Gs and W-3s), 29.elMW at Darlowo (Mi-14 and W-3) and 30.elMW at Cewice-Siemerowice (M-28).

Polish Army Aviation

Polish Army Aviation (Lotnictwo Wojsk Ladowych) includes 49.PSB (Attack Helicopter Regiment) at Pruszcz Gdanski (equipped with two Mi-24 squadrons, and two squadrons of Mi-2s). 56.PSB at Inowroclaw has a single squadron of Mi-24s and three Mi-2 squadrons. Under the command of the 25th Air Cavalry Brigade are 37.DL (Air Wing) at Leznica-Wielka (two squadrons of Mi-8s) and 66.DL at Tomaszów-Mazowiecki with three squadrons of W-3s.

Romania

Romanian Air Force

Romania was the first East European signatory of NATO's Partnership for Peace, and joined the alliance in 2004, and the Fortele Aerienne Române is now evolving to meet new requirements.

THE ROMANIAN AIR arm is now looking forward to receiving F-16s to replace the upgraded MiG-21 Lancers that spearhead the fighter arm at present. Five air bases are in regular use, and the air arm uses a group structure. Lancers serve with 711 and 712 Squadrons at Câmpia Turzii, which is also home to the 713rd Helicopter Squadron with IAR-330s. The 714th Helicopter Squadron reports to Câmpia Turzii but is based at Timisoara. More Lancers are found with 861 and 862 Squadrons at Borcea-Fetesti, parent base to the 863rd Helicopter Squadron with IAR-330s at Mihail Kogalniceanu. Final Lancer operator is the 951st Squadron at Bacau, co-located with the 205th Squadron, responsible for Lancer training, and the 952nd Squadron (IAR-330). The multi-mission IAR-330 SOCAT is assigned to the 904th and 905th Squadrons at Bucuresti-Otopeni. The latter base is also home to the transport fleet, with two squadrons of An-26/30s, C-27Js and C-130B/Hs, and the 903rd Squadron with IAR-330s. Training takes place at Boboc, where five squadrons fly Alouette III, An-2 IAK-52 and IAR-99 aircraft.

Specifications

Crew: 1
Powerplant: 1 x 60.8kN (14,550lb) thrust Tumanskii R-13-300 afterburning turbojet
Maximum speed: 2229km/h (1385mph)
Range: 1160km (721 miles)
Service ceiling: 17,500m (57,400ft)
Dimensions: span 7.15m (23ft 5.5in); length (including probe) 15.76m(51ft 8.5in); height 4.1m (13ft 5.5in)
Weight: 10,400kg (22,925lb) loaded
Armament: 1 x 23mm (0.90in) cannon, provision for about 1500kg (3307lb) of stores, including air-to-air missiles, rocket pods, napalm tanks, or drop tanks

Aerostar MiG-21MF Lancer A, 711 Squadron, Câmpia Turzii

A total of 71 air-to-ground Lancer As, 25 air-defence Lancer Cs and 14 Lancer B trainers were produced via upgrade. 711 Squadron at Câmpia Turzii (Baza 71 Aerianâ) is equipped with a mix of Lancer A and B versions. Co-located 712 Squadron flies Lancer Bs and Cs.

Specifications

Crew: 1
Powerplant: 2 x 81.4kN (18,298lb) Sarkisov RD-33 turbofans
Maximum speed: 2443km/h (1518mph)
Range: 1500km (932 miles)
Service ceiling: 17,000m (55,775ft)
Dimensions: span 11.36m (37ft 3.75in); length (including probe) 17.32m (56ft 10in); height 7.78m (25ft 6.25in)
Weight: 18,500kg (40,785lb) loaded
Armament: 1 x 30mm (1.18in) GSh-30 cannon, provision for up to 4500kg (9921lb) of stores

Mikoyan MiG-29, 1st Squadron, Grupul 57 (57th Fighter Regiment), Mihail Kogalniceanu

Formerly the pride of the Romanian Air Force, the 18 survivors of 20 MiG-29s (plus a single ex-Moldovan 'Fulcrum-C') were put into storage in 2003 after funding for their overhaul and upgrade was withheld.

Russia

Russian Air Force and Naval Aviation

In terms of numbers, the Russian air arms are among the most powerful in the world, but after years of under-funding Russia is only now making strenuous efforts to restructure its air force.

Among the key concerns of the Russian Air Force have been increasing flying hours and exercises, introduction of aircraft upgrades, and developing new combat aircraft. The last two objectives have been progressing only very slowly, although the Sukhoi T-50 new-generation fighter took to the air in 2010. Additionally, the strategic bomber force has significantly stepped up its tempo of activity.

Perhaps most significantly, the Russian Air Force is now on the verge of a major restructuring, replacing its Cold War-era organization with a new system centred around numbered air bases. The former Frontal Aviation is now designated as Tactical Aviation, and is responsible for all fighter, theatre bomber and attack types. In the future, the regiments indicated here (and many more besides them) will be organized around approximately 60 air bases. The previous structure was based on eight Air Armies, of which two were role-specific: the 37th Air Army with strategic bombers, and 61st Air Army with transport

Specifications

Crew: 1
Powerplant: 2 x 122.5kN (27,557lb) Lyul'ka AL-31M turbofans
Maximum speed: 2150km/h (1335mph)
Range: 500km (930 miles)
Service ceiling: 17,500m (57,400ft)
Dimensions: span 14.7m (48ft 2.75in); length 21.94m (71ft 11.5in); height 6.36m (20ft 10.25in)
Weight: 30,000kg (66,138lb) loaded
Armament: 1 x 30mm (1.18in) GSh-3101 cannon with 149 rounds; 10 external hardpoints with provision for 6000kg (13,228lb) of stores

Sukhoi Su-27UB, 206th Guards Fighter Aviation Regiment, Volzskiy

This Su-27UB was operated by the 206th Guards Fighter Regiment (IAP) of the Astrakhan Military Region. The unit was disbanded in 2002, and its Su-27s were taken over by the 562nd IAP at Krymsk. That unit was in turn re-designated as the 3rd Guards IAP.

Specifications

Crew: 1
Powerplant: 2 x 81.4kN (18,298lb) Sarkisov RD-33 turbofans
Maximum speed: 2443km/h (1518mph)
Range: 1500km (932 miles)
Service ceiling: 17,000m (55,775ft)
Dimensions: span 11.36m (37ft 3.75in); length (including probe) 17.32m (56ft 10in); height 7.78m (25ft 6.25in)
Weight: 18,500kg (40,785lb) loaded
Armament: 1 x 30mm (1.18in) GSh-30 cannon, provision for up to 4500kg (9921lb) of stores

Mikoyan MiG-29, 120th Guards Fighter Aviation Regiment 'Brest', Domna

This MiG-29 'Fulcrum-C' is operated by the 120th Guards IAP. Current plans call for the establishment of a new unit as Domna, the 6982nd Air Base, which will also receive a MiG-29 squadron transferred from the 28th Guards IAP at Andreapol.

Specifications

Crew: 2
Powerplant: 2 x 110.3kN (24,802lb) Lyul'ka AL-21F-3A turbojets
Maximum speed: 2316km/h (1439mph)
Range: 1050km (650 miles)
Service ceiling: 17,500m (57,415ft)
Dimensions: span 17.63m (57ft 10in) spread, 10.36m (34ft) swept; length 24.53m (80ft 5in); height 4.97m (16ft 0.75in)
Weight: 39,700kg (87,520lb) loaded
Armament: 1 x 23mm (0.9in) GSh-23-6 six-barrelled cannon; nine external pylons with provision for up to 8000kg (17,635lb) of stores

Sukhoi Su-24M, 455th Bomber Aviation Regiment, Baltimor

This Su-24M is operated by the 455th BAP, part of the 105th BAD. Normally based at Baltimor, it was stationed at Mozdok for combat operations against Georgia in August 2008.

aircraft. The remaining six armies were arranged geographically, and tactical aircraft were provided to Military Districts. The basic unit was the regiment, these being subordinate to divisions, and divisions in turn to air armies or air corps. The 37th and 61st Air Armies are to be remodelled as commands, answering to Air Force High Command.

In future, Brigades of Air and Space Defence will be assigned to Air and Air Defence Forces Commands. Each brigade will consist of various air bases – as well as air defence missile units and radar sites – and will provide airpower for several Military Districts. In each Military District, a maximum of two air bases will be dedicated to air defence fighters. The new-look Tactical Aviation will be based around 15 squadrons of Su-27s, 14 of Su-25s, 14 of Su-24s, 12 of MiG-31s, and 10 of MiG-29s.

In 2008, it was estimated that the six tactical armies were responsible for 380 MiG-29, 370 Su-27 and 230 MiG-31 fighters, 300 Su-24 bombers, 260

LONG-RANGE AVIATION FRONT-LINE UNITS

37th Strategic Air Army Moscow		
203rd Airborne Refuelling Aviation Regiment	Dyagilyevo	Il-78, Il-78M
22nd Heavy Bomber Aviation Division Engels		
121st Heavy Bomber Aviation Regiment	Engels	Tu-160
184th Heavy Bomber Aviation Regiment	Engels	Tu-95MS
52nd Heavy Bomber Aviation Regiment	Shaikovka	Tu-22M3
840th Heavy Bomber Aviation Regiment	Soltsy	Tu-22M3
326th Heavy Bomber Division Ukrainka		
79th Heavy Bomber Aviation Regiment	Ukrainka	Tu-95MS
182nd Heavy Bomber Aviation Regiment	Ukrainka	Tu-95MS
200th Heavy Bomber Aviation Regiment	Bobruisk	Tu-22M3, Tu-22MR
444th Heavy Bomber Aviation Regiment	Vozdvizhenka	Tu-22M3

Ilyushin Il-76

The backbone of the Russian Air Force's transport fleet is the Il-76. Older Il-76Ms are to be removed from service, leaving the air arm with around 120 examples of the definitive Il-76MD version operating from six different transport air bases.

CENTRALLY SUBORDINATED UNITS		
4th Centre for Combat Training and Aircrew Conversion	Lipetsk	Su-27, Su-27SM, Su-34, Su-25, Su-25SM, Su-39, Su-24M, Su-24M2, MiG-29, MiG-29SMT
344th Centre for Army Aviation Combat Training and Aircrew Conversion	Torzhok	Mi-24, Mi-28, Mi-8, Mi-26, Ka-50
185th Centre for Combat Training and Aircrew Conversion	Astrakhan	MiG-29
2457th Aviation Base for Long-range Airborne Early Aircraft	Ivanovo	A-50, A-50M

Su-25 attack aircraft, plus 100 Su-24MR and 40 MiG-25RB reconnaissance aircraft. Today numbers have dropped, with the Su-24 numerically the most important type, with around 300 in service, followed by over 200 each of the MiG-29, Su-25 and Su-27. In addition, the Russian Air Force maintained in 2008 some 1000 Mi-8, Mi-24 and Mi-26 helicopters, 300 trainers and 250 support aircraft.

Long-Range Aviation Command will have a strength based around approximately 170 Tu-22M3, Tu-95MS and Tu-160 bombers, with front-line assets based at Engels, Shaikovka, Belaya and Ukrainka. Soltsy is due to close and a new base will be established at Belaya, with Tu-22M3/MRs. There are plans afoot to introduce a new strategic bomber, but in the meantime, low-rate production of the Tu-160 has resumed, and Tu-95MS and Tu-160 aircraft

Specifications

Crew: 3
Powerplant: 2 x 1454kW (1950shp) Klimov TV3-117Mt turboshafts
Maximum speed: 260km/h (162mph)
Range: 450km (280 miles)
Service ceiling: 4500m (14,765ft)
Dimensions: rotor diameter 21.29m (69ft 10in); length 18.17m (59ft 7in); height 5.65m (18ft 6in)
Weight: 11,100kg (24,470lb) loaded
Armament: up to 1500kg (3300lb) of disposable stores on six hardpoints, including 57mm (2.24in) S-5 rockets, bombs, or 9M17 Phalanga ATGMs

Mil Mi-8, Army Aviation

Operated by an unknown unit of Army Aviation, the Mi-8 remains the workhorse of the rotary-wing fleet. The type is still being built for Russian use, with the latest orders being for the Mi-8MTV-5 combat transport versions with a rear loading ramp.

Specifications

Crew: 2–3
Powerplant: 2 x 1600kW (2200hp) Isotov TV3-117 turbines
Maximum speed: 335km/h (208mph)
Range: 450km (280 miles)
Service ceiling: 4500m (14,750ft)
Dimensions: span 6.5m (21ft 3in); length 17.5m (57ft 4in); height 6.5m (21ft 3in)
Weight: 12,000kg (26,500lb) loaded
Armament: 1 x 12.7mm (0.5in) Yakushev-Borzov gun, 4 x S-8 80mm (3.15in) rocket pods or up to 3460kg (7612lb) of rockets or missiles

Mil Mi-24, 27th Aviation Group, Army Aviation, Pristina

This Mi-24 was operated on behalf of KFOR (Kosovo Force), based at Pristina Airport, in 2000. Russian Air Force Mi-24s have also been deployed in a peacekeeping capacity to Freetown in Sierra Leone.

Mikoyan MiG-31B, 174th Guards Fighter Aviation Regiment, Monchegorsk

The MiG-31 remains the most powerful long-range interceptor available to Russia. This example was operated by the 174th GvIAP in around 1998. Part of the Leningrad Military District, this unit was disbanded in 2001.

Specifications

Crew: 2
Powerplant: 2 x 91kN (lb) thrust D-30F6 Turbofan
Maximum speed at altitude 17,500m (57,415ft): 2.83 Mach (3000km/h; 1864mph)
Range: 3300km (2050 miles)
Service ceiling: 20,600m (67,585ft)
Dimensions: span 13.464m (44ft 2in); length 22.69m (74ft 5in); height 6.15m (20ft 2in)
Weight: 46,200kg (101,854lb) loaded
Armament: 1 x 23mm (0.90in) GSh-6-23M six-barrel gun, various anti-aircraft missiles

Tupolev Tu-22M3

A highly capable asset (with no direct Western counterpart), older examples of the Tu-22M3 are already being withdrawn, and many have gone into storage. The type is also being transferred from Naval Aviation to Long-Range Aviation Command.

are being upgraded. By 2025-30, Russia hopes to double the fleet of front-line Tu-160s to 30 aircraft.

Military Transport Aviation Command will inherit the seven regiments of the 61st Air Army, (two will be disbanded). Fixed-wing transport strength will thereafter be focused at Ivanovo, Pskov, Seshtsha, Tver, Klin, Taganrog and Orenburg, with helicopters resident at Troitsk and Tshebenki.

Since 2002 Army Aviation has been part of the Air Force, with helicopter regiments incorporated as independent units within its structure. Russian Naval Aviation, headquartered in Moscow, divides

FIGHTER AVIATION REGIMENTS (IAP)		
9th IAP	Kilp-Yavr	Su-27
3rd IAP	Krymsk	Su-27
14th IAP	Khalino	MiG-29, MiG-29SMT
19th IAP	Millerovo	MiG-29
22nd IAP	Uglovaya	Su-27SM
23rd IAP	Dzemgi	Su-27SM
28th IAP	Andreapol	MiG-29
31st IAP	Zernograd	MiG-29
120th IAP	Domna	MiG-29
159th IAP	Besovets	Su-27
177th IAP	Lodeynoye Polye	Su-27
458th IAP	Savvatiya	MiG-31
530th IAP	Chuguyevka	MiG-31
712th IAP	Kansk	MiG-31
611th IAP	Dorokhovo	Su-27
764th IAP	Bolshoye Savino	MiG-31
790th IAP	Khotilovo	MiG-31

BOMBER AVIATION REGIMENTS (BAP)		
1st BAP	Lebyazhye	Su-24M
2nd BAP	Dzhida	Su-24M
67th BAP	Siverskii	Su-24M
277th BAP	Khurba	Su-24M
302nd BAP	Pereyaslavka	Su-24M, Su-24M2
455th BAP	Baltimor	Su-24M
523rd BAP	Vozhaevka	Su-24M, Su-24MR
559th BAP	Morozovsk	Su-24M
722nd BAP	Smuravyevo	Su-24M
959th BAP	Yeisk	Su-24M

Specifications

Crew: 1
Powerplant: 2 x 44.1kN (9921lb) Tumanskii R-195 turbojets
Maximum speed: 975km/h (606mph)
Range: 750km (466 miles)
Service ceiling: 7000m (22,965ft)
Dimensions: span 14.36m (47ft 1.5in); length 15.53m (50ft 11.5in); height 4.8m (15ft 9in)
Weight: 17,600kg (38,800lb) loaded
Armament: 1 x 30mm (1.18in) GSh-30-2 cannon; eight external pylons with provision for up to 4400kg (9700lb) of stores

Sukhoi Su-25, 899th Assault Aviation Regiment, Mozdok

Deployed from its home base of Buturlinovka to Mozdok during the conflict in Georgia in August 2008, this Su-25 was hit and badly damaged by a man-portable surface-to-air missile during the conflict. The 899th ShAP is subordinate to the 105th Assault Aviation Division.

Specifications

Crew: 1
Powerplant: 2 x 175kN (39,360lb thrust) unnamed NPO Saturn and FNPTS MMPP Salyut engine
Maximum speed: Mach 2.45 (2600km/h; 1615mph) at 17,000m (45,000ft)
Range: 5500km (3417 miles)
Service ceiling: 20,000m (65,616ft)
Dimensions: span 14m (46.6ft); length 19.8m (65.9ft); height 6.05m (19.8ft)
Weight: 26,000kg (57,320lb) loaded
Armament: No guns on prototype but provision for a cannon and two internal hardpoint bays

Sukhoi T-50, Prototype

Hopes for the future of the Russian Air Force's combat fleet rest with the T-50, which has been developed by Sukhoi under the Perspektivnyi Aviatsionnyi Kompleks Frontovoi Aviatsii, or Future Air Complex for Tactical Aviation initiative. Illustrated is the first prototype, which made its first flight in February 2010, before receiving this disruptive camouflage pattern.

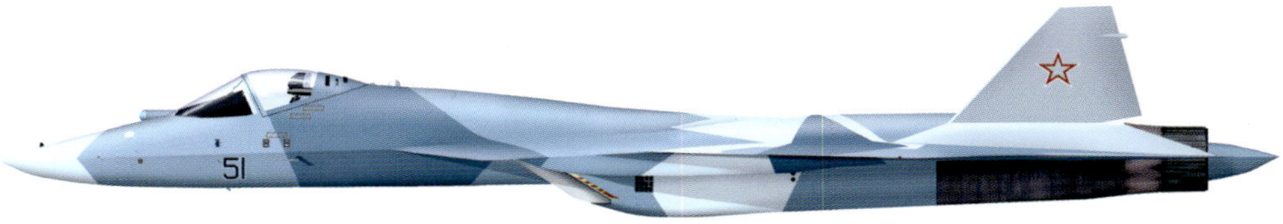

its assets between the Northern, Pacific, Baltic, Caspian and Black Sea Fleets. It also includes a number of direct-reporting units, and a carrier-capable regiment, the 279th OKIAP, that deploys Su-33s and Su-25UTGs aboard the carrier *Admiral Kuznetsov*. The Ka-27 is the primary shipborne helicopter, while land-based aircraft include Su-24 bombers/reconnaissance aircraft, Tu-142 and Il-38 patrol aircraft, Be-12 amphibians and Mi-14 helicopters, plus transports and trainers.

RECONNAISSANCE AVIATION REGIMENTS (RAP)		
11th RAP	Marinovka	Su-24MR
47th RAP	Shatalovo	Su-24MR, MiG-25RB
98th RAP	Monchegorsk	Su-24MR, MiG-25RB
313th RAP	Bada	Su-24MR
799th RAP	Varfolomyeevka	Su-24MR

ASSAULT AVIATION REGIMENTS (SHAP)		
18th ShAP	Galenki	Su-25
187th ShAP	Chernigovka	Su-25
266th ShAP	Step	Su-25
368th ShAP	Budyonnovsk	Su-25
461st ShAP	Krasnodar	Su-25
899th ShAP	Buturlinovka	Su-25
960th ShAP	Primorsko-Akhtarsk	Su-25

Serbia

Serbian Air Force

The Vazduhoplovstvo i protivvazdusna odbrana (ViPVO, or Serbian Air Force) emerged from the Yugoslavian civil war and the NATO bombing campaign of 1999 to be re-established in 2006.

Specifications

Crew: 1

Powerplant: 1 x 35.59kN (8000lb) Armstrong-Siddeley Sapphire turbojet engine

Maximum speed: 144km/h (710mph)

Range: 689km (490 miles)

Service ceiling: 15,240m (50,000ft)

Dimensions: span 10.26m (33ft 8in); length 13.98m (45ft 10.5in); height 4.02m (13ft 2in)

Weight: 8501kg (18,742lb) loaded

Armament: 4 x 30mm (1.18in) Aden cannon; up to 2722kg (6000lb) of bombs or rockets

Mikoyan MiG-29, 101st Fighter Squadron 'Knights', 204th Aviation Base, Batajnica

One of only four survivors out of the original 16 aircraft, this overhauled MiG-29 is now in service alongside MiG-21s at Batajnica, near Belgrade.

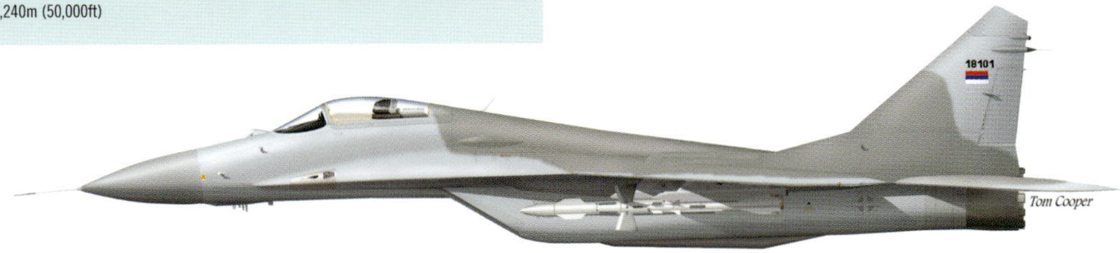

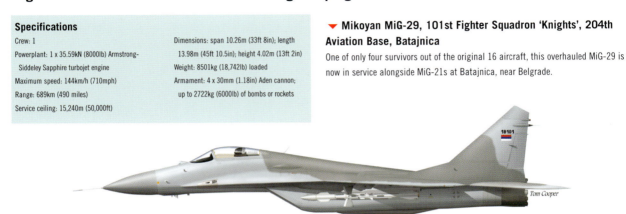

The equipment of the ViPVO is mainly inherited from the former Socialist Federal Republic of Yugoslavia's air arm, and is shared between two air bases: the 98th Aviation Base at Ladevci-Kraljevo and the 204th Aviation Base at Batajnica. The 98th Aviation Base incorporates the 241st Fighter-Bomber Squadron, 714th Combat Helicopter Squadron and the 2nd Reconnaissance Flight. The 119th Combat Helicopter Squadron operates from Nis under 98th Aviation Base command. Aircraft types comprise the J-22 Orao, G-4 Super Galeb, Utva 75, Gazelle, Mi-8 and An-2. At Batajnica are the 101st Fighter Squadron, 252nd Composite Squadron, 138th Composite Transport Squadron and the 2nd Reconnaissance Flight, equipped with the MiG-21, MiG-29, An-26, Mi-8, Yak-40, Utva 75, G-4 and Gazelle. Lasta 95 primary trainers are due to replace the Utva 75s in the same role.

Mikoyan-Gurevich MiG-21bis

Serbian MiG-21bis fighters and two-seat MiG-21UM combat trainers are flown by the 204th Aviation Base's 101st Fighter Squadron, alongside MiG-29s. The MiG-21s are used for Quick Reaction Alert interception duty, for which they are armed with R-60 missiles and onboard cannon.

Slovakia

Slovak Air Force and Air Defence Force

The Velitelstvo Vzdusnych Sil was formed in 1993 after the division of Czechoslovakia, and received a proportion of the former Czechoslovakian Air Force inventory.

THE MAJOR BASES of the Slovak Air Force are Sliac, Malacky-Kuchyna and Presov. Headquarters, and the Air Operation Control Centre, are at Zvolen. The air arm has reported to NATO since Slovakia joined the alliance in 2004. Sliac is the Slovak fighter base, and is home to the Mixed Air Wing. This organization accommodates a squadron of 12 upgraded MiG-29s (including a pair of two-seaters) and a squadron of 15 L-39 jet trainers. At Malacky-Kuchyna can be found the Air Transport Wing, responsible for a single squadron of two An-26s (due to be replaced by C-27Js), and one of L-410s in various configurations. Helicopter operations are centred at Presov, from where the Mixed Helicopter Wing hosts three squadrons equipped with the Mi-24, Mi-17 and Mi-2 respectively. A SAR unit with Mi-8/17s is also active at Presov. Air Force structure also includes an air defence missile brigade at Nitra.

Slovenia

Slovenian Air Defence and Aviation Brigade

Part of NATO since 2004, Slovenia maintains a small but well-equipped air arm that was established following its declaration of independence from the Yugoslav Federation in 1991.

WITH NATO RESPONSIBLE for air defence of Slovenia, the air arm focuses on support of the ground forces, SAR and training. The three flying units comprise the 15th Helicopter Battalion, the Flight School, and the Air Transport Section. The Flight School at Cerklje ob Krki is responsible for basic and advanced training, with Zlin 143, Zlin 242, Bell 206 and PC-9 aircraft. The Air Transport Section, also at Cerklje ob Krki, uses two PC-6s and one L-410. Previously, the 15th Helicopter Battalion operated from Brnik, with a fleet of eight Bell 412 and four AS532 helicopters. With the exception of a single SAR Bell 412 at Brnik, all other helicopters have now moved to Cerklje ob Krki.

Specifications

Crew: 1–2	Service ceiling: 11,580m (37,992ft)
Powerplant: 1 x 857kW (1149hp) Pratt & Whitney Canada PT6A-62 turboprop	Dimensions: span 10.11m (33ft 2in); length 10.69m (35ft 1in); height 3.26m (10ft 8in)
Maximum speed: 593km/h (368mph)	
Range: 1593km (990 miles)	Weight: 3200kg (7055lb) loaded

Pilatus PC-9M, Air Force Military School, Cerklje ob Krki

Slovenia's PC-9 fleet includes three standard aircraft and nine PC-9M Hudournik (Swift) aircraft, upgraded by RADOM of Israel and featuring head-up displays, weapons systems and advanced communications.

Ukraine

Ukrainian Air Force, Army Aviation and Navy

Created through the amalgamation of the former Air Force and Air Defence Force, the Air Force of the Armed Forces of Ukraine is complemented by separate Army and Navy air components.

Specifications

Crew: 1

Powerplant: 2 x 81.4kN (18,298lb) Sarkisov RD-33 turbofans

Maximum speed: 2443km/h (1518mph)

Range: 1500km (932 miles)

Service ceiling: 17,000m (55,775ft)

Dimensions: span 11.36m (37ft 3.75in); length (including probe) 17.32m (56ft 10in); height 7.78m (25ft 6.25in)

Weight: 18,500kg (40,785lb) loaded

Armament: 1 x 30mm (1.18in) GSh-30 cannon, provision for up to 4500kg (9921lb) of stores

▼ Mikoyan MiG-29, 9th Fighter Aviation Regiment, Ozerne

This MiG-29 of the 9th IAP is based at Ozerne, in the Zhitomyr region. The unit is part of Air Command Centre. Of a reported 80 MiG-29s of various subtypes in Ukrainian service, a handful have been locally upgraded to MiG-29MU1 standard, with improved weapons and avionics.

HEADQUARTERED AT VINNITSA, the Ukrainian Air Force is organized on the basis of three air commands: the Air Command South headquartered at Odessa; Air Command West (Lviv); and Air Command Centre (Vasilkiv); plus a tactical command in Crimea. Each command is responsible for bases and their attendant regiments. From its original strength of around 2800 aircraft and helicopters in 1992, the air arm has been considerable downsized, and in 2003 numbered just under 400 combat aircraft in 10 regiments. By 2015, a force of 190 aircraft of all types is projected.

Air defence is maintained by one fighter regiment with Su-27s (at Mirgorod, with another possibly at Ozerne) and four with MiG-29s (Belbek, Ivano-Frankivsk, Ozerne and Vasilkiv). A bomber regiment equipped with Su-24Ms is located at Starokostyantiniv, along with a squadron of Su-24MRs, while two attack regiments fly the Su-25 (Chortkiv and Kulbakino).

Transport is handled by the 7th Military Transport Aviation Division, which includes a single regiment equipped with the Il-76 at Melitopol. Other transport types are based at Borispol and Gavryshevka, and include An-12s, An-24/26/30s, a pair of Tu-134s, and Mi-8 helicopters.

Primary training is conducted by the Kharkiv Institute, with three aviation colleges, and a combat training centre. Tuition begins on the Yak-52, students later progressing to the L-39 at Chuguyiv. Air force Mi-2s train Army Aviation aircrews.

Army Aviation

Ukrainian Army Aviation consists of three brigades of two mixed helicopter squadrons each. Assets are divided geographically between two commands: Army Command West (HQ Lviv) and South (HQ Odessa). Army Command West incorporates the 3rd Brigade at Brody and the 7th Brigade at Novi Kaliniv. Army Command South is responsible for the 11th Brigade at Kherson and two independent squadrons. Types in service comprise various subtypes of Mi-8/9 and Mi-24, plus heavylift Mi-26s. Certain squadrons are assigned to a Rapid Reaction Force, and others have deployed on international peacekeeping assignments.

The Ukrainian Navy maintains a single major aviation base at Saki, from where it operates a mixed brigade consisting of Ka-25, Ka-27/29 and Mi-14 maritime helicopters, plus An-12s, An-26s and Mi-8s for transport. There is also a squadron of Be-12 maritime patrol amphibians in use.

MONGOLIA
KAZAKHSTAN
MONGOLIA
UZBEKISTAN
KYRGYZSTAN
GEORGIA
ARMENIA
AZERBAIJAN
TURKMENISTAN
TAJIKISTAN
SYRIA
LEBANON
ISRAEL
IRAQ
IRAN
AFGHANISTAN
JORDAN
KUWAIT
BAHRAIN
QATAR
SAUDI ARABIA
U.A.E.
OMAN
YEMEN
ARABIAN SEA
INDIAN OCEAN

Chapter 5

Central and Western Asia and the Middle East

Militarily, the region of central and western Asia is dominated by the Middle East, with its history of conflict and its position as the most profitable arms market in the world. This is reflected in its highly equipped air forces, although a very different situation is found among the former Soviet states further to the east, and Afghanistan, scene to successive conflicts over the last three decades. In addition to the continuing conflict in Iraq, and the ongoing Israel-Palestine confrontation, airpower has recently been deployed in combat by Lebanon, Saudi Arabia and Yemen, as well as in Georgia to the north of the region.

Afghanistan

Afghan National Army Air Corps

Following the launch of Coalition military operations in Afghanistan in 2001 and the subsequent collapse of the Taliban, the Afghan National Army Air Corps has been established with U.S. help.

With a strength based around 36 Mi-17 and Mi-35 helicopters and eight An-26/32 and G222 fixed-wing transport aircraft, the ANAAC is divided into two wings – in Kabul in the north, and in Kandahar in the south. By 2009, the ANAAC had 3000 personnel en route to its goal of over 7000.

Specifications

Crew: 1

Powerplant: 1 x 73.5kN (16,535lb) Tumanskii R-25 turbojet

Maximum speed: 2229km/h (1385mph)

Range: 1160km (721 miles)

Service ceiling: 17,500m (57,400ft)

Dimensions: span 7.15m (23ft 5.5in); length (including probe) 15.76m (51ft 8.5in); height 4.1m (13ft 5.5in)

Weight: 10,400kg (22,925lb) loaded

Armament: 1 x 23mm (0.9in) GSh-23 twin-barrel cannon in underbelly pack, provision for about 1500kg (3307kg) of stores

Mikoyan-Gurevich MiG-21bis, ANAAC

The ANAAC operates a handful of MiG-21s for training purposes. Currently, the focus of ANAAC activities is on supply missions between military installations.

Armenia

Armenian Air Force

Economic problems have stifled the development of the Armenian air force, which during the 1990s saw combat against Azerbaijan over the disputed region of Nagorno-Karabakh.

At the end of the Cold War, Armenia officially possessed just three combat aircraft and 13 combat helicopters. Armenia's air arm now includes a handful of An-2, An-24/32 and Il-76 transports, MiG-25PD, Su-25 and L-39 jets, plus Mi-8 and Mi-24 helicopters, and Yak 18 and Yak-52 trainers.

Azerbaijan

Azeri Air Force

The Azeri air force was left with only a handful of combat types following the collapse of the USSR, but has expanded to include fixed- and rotary-wing equipment from a variety of sources.

The backbone of the Azeri air force is provided by a small number of MiG-29 fighters and Su-17M attack aircraft, supported by larger numbers of Su-24s, Su-25s and L-39s, the latter used for both light attack and training. The helicopter fleet is based around Mi-8s and Mi-24s.

Bahrain

Royal Bahraini Air Force

Independent since 1971, the small kingdom of Bahrain is defended by a modern fleet of aircraft, with RBAF operations concentrated at air bases at Isa and Manama.

Fighter operations for the RBAF (formerly known as the Bahrain Ameri Air Force – BAAF) are focused at the purpose-built Isa air base, home to No. 6 Squadron with F-5E/F jets, and two F-16C/D units (Nos 1 and 2 Squadrons). The most recent Bahraini F-16s are Block 40D aircraft procured under the Peace Crown II deal in 1998.

Flight training is conducted at Isa air base on six Hawk Mk129s ordered in 2003, from which students progress after time on Firefly primary trainers.

The RBAF helicopter fleet at Rifa'a comprises AH-1E attack helicopters, supported by AB212s, Bell 412s (on order) and BO105s. A total of three UH-60s provide a medium-lift helicopter capability, with another eight examples on order. Single examples of the BAe 146 and S-92 serve in the VIP transport role.

Manama air base (part of Bahrain International Airport), and located on Muharraq Island, was formerly the BAAF's main fighter base, but today supports the Bahrain Amiri Royal Flight.

Sikorsky S-92A

The RBAF operates a single S-92 as a VIP transport, seen here landing on board the aircraft carrier USS *Dwight D. Eisenhower.* The helicopter was purchased new from the manufacturer in 2008 and now serves with No. 9 Squadron, part of the Helicopter Wing at Rifa'a air base.

Specifications

Crew: 1
Powerplant: 1 x 126.7kN (28,500lb) thrust Pratt & Whitney F100-PW-229 afterburning turbofan
Maximum speed: 2177km/h (1353mph)
Range: 3862km (2400 miles)
Service ceiling: 15,240m (49,000ft)
Dimensions: span 9.45m (31ft); length 15.09m (49ft 6in); height 5.09m (16ft 8in)
Weight: 19,187kg (42,300lb) loaded
Armament: 1 x GE M61A1 20mm (0.79in) multi-barrelled cannon, wingtip missile stations; 7 external hardpoints with provision for up to 9276kg (20,450lb) of stores

Lockheed Martin F-16C Fighting Falcon, No. 1 Fighter Squadron, Manama AB

F-16C 90-0031 was delivered to the RBAF in July 1990, part of an initial order for eight F-16Cs and four F-16Ds placed in 1987. The two F-16 squadrons combine with the F-5E/F squadron to form the 1st Fighter Wing.

Georgia

GEORGIAN AIR FORCE

Following the August 2008 war fought against Russia over the disputed region of South Ossetia, the precise status of the Georgian Air Force must now be considered uncertain.

ESTABLISHED FOLLOWING THE demise of the USSR, the Georgian Air Force saw action in the 1990s after the breakaway republic of Abkhazia declared independence. Today, the air force includes around 3000 personnel, fixed- and rotary-wing aircraft and air defence missile units. Key air bases are located at Alekseyevka and Marneuli. The inventory includes Su-25 (including upgraded Su-25KM) attack aircraft, some of which were locally built in Tbilisi, L-39 jet trainers, Yak-52 piston-engined trainers, An-2, An-24 and Tu-134 transports, as well as Mi-2, Mi-8, Mi-14 Mi-24 and UH-1H helicopters, the latter provided as military aid by Turkey and the USA. A number of losses were sustained during the course of the brief South Ossetian War, both to Russian forces and through 'friendly fire', and reports suggest that the air force may be integrated within the structure of Georgia's land forces in the future.

Iraq

IRAQI AIR FORCE

In the wake of the U.S.-led invasion in 2003, the Iraqi Air Force is being rebuilt, with a focus on counter-insurgency and transport assets to support efforts against the insurgency campaign.

THE NEW-LOOK IRAQI air arm was re-established by the Coalition Provisional Authority (CPA), and now includes Mi-17V-5/171s used for special operations, King Air 350ER and Cessna 208 transports, some with ISR mission payloads, AT-6B COIN aircraft, and armed Bell 407 helicopters.

There are four active air bases (New Al Muthanna, Kirkuk, Basrah, and Taji), with five more bases under construction. Aircraft are operated by nine squadrons, with three more being established. The current squadrons comprise three for reconnaissance, one fixed-wing training, one helicopter training, one transport, one utility helicopter, one transport helicopter, and one special operations squadron.

Specifications

Crew: 5
Powerplant: 4 x 3021kW (4050hp) Allison T56-A-7A turboprop engines
Maximum speed: 547km/h (340mph)
Range: 3896km (2420 miles)
Service ceiling: 7010m (23,000ft)
Dimensions: span 40.4m (132ft 7in); length 29.8m (97ft 9in); height 11.7m (38ft 6in)
Weight: 79,375kg (175,000lb) loaded

Lockheed C-130E Hercules, No. 23 Transport Squadron, New Al Muthanna AB

Three Iraqi Air Force C-130Es are due to be joined by six new C-130Js, with deliveries planned between 2012 and 2014.

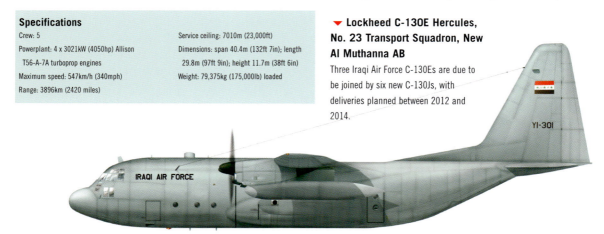

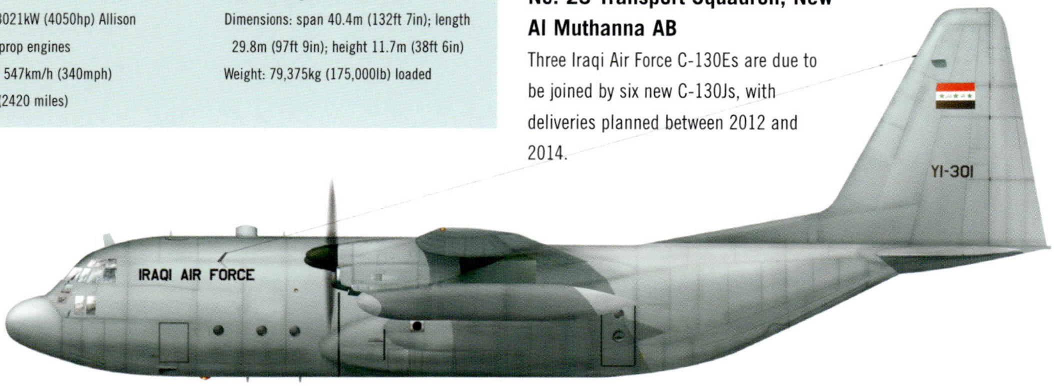

Iran

Islamic Republic of Iran Air Force, Naval and Army Aviation

Once the most powerful air arm in the Middle East, today's IRIAF remains a potent and increasingly self-sufficient force, backed up by the Islamic Revolution Guards Corps Air Force.

The primary role of the IRIAF is to defend Iranian airspace, but the air arm can also undertake offensive operations and power projection beyond its own borders. The IRGCAF air arm, meanwhile, focuses on close support for the Islamic Revolution Guards Corps. Naval aviation is provided by the Islamic Republic of Iran Naval Aviation, while army airpower is operated by a separate organization.

▲ **Lockheed C-130H Hercules**

Iran maintains a fleet of around 20 C-130E/Hs, which are mainly based at TFB.1 Mehrabad, the centre of IRIAF tactical transport operations, with other examples observed at Shiraz. Reflecting the importance of the airlifter within the IRIAF is the fact that much of the fleet is being overhauled locally.

The IRIAF strike force is headed by 32 Su-24MKs used by two squadrons. The F-4E is the most important fighter type, with at least six squadrons equipped with about 64 examples. Long-range missions by Su-24s and F-4s are supported by Boeing 707-3J9C tankers, which also have a designated airborne command post role.

Air defence force

In line with a new defensive posture, the IRIAF is fielding a larger number of dispersed air defence squadrons, with assets able to be stationed around some 60 airfields across the country. The premier interceptor remains the F-14A, 44 of which are available within four squadrons. Supporting the Tomcat in the air defence role are approximately 12 F-4Ds, some 20 MiG-29s, and 16 Mirage F1s, although the latter may be used mainly for training.

Additional combat assets comprise around 60 F-5E/Fs and some 35 Shenyang F-7Ns, which serve as advanced trainers, with a secondary interception role.

The IRGCAF is the organic air arm of the IRGC, and uses transport aircraft to deploy rapid-reaction forces, and combat types for close air support. IRGCAF equipment includes 10 Su-25 attack jets, four Il-76 and 11 An-74 transports, some 13 EMB-

Specifications

Crew: 2
Powerplant: 2 x 92.9kN (20,900lb) Pratt & Whitney TF30-P-412A turbofan engines
Maximum speed: 2517km/h (1564mph)
Range: about 3220km (2000 miles)
Service ceiling: 17,070m (56,000ft)
Dimensions: span 19.55m (64ft 1.5in) unswept; 11.65m (38ft 2.5in) swept; length 19.1m (62ft 8in); height 4.88m (16ft)
Weight: 33,724kg (74,349lb) loaded
Armament: 1 x 20mm (0.79in) M61A1 Vulcan rotary cannon; external pylons for a combination of AIM-7 Sparrow medium range air-to-air missiles, AIM-9 medium range air-to-air missiles, and AIM-54 Phoenix long range air-to-air missiles

▼ **Grumman F-14A Tomcat, TFB.8 Shahid Baba'ie**

Recently overhauled by Iranian Aircraft Industries at Mehrabad, F-14A 3-6073 is currently serving at TFB.8 Shahid Baba'ie AB, near Esfahan. The aircraft can now be armed with the AIM-23C Sejil air-to-air missile, a locally manufactured variant of the I-HAWK surface-to-air missile.

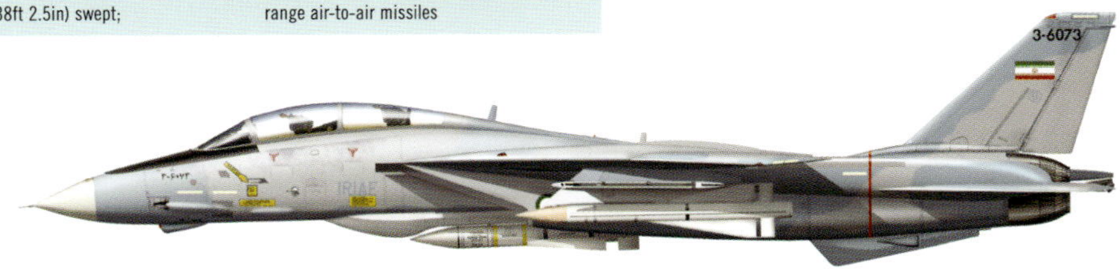

Specifications

Crew: 2
Powerplant: 2 x 79.6kN (17,900lb) General Electric J79-GE-17 turbojets
Maximum speed: 2390km/h (1485mph)
Range: 817km (1750 miles)
Service ceiling: 19,685m (60,000ft)
Dimensions: span 11.7m (38ft 5in); length 17.76m (58ft 3in); height 4.96m (16ft 3in)
Weight: 26,308kg (58,000lb) loaded
Armament: 1 x 20mm (0.78in) M61A1 Vulcan cannon and 4 x AIM-7 Sparrow recessed under fuselage or other weapons up to 1370kg (3020lb) on centreline pylon; four wing pylons for two AIM-7, or four AIM-9

McDonnell Douglas F-4E Phantom II, 61st TFS, TFB.6 Bushehr

This F-4E is depicted carrying the indigenous Sattar-3 laser-guided missile together with an associated laser-marker. Phantoms serve alongside F-14s at Bushehr, in one of Iran's most strategically vital areas, and at least two examples of each fighter are kept on permanent alert at the base.

ISLAMIC REPUBLIC OF IRAN AIR FORCE COMBAT AND TRANSPORT UNITS

TFB.1 Tehran-Mehrabad

11th TFS	MiG-29, MiG-29UB
11th and 12th TS	C-130H
Unknown TS	Boeing 747-2J9F
Unknown TS	Boeing 707-3J9C

* a total of five Transport Squadrons operate from Mehrabad.

TFB.2 Tabriz

21st and 22nd TFS	F-5E/F
23rd TFS	MiG-29, MiG-29UB

* a total of four Tactical Fighter Squadrons operate from Tabriz.

TFB.3 Nojeh, Hamedan

31st, 32nd, 33rd TFS	F-4E, RF-4E
Unknown TFS	F-4E

TFB.4 Defzul-Vahdati

41st, 42nd, 43rd TFS	F-5E/F

TFB.5 Ardestani

51st, 52nd, 53rd TFS	F-7N/FT-7

TFB.6 Bushehr

61st and 62nd TFS	F-4E
Unknown TFS	F-14A

TFB.7 Dastghaib, Shiraz

71st and 72nd TFS	Su-24MK
Unknown squadron	P-3F

TFB.8 Shahid Baba'ie

81st, 82nd and 83rd TFS	F-14A

TFB.9 Bandar Abbas

91st or 92nd TFS	F-4E

TFB.10 Kangan (Chabahar)

101st TFS	F-4D
Unknown TFS	F-4D

TFB.12 Asyaee, Masjed-e Soleyman

No permanently assigned units

TFB.13 Gayem al-Mohammad

Unknown TFS	type unknown

TFB.14 Hashemi Nejad

Two fighter squadrons	Mirage F1EQ

Islamic Revolution Guards Corps Air Force Combat Units

Transport Wing	Il-76MD, An-74TK	Mehrabad
Helicopter Wing Fighter Wing	Su-25K/UBK, EMB-312	Shiraz and Zahedan
	Mi-171, AH-1	Mehrabad

312 Tucano turboprop trainers, approximately 30 Mi-171 assault helicopters, and AH-1 attack helicopters.

Although the exact nature of the IRIAF's order of battle remains unknown, organization is based around Tactical Fighter Bases (TFBs). Each TFB has a number of flying squadrons permanently attached. The TFB operates according to a wing structure, which may include up to six squadrons. Squadrons are assigned to TFBs as required, with TFBs therefore having a flexible, mixed-force structure.

Islamic Republic of Iran Naval Aviation maintains a force of fixed-wing types and helicopters, with AB205s, AB206s, AB212s, ASH-3Ds, Falcon 20s, F27s and Shrike Commanders likely operating from bases at Bushehr, Shiraz and Bandar Abbas.

Islamic Republic of Iran Army Aviation primarily operates helicopters, including AB205s, AB206s, AH-1s, Bell 214s and CH-47s, with fixed-wing assets including O-2s. Bases are believed to include Bakhtaran, Isfahan, Kerman and Tehran.

▲ Lockheed P-3F Orion

The P-3F variant was developed specifically for the then Imperial Iranian Air Force. Four examples are reported to remain in service in the maritime patrol role, and these have been outfitted with locally developed electro-optical sensors and are believed to have been equipped to launch Chinese-made anti-ship missiles.

Specifications

Crew: 1
Powerplant: 2 x 22.2kN (5000lb) General Electric J85-GE-21B turbojets
Maximum speed: 1741km/h (1082mph)
Range: 306km (190 miles)
Service ceiling: 15,790m (51,800ft)
Dimensions: span 8.13m (26ft 8in); length 14.45m (47ft 4.75in); height 4.07m (13ft 4.25in)
Weight: 11,214kg (24,722lb) loaded
Armament: 2 x 20mm (0.78in) cannon; 2 x air-to-air missiles, five external pylons with provision for 3175kg (7000lb) of stores, including missiles, bombs and ECM pods

▼ IAMI (Northrop) F-5E Saeqeh, TFB.2 Tabriz

The former first prototype for the Saeqeh programme, this jet is now in service at TFB.2. Iran has developed two indigenous upgrades of the F-5E/F, the Saeqeh and Azarakhsh, apparently with the eventual aim of launching local production of a reverse-engineered version.

Specifications

Crew: 2
Powerplant: 2 x 110.3kN (24,802lb) Lyul'ka AL-21F-3A turbojets
Maximum speed: 2316km/h (1439mph)
Combat radius: 1050km (650 miles)
Service ceiling: 17,500m (57,415ft)
Dimensions: span 17.63m (57ft 10in) spread, 10.36m (34ft) swept; length 24.53m (80ft 5in); height 4.97m (16ft 0.75in)
Weight: 39,700kg (87,520lb) loaded
Armament: 1 x 23mm (0.9in) GSh-23-6 six-barrelled cannon; nine external pylons with provision for up to 8000kg (17,635lb) of stores

▼ Sukhoi Su-24MK, 71st TFS, TFB.7 Shiraz

3-6853 is one of 24 ex-Iraqi Air Force Su-24s that were evacuated to Iran from Iraq in 1991. Another 12 Su-24s were purchased directly from the USSR in 1990. Armed with indigenous and Chinese-made weapons, the IRIAF Su-24s can be refuelled in flight by 707 and 747 tankers.

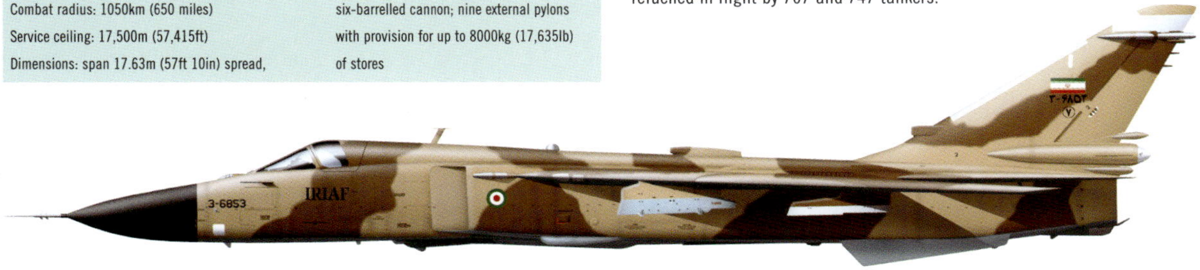

Israel

Israeli Air and Space Force

One of the world's most experienced air arms in terms of combat operations, the IASF occupies a unique position in the Middle East, operating some of the world's most advanced warplanes.

ONCE DESIGNATED the Israeli Defence Force/Air Force, the Israeli air arm was renamed in 2005 to reflect its dual air and space mission. Originally established in 1947, as the air component of the Jewish resistance movement, the antecedents of today's IASF fought with distinction in successive Middle East conflicts during which the very existence of Israel was under threat. The constant threat of terrorist action and insurgency in the Gaza Strip and Golan Heights, combined with geopolitical tensions within the region, ensure that the IASF remains at a high level of readiness.

The backbone of the IASF's combat units are numerous versions and subversions of the F-15 and F-16, the total quantity of both types amounting to around 360 aircraft. They are responsible for air defence, long-range strike and interdiction duties. The acquisition of new types has added the F-15I and F-16I strike aircraft (both of which were developed to meet specific Israeli requirements), Beech 200, special missions Gulfstream 550s (comprising the Eitam airborne early warning and Shavit special electronic missions aircraft), AH-64D attack helicopter and Eitan UAV to the IASF fleet, while older aircraft are being upgraded locally. Most combat types are equipped with Israeli-produced electronic warfare equipment and weaponry. The 20 AH-64Ds join an

Specifications

Crew: 1
Powerplant: 2 x 77.62kN (17,450lbf) (dry thrust) Pratt & Whitney F100-PW-220 turbofans
Maximum speed: 2655km/h (1650mph)
Range: 5550km (3450 miles)
Service ceiling: 20,000m (65,000ft)
Dimensions: span 13.05m (42ft 9.75in); length 19.43in (63ft 9in); height 5.63m (18ft 5in)
Weight: 20,200kg (44,500lb) loaded
Armament: 1 x 20mm (0.79in) M61A1 cannon, provision for 7300kg (16,000lb) of stores

McDonnell Douglas F-15C Eagle, 148 Squadron, Tel Nof

Israeli F-15C serial 640, nicknamed 'Commando', was active during 1982–85 before being re-serialled as 840. As originally coded, it was officially credited with 3.5 victories in the early 1980s (although six kill markings were originally applied, as seen here). It now serves with 106 Squadron.

Specifications

Crew: 1
Powerplant: 1 x 126.7kN (28,500lb) thrust Pratt & Whitney F100-PW-229 afterburning turbofan
Maximum speed: 2177km/h (1353mph)
Range: 3862km (2400 miles)
Service ceiling: 15,240m (49,000ft)
Dimensions: span 9.45m (31ft); length 15.09m (49ft 6in); height 5.09m (16ft 8in)
Weight: 19,187kg (42,300lb) loaded
Armament: 1 x GE M61A1 20mm (0.79in) cannon, wingtip missile stations; seven external hardpoints with provision for up to 9276kg (20,450lb) of stores

General Dynamics F-16C Fighting Falcon, 110 Squadron 'The Knights of the North', Ramat David

This F-16C Block 30 wears one kill marking associated with the destruction of a Hezbollah Ababil UAV in August 2006. The jet carries a mixed air-to-air load of AIM-9 Sidewinder and (underwing) Python 4 missiles.

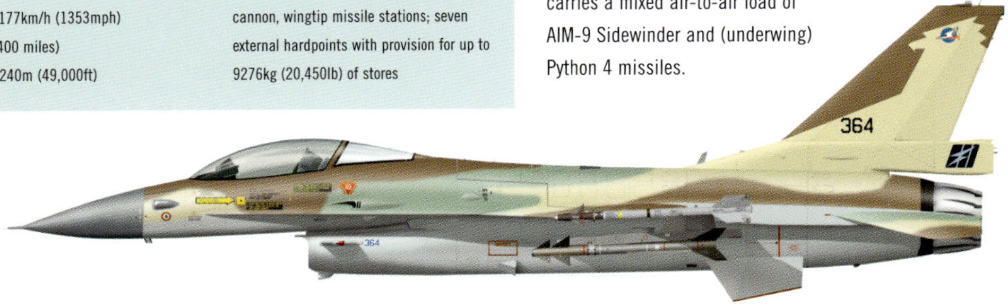

ISRAELI AIR AND SPACE FORCE

F-15 Units

69 Squadron	F-15I	Hatzerim, Southern Command
106 Squadron	F-15B/C/D	Tel Nof, Central Command
133 Squadron	F-15B/C/D	Tel Nof, Central Command
601/FTC	F-15A/B/C/D/I	Tel Nof, Central Command

F-16 Units

101 Squadron	F-16C	Hatzor, Central Command
105 Squadron	F-16D	Hatzor, Central Command
107 Squadron	F-16I	Hatzerim, Central Command
109 Squadron	F-16D	Ramat David, Northern Command
110 Squadron	F-16C	Ramat David, Northern Command
115 Squadron	F-16A/B	Ovda, Southern Command
116 Squadron	F-16A/B	Nevatim, Southern Command
117 Squadron	F-16C	Ramat David, Northern Command
119 Squadron	F-16I	Ramon, Southern Command
140 Squadron	F-16A/B	Nevatim, Southern Command
201 Squadron	F-16I	Ramon, Southern Command
253 Squadron	F-16I	Ramon, Southern Command

▲ McDonnell Douglas F-15D Eagle

Maintainers conduct post-flight checks on an IASF F-15D Baz (Buzzard) at Lajes, Azores, while deploying to the U.S. for a Red Flag training exercise. The aircraft, which serves with 106 Squadron 'The Point of the Spear', is nicknamed 'The Rose of the Winds'.

extensive roster of attack helicopter types, numbering around 30 AH-1Q/Ss and 28 AH-64As. Almost certainly reflecting the lessons of the 2006 Lebanon War, the IASF is also testing an armed version of the UH-60 transport helicopter, with a view to upgrading more of the S-70/UH-60 fleet.

Future requirements

Looking ahead, Israel hopes to induct the F-35 to replace earlier F-16s, and is also examining future airlift requirements, with C-130Js likely to be ordered, and the V-22 tilt-rotor assault transport

Specifications

Crew: 1
Powerplant: 1 x 126.7kN (28,500lb) thrust Pratt & Whitney F100-PW-229 turbofan
Maximum speed: 2177km/h (1353mph)
Range: 3862km (2400 miles)
Service ceiling: 15,240m (49,000ft)
Dimensions: span 9.45m (31ft); length 15.09m (49ft 6in); height 5.09m (16ft 8in)
Weight: 19,187kg (42,300lb) loaded
Armament: 1 x GE M61A1 20mm (0.79in) multi-barrelled cannon, wingtip missile Python 4; seven external hardpoints with provision for up to 9276kg (20,450lb) of stores

▼ Lockheed Martin F-16D Fighting Falcon, 109 'The Valley' Squadron, Ramat David

A Block 30 F-16D, serial 074 wears one kill marking for a Hezbollah UAV shot down in July 2006. In Israeli service, the F-16C/D is known by the name Barak (Lightning). This aircraft carries an indigenous Python 4 missile on the wingtip.

Specifications

Crew: 6
Powerplant: 2 x 2127kW (2852shp) GE T64-GE turboshafts
Maximum speed: 305km/h (189mph)
Range: 870km (540 miles)
Dimensions: main rotor diameter 22.02m (72ft 3in); length 20.47m (67ft 2in); height 7.6m (24ft 11in)
Weight: 18,370kg (40,500lb) loaded

Sikorsky CH-53A, 114 Squadron 'The Night Leaders', Tel Nof

Known locally as the Yasur (Petrel), the CH-53 is the IASF's most capable transport helicopter. The fleet, previously upgraded to CH-53 2000 standard, is now being upgraded to 2025 standard, which extends service life through replacement of structural and dynamic components.

Specifications

Crew: 2
Powerplant: 1 x 1300 kW (1800shp) Lycoming T53-L-703 turboshaft
Maximum speed: 277km/h (172mph)
Range: 510km (315 miles)
Service ceiling: 3720m (12,200ft)
Dimensions: rotor diameter 13.6m (44ft); length 16.1m (53ft); height 4.1m (13ft 5in)
Weight: 4500kg (10,000lb) loaded
Armament: 1 x 20mm (0.78in) M197 cannon; 7–19 x 70mm (2.75in) Hydra 70 rockets; 4 or 8 x TOW missiles

Bell AH-1F Cobra, 161 'The First Attack' Squadron, Palmachim

Israeli Cobras are known by the name Tsefa (Viper). AH-1F serial 393 was at Palmachim in 2004, although the unit is now thought to be based at Ovda. Once fielded as a tank-hunter, the AH-1 is now increasingly used for anti-terrorist missions.

under examination as a potential CH-53 replacement. The IASF also requires a new jet trainer to replace an ageing fleet of A-4s. Basic and primary training is conducted using Tzukits (modernized and rebuilt Magisters,), and T-6As, 25 of which have been ordered, and privately operated Grob 120s.

The structure of the IASF is based around semi-autonomous wings distributed across the country and normally consisting of around three squadrons each, plus co-located SAR and liaison flights. Current strength comprises around 750 aircraft organized within approximately 45 operational squadrons (including squadrons equipped with intermediate-range ballistic missiles and UAVs) and eight reserve squadrons. The squadrons are located at nine major air bases (Hatzerim, Hatzor, Nevatim, Ovda, Palmachim, Ramat David, Ramon, Sde Dov and Tel Nof), while numerous other reserve air bases around the country are available to support detachments or to serve as forward operating locations. Liaison and transport types also regularly operate from civil airfields.

Air support of maritime units is entrusted to the IASF, which maintains a single joint air force/navy squadron equipped with five AS565 helicopters. Meanwhile, three fixed-wing IAI 1124 Shahaf aircraft are outfitted for maritime patrol duties.

▲ **Lockheed Martin F-16I Fighting Falcon**

The two-seat F-16I Sufa (Storm) has emerged as the backbone of the IASF's fixed-wing combat fleet. This F-16I is from 253 'The Negev' Squadron, based at Ramon. The use of upper fuselage conformal fuel tanks means the F-16I has almost the same combat radius as the F-15I strike aircraft.

SUPPORT AND TRANSPORT UNITS

100 Squadron	Beech 200	Sde Dov, Transport Command
103 Squadron	C-130E, K/C-130H	Tel Aviv, Transport Command
120 Squadron	Boeing 707, IAI 1124N	Tel Aviv, Transport Command
122 Squadron	Gulfstream 550	Tel Aviv,Transport Command
131 Squadron	C-130E, K/C-130H	Tel Aviv, Transport Command
135 Squadron	Beech 200, Beech Bonanza	Sde Dov, Transport Command
166 Squadron	Hermes 450	Palmachim, Southern Command
191 Squadron	RC-12D/K	Sde Dov, Transport Command
200 Squadron	Heron 1	Palmachim, Southern Command

HELICOPTER UNITS

113 Squadron	AH-64D	Ramon, Southern Command
114 Squadron	CH-53	Tel Nof, Central Command
118 Squadron	CH-53	Tel Nof, Central Command
123 Squadron	S-70A	Hatzerim, Southern Command
124 Squadron	UH-60A, S-70A	Palmachim*, Southern Command
* detachments at Bezet and Haifa		
125 Squadron	Bell 206, OH-58B	Sde Dov, Transport Command
160 Squadron	AH-1E/F	Palmachim, Southern Command
* detachments at Biraneet		
161 Squadron	AH-1E/F	Ovda, Southern Command
190 Squadron	AH-64D	Ramon, Southern Command
193 Squadron	AS565	Ramat David

TRAINING UNITS

FTS	TA/A-4N, Bell 206, Grob 120, Tzukit, AH-1E, T-6A	Hatzerim, Training Command
102 Squadron	TA/A-4N	Hatzerim, Training Command

Jordan

ROYAL JORDANIAN AIR FORCE

Jordan once relied on Saudi Arabia to help fund the equipment of its RJAF, although the current fleet includes a significant proportion of U.S.-surplus combat jets, transports and helicopters.

THE EQUIPMENT OF the RJAF was upgraded after relations with the USA were re-established in the mid-1990s, permitting induction of C-130H transports, UH-1H helicopters, and USAF-surplus F-16A/Bs. Sixteen of the latter were acquired initially, followed in 2003 by another 17 examples. The F-16s now represent the most capable equipment within the RJAF, supported by Mirage F1s and F-5E/Fs, the latter also used for advanced training. An Attack Helicopter Wing maintains two AH-1F/S squadrons, and combat types are part of Operations Command, with bases at Amman-Marka, Al Jafr, Al Matar, Al Azraq and H5. Training Command operates from King Hussein Air College. A Royal Flight operates from Amman-Marka, also home to a display team with Extra 300s. Military transports include fixed-wing C-295s, C-212s and CN-235s, plus AS332, S-70 and UH-1 helicopters.

Specifications

Crew: 1
Powerplant: 1 x 105.7kN (23,770lb) Pratt & Whitney F100-PW-200 turbofan
Maximum speed: 2142km/h (1320mph)
Range: 925km (525 miles)
Service ceiling: 15,240m (50,000ft)
Dimensions: span 9.45m (31ft); length 15.09m (49ft 6in); height 5.09m (16ft 8in)
Weight: 16,057kg (35,400lb) loaded
Armament: 1 x GE M61A1 20mm (0.79in) multi-barrelled cannon, wingtip missile stations; provision for 9276kg (20,450lb) of stores

Lockheed Martin F-16A Fighting Falcon, No. 2 Squadron, Al Azraq/As Shaheed Muwaffaq al Salti AB

A Block 15 ADF F-16A, 80-0546 has been operated by No. 2 Squadron since 1998. The F-16s were acquired as replacements for the Mirage F1 fleet, although today the Mirage remains in service with No. 1 Squadron, which is based alongside the two F-16 units (Nos 2 and 6 Squadrons) at Al Azraq/As Shaheed Muwaffaq al Salti AB.

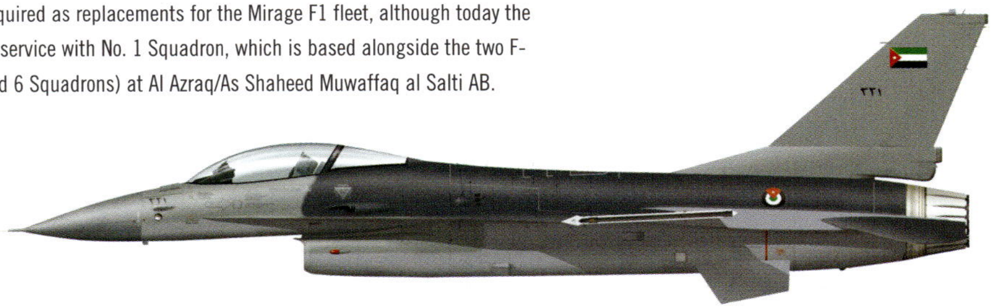

Kuwait

KUWAIT AIR FORCE

Invasion by Iraq in 1990 saw the KAF subsequently receive advanced new aircraft, and the current fleet, although relatively small, operates modern and capable equipment.

ORIGINALLY ESTABLISHED AS the Kuwait Air Force and Air Defence in 1961, at the time of the 1991 Gulf War, the Kuwaiti air arm was spearheaded by Mirage F1 fighters and A-4KU attack jets and had been re-named as the al-Quwwat al-Jawwiya al-Kuwaitiya (Kuwait Air Force). Today, the air arm is equipped with more potent F/A-18 Hornets, of which 32 single-seat F/A-18Cs and eight two-seat F/A-18Ds serve with Nos 9 and 25 Squadrons at Ahmed al Jaber, one of three bases in regular use. A total of 16 AH-64D attack helicopters began to be delivered in 2006.

Kuwait IAP is the centre of KAF transport operations, with No. 41 Squadron's six L-100-30 Hercules, and a VIP Transport Flight equipped with A300s, A310s and Gulfstream IV and V types, as well as S-92A helicopters.

The training fleet is based around nine Hawk Mk64s and eight Tucano Mk52s of the Flight Training Centre at Ali al Salem, these types operated by Nos 12 and 19 Squadrons, respectively. The same base is home to the helicopter fleet, comprising No. 32 Squadron with SA330Hs, No. 33 Squadron with SA342Ks, No. 62 Squadron with AS332B/Ms and AS532s, and the AH-64Ds of No. 88 Squadron.

Kuwait also maintains a Police Helicopter Wing with a fleet consisting of EC135 and AS365 types. The Police Helicopter Wing operated SA330 and SA342 helicopters in the past, but these are now likely withdrawn.

Lebanon

Lebanese Air Force

Plagued by civil war during the 1980s, and more recently the scene of Israel's anti-Hezbollah operations, the Lebanese Air Force maintains a small but active force of combat aircraft.

The current capabilities of the Lebanese Air Force (LAF) are vested in a fleet of rotary-wing aircraft acquired from various sources, plus a token force of four Hunter jet fighters at Rayak, the first of which originally arrived in Lebanon in 1959.

Also still in use are around 10 ex-UAE SA342L anti-tank helicopters, flown by No. 8 Squadron at Beirut. The receipt of 16 UH-1H helicopters from U.S. Army surplus in 1995 allowed the formation of two more squadrons at Beirut. These aircraft are also used in an offensive role, fitted with locally with bomb racks, and can be found equipping Nos 10 and 11 Squadrons at Beirut, No. 12 Squadron at Rayak and No. 14 Squadron at Kleyate.

In 2005 a training unit, No. 15 Squadron, was created at Rayak, co-located with the aviation school and equipped with four Robinson R44 helicopters.

The LAF has its headquarters in Beirut, while individual air bases are headed by an independent commander responsible for a Technical Wing and an Air Wing, the latter incorporating flying squadrons.

The LAF is hopeful of receiving Mi-24 attack helicopters, 10 of which were offered by Russia in 2010. If delivered, these will serve alongside around seven AB212 and SA330 helicopters, returned to service after they had been refurbished with financial assistance from Qatar. One AW139 is also in service for VIP transport, while the only other fixed-wing asset is a single armed Cessna 208 transport.

Specifications

Crew: 1

Powerplant: 1 x 45.13kN (10,145lb) thrust Rolls-Royce Avon 207 turbojet engine

Maximum speed: 1144km/h (710mph)

Range: 689km (490 miles)

Service ceiling: 15,240m (50,000ft)

Dimensions: span 10.26m (33ft 8in); length 13.98m (45ft 10.5in); height 4.02m (13ft 2in)

Weight: 17,750kg (24,600lb) loaded

Armament: 4 x 30mm (1.18in) Aden Cannon; up to 2722kg (6000lb) of bombs or rockets; AIM-9 Sidewinder AAMs or AGM-65 ASMs

▼ Hawker Hunter F70A, No. 2 Squadron, Rayak

Lebanon's first Hunters were delivered in 1959 to equip the No. 1 Squadron at Khalde, and the type saw action in the Six-Day War of 1967. Grounded in 1994, the Hunter remained in storage for many years, but a handful of the jets were returned to operational service in 2008.

Kazakhstan

Kazakhstan Air Force

Based on equipment inherited from the USSR, the Kazakhstan air force is small but relatively well equipped, although a lack of funds has allowed only limited upgrade of the inventory.

MAJOR BASES ARE at Taldy Kurgan (MiG-27s) and Karaganda (MiG-31s, MiG-29s and Su-27s), and Almaty, which is home to the transport fleet, with An-12s and An-24/26s. Aktau houses Su-27s and Su-25s, while Shetygen supports Su-24s and MiG-29s, with the latter type also at Lugovoye. Utsharal and Taras are major helicopter bases, with Mi-8/17s, Mi-24s and Mi-26s. A reconnaissance regiment (MiG-25RBs and Su-24MRs) is at Balkash, while a border guard air fleet is at Almaty-Boralday.

Kyrgyzstan

Kyrgyzstan Air Force

With the break-up of the USSR, Kyrgyzstan was left with a former Soviet flight training school on its territory. Today, the Kyrgyzstan air force is reported to maintain two units.

THE CURRENT STRUCTURE of the Kyrgyzstan Air Force is likely based around a single transport unit and a training squadron, the latter a hangover from the previous Soviet training facility at Frunze. The current Kyrgyzstan Air Force training squadron is equipped with L-39s. The transport squadron is responsible for a mixed fleet of An-12s, An-26s and Mi-8s, plus VIP-configured Tu-154s and Yak-40s. Around nine Mi-24 assault helicopters are reportedly active, although 48 MiG-21 fighters are now stored.

Mongolia

Mongolian People's Air Force

Formerly organized along Soviet lines, the Mongolian air arm is controlled by the army, although economic problems mean that much of its fleet is now non-operational.

THE ASSETS OF the small Mongolian armed forces were divided into five branches in 1993, a year after Soviet forces left the country. These comprise the General Purpose Troops, Air Defence Forces, Construction Corps, Civil Defence and Mobilization Reserves. A separate body is responsible for internal security and border protection.

The last jet fighters to be received were MiG-21s that were delivered in the late 1970s, and the fleet must now be presumed to be grounded at Sainshand, although reports suggest there may have been efforts to return at least some of the aircraft to flying order. The most potent combat equipment is the Mi-24, although only four are reported to be in use at Nalayh, supported by around 25 Mi-8s.

A transport capability is provided by a small number of An-24/26 and Y-12 aircraft, together with around 10 An-2 utility aircraft. Around 80 airfields are available across the country, although the most important of these is at Ulan Bator – which is the centre of air force fixed-wing and helicopter transport operations – as well as at Altai and Choilbalsan.

Oman

Royal Air Force of Oman

Originally formed as the Sultan of Oman's Air Force in 1959 with assistance from the UK, the RAFO adopted its current name in 1990 and is today undergoing re-equipment and upgrade.

The cutting edge of RAFO airpower is provided by the fast-jet units at Thumrait. The three front-line units at the base are responsible for 16 Jaguars, first ordered in 1977 and since upgraded to Jaguar 97 standard. Meanwhile, 20 Squadron is equipped with eight single-seat multi-role F-16Cs and four two-seat F-16Ds that were ordered in 2002. Looking to the future, the RAFO hopes to replace its last Jaguars by 2010, with the Typhoon seen as a likely successor.

Transport arm

The RAFO transport fleet is headquartered at Seeb and consists of three C-130Hs (a single C-130J is also on order), one BAC 111 and a single Airbus A320, with another A320 due to arrive to allow the BAC 111 to be retired. Also at Seeb is a single Skyvan and three Seavans used for maritime patrol, and also due for replacement in the near term. A further three Skyvans are still in use at Salalah.

A new base is being built at Al Musana, and this installation has received the helicopters that were formerly based at Seeb. No. 14 Squadron is in the process of re-equipping with 20 NH90s, allowing the retirement of older helicopter models and the Skyvan. Helicopter training is conducted at Salalah using the Bell 206s of 3 Squadron.

Masirah Island is home to RAFO pilot training, supporting 12 PC-9(M) turboprop trainers and Super Mushshak primary trainers, divided into two flights. Advanced training and air defence are the roles of 6 Squadron's 11 single-seat Hawk Mk203s and four two-seat Hawk Mk103s. Masirah also supports a SAR detachment with Lynx Mk120s.

ROYAL AIR FORCE OF OMAN

1 Squadron	Super Mushshak, PC-9	Masirah
2 Squadron	Skyvan/Seavan	Seeb
3 Squadron	Lynx Mk120, Bell 206	Salalah
4 Squadron	BAC 111, A320	Seeb
5 Squadron	Skyvan	Salalah
6 Squadron	Hawk Mk103/203	Masirah
8 Squadron	Jaguar	Thumrait
14 Squadron	AB205, SA330, AS332	Al Musanah*
* SAR detachment at Khasab.		
15 Squadron	Lynx Mk120	Al Musanah*
* SAR detachment at Masirah.		
16 Squadron	C-130H	Seeb
18 Squadron	F-16C/D	Thumrait
20 Squadron	Jaguar S/B	Thumrait

Specifications

Crew: 2
Powerplant: 1 x 131kN (29,400lbf) F110-GE-129
Maximum speed: 2177km/h (1353mph)
Range: 3862km (2400 miles)
Service ceiling: 15,240m (49,000ft)
Dimensions: span 9.45m (31ft); length 15.09m (49ft 6in); height 5.09m (16ft 8in)
Weight: 19,187kg (42,300lb) loaded
Armament: 1 x 20mm (0.79in) GEc M61A1 multi-barrelled cannon, seven external hardpoints with provision for up to 9276kg (20,450lb) of stores

Lockheed Martin F-16D Fighting Falcon, 18 Squadron, Thumrait

This two-seat F-16D Block 50 is one of four purchased by Oman, for use with 18 Squadron. The aircraft are multi-role, and can also be used for anti-shipping.

Specifications

Crew: 2 or 3
Powerplant: 2 x 835kW (1120shp) Rolls-Royce Gem turboshafts
Maximum speed: 324km/h (201mph)
Range: 528km (328 miles)
Dimensions: rotor diameter 12.80m (42ft); length 15.241m (50ft); height 3.734m (12.25ft)
Weight: 5330kg (11,750lb) loaded
Armament: 1 x 7.62mm (0.3in) heavy machine gun, 2 x 70mm (2.76in) rocket pods

AgustaWestland Lynx Mk120, 15 Squadron, Al Musanah

Based at Al Musanah, 15 Squadron also maintains a permanent SAR detachment at the RAFO training base at Masirah. The Lynx is also flown by 3 Squadron at Salalah, the most southerly RAFO base, where the type is used for training alongside the Bell 206.

Specifications

Crew: 1
Powerplant: 2 x 37.3kN (8400lb) Rolls-Royce/Turbomeca Adour Mk 811 turbofans
Maximum speed: 1699km/h (1056mph)
Range: 537km (334 miles)
Service ceiling: 14,000m (46,000ft)
Dimensions: span 8.69m (28ft 6in); length 16.83m (55ft 2.5in); height 4.89m (16ft 0.5in)
Weight: 15,700kg (34,613lb) loaded
Armament: 2 x 30mm(1.18in) Aden Mk.4 cannon; provision for 4763kg (10,500lb) of stores

SEPECAT Jaguar S, 8 Squadron, Thumrait

This is an example from the first batch of Jaguar Internationals delivered to Oman starting in 1977. Although the Omani fleet was upgraded to Jaguar 97 standard, with expanded weapons options and improved navigation equipment, retirement of the Jaguar is imminent.

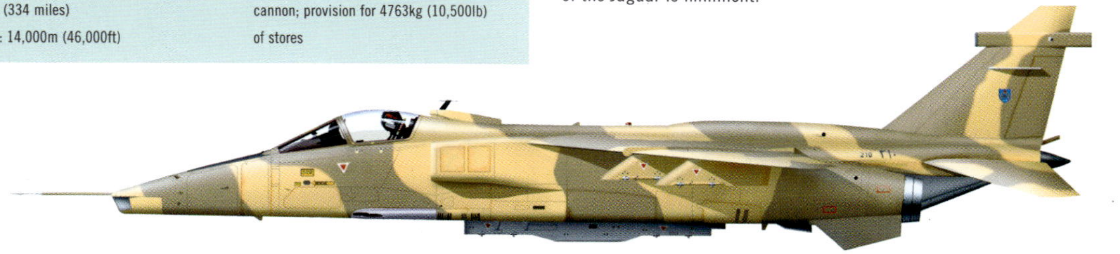

Qatar

Qatar Emiri Air Force

The foundations of the modern-day QAEF were laid in 1974, when the Public Security Forces of the newly independent Qatar established an Air Wing, mainly equipped with helicopters.

In its current guise, the QAEF relies primarily on equipment supplied by France and the UK, although Qatar now shows signs of turning increasingly to the USA for new aircraft. British-supplied equipment consists of nine Commando Mk2/3 helicopters. The Commandos equip two squadrons at Doha International Airport, Nos 8 and 9 Squadrons, tasked with anti-surface warfare and assault transport, respectively. The QAEF hoped to add 18 Hawk Mk100s to its inventory, but limited budgets mean that this deal has been put on hold.

The French contribution to the QAEF comprises six Alpha Jets for light attack and training, and about a dozen SA342 close-support helicopters serving with No. 6 Squadron at Doha. The Alpha Jet fleet is the responsibility of No. 11 Squadron at Doha, which concentrates on close support. The arrival of nine single-seat Mirage 2000-5EDA and three two-seat Mirage 2000-5DDA multi-role fighters in 1997 allowed the

Specifications

Crew: 1
Powerplant: 2 x 97kN (21,834lb) SNECMA M53-P2 turbofan
Maximum speed:2338km/h (1453mph)
Range: 1480km (920 miles)
Service ceiling: 18,000m (59,055ft)
Dimensions: span 9.13m (29ft 11.5in); length 14.36m (47ft 1.25in); height 5.2m (17ft 0.75in)
Weight: 17,000kg (37,480lb) loaded
Armament: 1 x DEFA 554 cannon; nine external pylons with provision for up to 6300kg (13,889lb) of stores

▼ **Dassault Mirage 2000-5EDA, No. 7 Squadron, Doha**

The QAEF operates three Mirage 2000 Mk5 DDA two-seaters and nine Mirage 2000 Mk5 EDA single-seat, multi-role fighters with No. 7 Air Superiority Squadron at Doha, where they form part of No. 1 Fighter Wing.

transfer of the QAEF's Mirage F1s to Spain. The Mirage fleet, also stationed at Doha, is operated by No. 7 Squadron, with air defence as a primary task. Latest helicopter to enter service is the AW139, with a total of 18 on order for use in the utility transport role.

New airlifters

Recently, the QAEF has set about establishing a strategic and intra-theatre airlift capability, with the purchase of four C-17A transports. Two C-17s were in service by 2010, and the QAEF is also to receive four C-130J-30 airlifters from 2011. These new aircraft will serve with a newly established transport squadron at Doha.

In addition to front-line assets, the government maintains a Qatar Amiri Flight responsible for a fleet of VIP aircraft based on the civilian side of Doha IAP. Qatar Emiri Flight aircraft include examples of the Airbus A310, A319, A320 and A340, Boeing 707, 727 and 747SP, and the Falcon 900.

▲ **Boeing C-17A Globemaster III**

The first Middle East nation to order the type, Qatar is assembling a fleet of four C-17A airlifters, after placing an order in 2008. The second example was delivered in Qatar Airways colours. 2008 also saw Qatar sign contracts for four C-130J airlifters and 18 AW139 medium helicopters.

Saudi Arabia

Royal Saudi Air Force, Army Aviation Command and Naval Air Arm

The largest country on the Arabian peninsula, Saudi Arabia entrusts its defence to the RSAF, one of the best-equipped air arms in the world, as well as separate Army and Navy air components.

THE UNITS OF the RSAF have long been engaged in a rolling series of capability upgrades, with major procurement programmes ensuring regular receipt of new and advanced warplanes. Numerically, the F-15 is the most important combat jet, with 57 single-seat F-15Cs and 25 two-seat F-15Ds serving in the air defence role (in which they are supported by five E-3A airborne early warning platforms) and 71 F-15S used for strike. The exact status of the 24 air defence-configured Tornado ADVs is uncertain, but 87 upgraded Tornado IDS interdictors remain in use. Despite its age, the F-5 remains in service in quantity, variants comprising the F-5A (83 examples) for air defence, and the F-5B (37) for training. New fighter equipment is arriving in the form of 72 Typhoons.

The RSAF transport fleet can call upon 30 C-130E/Hs, seven KC-130Hs and six Lockheed L-100-30s, with six A330 tanker/transports due to be delivered starting in 2011 to supersede seven KE-3As. The training component is based on the Hawk, the

Specifications

Crew: 2
Powerplant: 2 x 90kN (20,250lb) Eurojet EJ200 turbofans
Maximum speed: 2125km/h (1321mph)
Range: 2900km (1840 miles)
Service ceiling: 19,810m (65,000ft)
Dimensions: span 10.5m (34ft 5.5in); length 16.0m (52ft 6in); height 4m (13ft 1.5in)
Weight: 23,000kg (50,705lb) loaded
Armament: 1 x 27mm (1.06in) Mauser cannon; 13 fuselage hardpoints for a wide variety of stores

Eurofighter Typhoon, No. 10 Squadron, King Fahd AB, Taif

Saudi Arabia ordered a total of 72 EF2000 Typhoons, including 48 Tranche 2 and 24 Tranche 3 jets, and the first of these are entering service with No. 10 Squadron. The eventual Typhoon order for the RSAF may reach 100 aircraft.

Specifications

Crew: 2
Powerplant: 2 x 40.5kN (9104lbf) dry thrust Turbo-Union RB199-34R Augmented Turbofans
Maximum speed: Mach 2.27 (2338km/h; 1452mph)
Range: 1390km (869 miles)
Service ceiling: 15,240m (50,000ft)
Dimensions: span 13.91m (45.6ft) unswept, 8.6m (28.2ft) (swept); length 18.7m (61.3ft); height 5.95m (19.5ft)
Weight: 21,546kg (47,500lb) loaded
Armament: 1 x internal Mauser BK-27 and 10 hardpoints holding up to 9000kg (19,800 lb)

Panavia Tornado IDS, No. 75 Squadron, 11 Wing, King Abdullah Aziz AB, Dharan

Alongside F-15S jets, RSAF Tornado IDS strike aircraft have seen action against Houthi insurgents in Yemen and along the Saudi-Yemen border. RSAF Tornado IDS have been upgraded to a standard similar to the RAF's Tornado GR4.

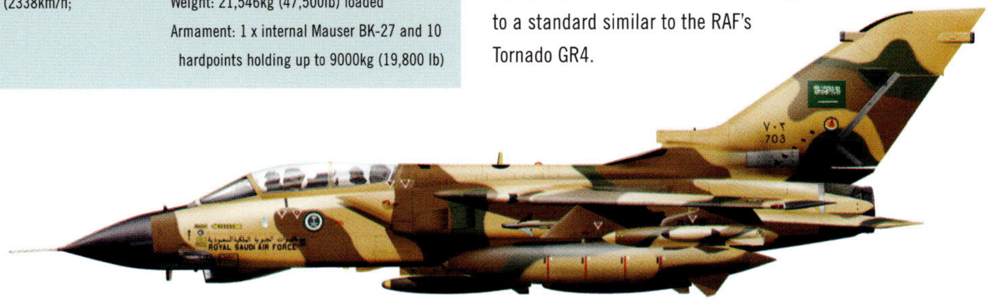

ROYAL SAUDI AIR FORCE

King Abdullah Aziz AB, Dharan

3 Wing	
No. 13 Squadron	F-15C/D
No. 92 Squadron	F-15S
No. 44 Squadron	Bell 412
11 Wing	
No. 7 Squadron	Tornado IDS
No. 35 Squadron	Jetstream 31
No. 75 Squadron	Tornado IDS
No. 83 Squadron	Tornado IDS

King Fahd AB, Taif

2 Wing	
No. 3 Squadron	F-5E/F*
No. 5 Squadron	F-15C/D
No. 10 Squadron	Typhoon
No. 14 Squadron	AB212, Bell 412
No. 12 Squadron det	AB212
No. 17 Squadron	F-5E/F
No. 34 Squadron	F-15C/D

* may have been disbanded.

King Khalid AB, Riyadh

4 Wing	
No. 1 Squadron (Royal Flight)	VC-130H, C-130H, L-100-30 Hercules, CN235, BAe 125, A340, AS61, Learjet 35, Boeing 707, Boeing 737, Boeing 747, MD-11, Gulfstream 1159, Cessna 550

King Faisal Air Academy

No. 8 Squadron	Cessna 172, Super Mushshak
No. 9 Squadron	PC-9
No. 22 Squadron	PC-9

King Khalid AB, Khamis Mushait

5 Wing	
No. 6 Squadron	F-15S
No. 15 Squadron	F-5E/F*
* may have been disbanded.	
No. 55 Squadron	F-15S
No. 99 Squadron	AS532
No. 14 Squadron det	AB212, Bell 412

Lockheed C-130H Hercules

The RSAF maintains a large fleet of Hercules, including C-130E/H tactical transports,KC-130H air-to-air refuelling tankers, VIP-configured VC-130H personnel transports and civilian-standard L-100-30 cargo transports. Seen here moments before airdropping a cargo load, this C-130H serves with No. 16 Squadron at Jeddah.

Prince Sultan AB, Al Kharj	
6 Wing	
No. 18 Squadron	E-3A, KE-3A
No. 71 Squadron	RE-3A
No. 32 Squadron	KC-130H
King Faisal AB, Tabuk	
7 Wing	
No. 2 Squadron	F-15C/D
No. 21 Squadron	Hawk T65
No. 37 Squadron	Hawk T65
No. 79 Squadron	Hawk T65A
No. 88 Squadron	Hawk T65/65A
Prince Abdullah AB, Jeddah	
8 Wing	
No. 4 Squadron	C-130E/H
No. 16 Squadron	C-130E/H
No. 20 Squadron	C-130E/H
King Khalid Military City, Hafar Al Batin	
No. 12 Squadron	AB212

turboprop PC-9, the piston-engined Mushshak and Cessna 172, and the Jetstream crew trainer.

RSAF helicopter arm

RSAF helicopter forces are represented by around 30 AB212s used for search and rescue and utility, 12 AS532s for combat search and rescue, a handful of AS-61A VIP transports, 24 Bell 205 and 16 Bell 412 utility transports and 12 SA365s for medical evacuation. A total of 22 UH-60Ls are on order.

The Royal Saudi Land Forces began operating aircraft in 1986 and its inventory now comprises 12 AH-64A attack helicopters and 12 Bell 406 Combat Scouts, 12 S-70As and 18 VH-60L VIP transports.

The Royal Saudi Naval Forces are responsible for 20 AS332s and 12 SA365s, with AS565s on order for use on board Saudi warships.

Specifications

Crew: 1

Powerplant: 2 x 77.62kN (17,450lbf) (dry thrust) Pratt & Whitney F100-PW-220 turbofans

Maximum speed: 2655km/h (1650mph)

Range: 5550km (3450 miles)

Service ceiling: 20,000m (65,000ft)

Dimensions: span 13.05m (42ft 9.75in); length 19.43in (63ft 9in); height 5.63m (18ft 5in)

Weight: 20,200kg (44,500lb) loaded

Armament: 1 x 20mm (0.79in) M61A1 cannon, provision for up to 7300kg (16,000lb) of stores, including missiles, bombs, tanks, pods and rockets

▼ McDonnell Douglas F-15C Eagle, No. 13 Squadron, 3 Wing, King Abdullah Aziz AB, Dharan

This Eagle was flown by the RSAF's Captain Ayed Salah al-Shamrani when he used AIM-9P Sidewinder missiles to shoot down two Iraqi Mirage F1EQ fighters during the 1991 Gulf War.

Specifications

Crew: 2

Powerplant: 1 x 29kN (6500lbf) Rolls-Royce Adour Mk.861 turbofan with FADEC

Maximum speed: .84 Mach (1028km/h; 638mph)

Range: 2520km (1565 miles)

Service ceiling: 13,565m (44,500ft)

Dimensions: span 9.94m (32ft 7in); length 12.43m (40ft 9in); height 3.98m (13ft 1in)

Weight: 9100kg (20,000lb) loaded

Armament: 4 x 12.7mm (0.5in) M-3 MGs; up to 19,504kg (43,000lb) of bombs

▼ BAe Hawk T65, No. 21 Squadron, 7 Wing, King Faisal AB, Tabuk

Saudi Arabia's Hawk advanced trainers operate within four squadrons at Tabuk. A total of 50 aircraft are in service, including both Mk65 and Mk65A versions, and the type equips the Saudi Hawks aerobatic display team, part of No. 88 Squadron.

Syria

Syrian Arab Air Force

Equipped almost exclusively with aircraft of Soviet origin, the SyAAF maintains a low profile, but now appears to be in a state of transition, with upgrade and restructuring efforts under way.

One of the world's most secretive air arms, the situation regarding the status of the SyAAF is made more confused by reforms implemented by the military in 2004, and further reorganization following the 2006 Lebanon War. The accompanying order of battle must be regarded as provisional, as some units have few, or no aircraft currently assigned.

Of the squadrons and brigades listed, a number have almost certainly been disbanded altogether, and the latest reports suggest that the SyAAF inventory is based on approximately 60 MiG-21s, 60-80 MiG-23s, and some 20 MiG-25s of various subtypes. Arguably the most potent type in the SyAAF inventory is the Su-24MK interdictor, of which an estimated 20 examples are in operational use.

Local upgrade

The SyAAF has upgraded their Soviet-era aircraft with new navigation/attack systems and weapons. Such upgrades have been undertaken within Syria since 2004, resulting in the modernization of MiG-21bis and MiG-23MF/ML fighters. Similar upgrades have provided MiG-23BNs with new precision weaponry and Western electronic warfare equipment.

Specifications

Crew: 1
Powerplant: 2 x 81.4kN (18,298lb) Sarkisov RD-33 turbofans
Maximum speed: 2443km/h (1518mph)
Range: 1500km (932 miles)
Service ceiling: 17,000m (55,775ft)
Dimensions: span 11.36m (37ft 3.75in); length (including probe) 17.32m (56ft 10in); height 7.78m (25ft 6.25in)
Weight: 18,500kg (40,785lb) loaded
Armament: 1 x 30mm (1.18in) GSh-30 cannon, provision for up to 4500kg (9921lb) of stores

▼ Mikoyan MiG-29, 698 Squadron, T-4/Tsaykal

The T-4/Tsaykal-based 698 Squadron remains the only SyAAF unit operating MiG-29s. This aircraft displays a typical air defence armament of radar-guided R-27R and heat-seeking R-60 air-to-air missiles.

Specifications

Crew: 2
Powerplant: 2 x 75kN (16,860lbf) dry thrust Saturn/Lyulka AL-21F-3A turbojets
Maximum speed: Mach 1.07 (1315km/h; 815mph) at sea level
Range: 2775km (1725 miles)
Service ceiling: 11,000m (36,090ft)
Dimensions: span 17.64m (57ft 10in) extended, 10.37m (34ft) max sweep; length 22.53m (73ft 11in); height 6.19m (20ft 4in)
Weight: 38,040kg (83,865lb) loaded
Armament: 1 x GSh-6-23 cannon, plus up to 8000kg (17,640lb) ordnance on 8 hardpoints

▼ Sukhoi Su-24MK, 819 Squadron, Tiyas

This is one of only a few Syrian Su-24MKs that remain operational with 819 Squadron, much of the fleet being in storage. The Su-24s are prized by the SyAAF for their ability to deliver precision-guided weapons, although advanced munitions have now also been integrated on upgraded MiG-23BNs.

The airlift of Syrian military personnel and equipment is traditionally entrusted to civil-registered Syrian aircraft, including An-24/26s and Il-76s. Other civilian-marked aircraft that have been identified as taking part in military missions include Falcon 20, Piper Navajo, Tu-134 and Yak-40 types.

The Syrian Arab Navy also maintains a small rotary-wing fleet for anti-submarine warfare, this operating Ka-28s and Mi-14s based at Latakia.

SYRIAN ARAB AIR FORCE

14 Brigade		
678 Squadron	MiG-23M/UB	Abu ad-Duhor
697 Squadron	MiG-23M/UB	Tsaykal
680 Squadron	MiG-21MF/UM	Hamah
24 Brigade		
8 Squadron	MiG-21MF	Dayr az-Zawr
10 Squadron	MiG-21PF/MF/UM	Jirah
12 Squadron	MiG-21MF/UM	Taboa
67 Brigade		
67 Squadron	MiG-23ML/UB	Dmeyr
679 Squadron	MiG-23ML/UB	Dmeyr
675 Squadron	MiG-23M/UB	Dmeyr
70 Brigade		
1 Squadron	MiG-25PD/PU	T4
5 Squadron	MiG-25PD/PU	T4
7 OCU	MiG-25PD/PU/RB	T4 and Shayrat
9 Squadron	MiG-23M/UB, MiG-25RB/PU	Shayrat
73 Brigade		
945 Squadron	MiG-21bis/UM	Khalkhala
946 Squadron	MiG-21bis/UM	Khalkhala
Unknown squadron	MiG-21PF/RF	Khalkhala
SAR Flight	Ka-25BSh	Khalkhala
86 Brigade		
825 Squadron	MiG-21bis/UM	al-Qusayr
826 Squadron	MiG-21bis/UM	al-Qusayr
1 Brigade		
697 Squadron	MiG-29/MiG-29UB	Tsaykal
698 Squadron	MiG-29/MiG-29UB	Tsaykal
699 Squadron	MiG-29/MiG-29UB	Tsaykal
17 Brigade		
695 Squadron	MiG-23BN/UB	an-Nassiriyah
695 Squadron	MiG-23BN/UB	an-Nassiriyah
30 Brigade		
77 Squadron	MiG-23ML/UB	Blei
50 Brigade		
677 OCU	Su-20, Su-22M4K/UM	Shayrat
685 Squadron	Su-22M3K/UM3K	Shayrat
81 Brigade		
819 Squadron	Su-24MK	Tiyas
820 Squadron	Su-22M4K/UM3K	Tiyas
827 Squadron	Su-22M-4K/UM-3K	Tiyas
59 Brigade		
525 Squadron	Mi-8M/MT	Marj as-Sultan
532 Squadron	Mi-2/8/17	Marj as-Sultan
537 Squadron	Mi-2/8/17	Marj as-Sultan
63 Brigade		
253 Squadron	Mi-8	Afis
255 Squadron	Mi-8	Afis
64 Brigade		
765 Squadron	Mi-24	as-Sweyda
766 Squadron	Mi-24	as-Sweyda
Unknown brigade		
767 Squadron	Mi-24	Blei
976 Squadron	SA342L	al-Mazzeh
977 Squadron	SA342L	al-Mazzeh
Unknown squadron	Mi-17	al-Mazzeh
909 Squadron	Mi-8PP	al-Mazzeh*
* probably disbanded.		
77 Brigade		
Unknown squadron	Mi-8	Nayrab (Aleppo)
Unknown squadron	Mi-8	Nayrab (Aleppo)
Unknown brigade		
522 Squadron	PA-38, An-24/26	Damascus IAP
565 Squadron	Yak-40	Damascus IAP
575 Squadron	Falcon 20	Damascus IAP
577 Squadron	SA342L	Damascus IAP
585 Squadron	Boeing 727, Il-76MD	Damascus IAP

Tajikistan

Tajikistan Air Force

Tajikistan's tiny air arm comprises a helicopter component and a VIP flight. Currently, fewer than 20 aircraft of all types are estimated to be operated by this former Soviet republic.

THE MOST CAPABLE combat aircraft operated by the Tajikistan Air Force is the Mi-24 assault helicopter, although no more than four examples are reported as operational. Around 15 Mi-8/17 transport helicopters are available, together with a single VIP-configured Tu-134 operated on behalf of the government. Operations are centred on the former Soviet air base at Dushanbe.

Turkmenistan

Turkmenistan Air Force

Emerging from the Soviet bloc in 1991, oil-rich Turkmenistan established its Air and Air Defence Forces on the basis of the 73rd Air Army, inherited from the former USSR.

APPARENTLY BASED AROUND approximately four regiments of combat aircraft, plus a training unit and a VIP transport flight, the Turkmenistan Air Force was formerly spearheaded by the 107th Fighter Regiment, operating MiG-25 and MiG-23 interceptors from Akdepe, though both are now reportedly retired from service. The 55th Fighter Regiment is also reported to have discarded the MiG-23s it formerly flew from Nebit-Dag. Replacing the MiG-25s at the sharp end of the air arm are the approximately 24 MiG-29s of the 67th Fighter Regiment at Mary. The MiG-29s may operate within a mixed regiment alongside a small number of Su-17M attack aircraft. Other offensive assets include around 20 Su-25s, plus a handful of Su-25 combat trainers.

A mixed transport regiment of the Turkmenistan Air Force is based at Ashkabad, equipped with a single An-24, plus several Mi-8s and Mi-24s.

Pilot training is handled by an unknown training unit at Chardzou. This unit previously operated two-seat MiG-21UMs, but its fleet is likely now to be based around a small number of L-39s.

The VIP transport squadron at Almaty operates Boeing 737 and BAe 125, supplied by the West.

Specifications

Crew: 1
Powerplant: 2 x 81.4kN (18,298lb) Sarkisov RD-33 turbofans
Maximum speed: 2443km/h (1518mph)
Range: 1500km (932 miles)
Service ceiling: 17,000m (55,775ft)
Dimensions: span 11.36m (37ft 3.75in); length (including probe) 17.32m (56ft 10in); height 7.78m (25ft 6.25in)
Weight: 18,500kg (40,785lb) loaded
Armament: 1 x 30mm (1.18in) GSh-30 cannon, provision for up to 4500kg (9921lb) of stores

MiG-29, 67th Fighter Regiment, Mary-2

With MiG-25s and MiG-23s now stored, the MiG-29 (mainly 9.13 'Fulcrum-C' versions) represents the most potent air defence fighter in the Turkmenistan Air Force inventory. The jets are based at Mary, which was a major Soviet aviation training centre during the Cold War.

United Arab Emirates

United Arab Emirates Air Force

With its headquarters in Bateen, Abu Dhabi, the United Arab Emirates Air Force and Air Defence consists of two commands, one each in Abu Dhabi and Dubai, and around 1800 personnel.

Typical of advanced equipment operated by the UAEAF are F-16E/F Desert Falcon and Mirage 2000-9 fighters, and AH-64A attack helicopters.

Fighter forces are centred on Al Dhafra air base in Abu Dhabi, part of Western Air Command. This base supports both the 79 Block 60 F-16E/Fs (one example having been lost) and a reported total of 46 Mirage 2000s (although a squadron of the latter may be detached to Al Safran air base). Al Dhafra is also home to the AH-64 fleet and will likely receive two Saab 340 airborne early warning aircraft on order.

Flight training for the UAEAF is undertaken at Al Ain Air, where various units are equipped with Hawk Mk63s, MB339s, PC-7s (to be replaced by PC-21s) and Grob 115s. More advanced training equipment has been ordered in the form of 48 M-346s, 20 of which will also be equipped for light attack.

Transport capability will be boosted by the arrival of six C-17As and 12 C-130Js, together with three A330s configured as tanker/transports. In the meantime, the UAEAF relies on five of the older C-130H-30 and six CN235s, both types operating from Bateen. Central Air Command, which provides the Dubai Air Force, maintains units at Dubai International Airport and Minhad. Dubai houses Transport Command, while Minhad supports the Hawk Mk102 trainers of 102 Squadron, together with a Transport Squadron. Transport assets at Minhad comprise C-130s and L-100-30s. The Air Academy operates AB206s and six MB339s from Minhad. Special Operations Command at Sas al Nakhil operates ex-Libyan CH-47Cs, as well as eight fixed-wing Cessna 208s.

Naval helicopters

The UAE Navy has a separate air arm that operates helicopters. Naval Squadron AS332s and AS565s are both based at Bateen, while the UAEAF operates four DHC-8s for maritime patrol.

Army Command, with its HQ at Abu Dhabi, incorporates the 10th Army Aviation Brigade. Based at Al Dhafra air base, the 10th Brigade is equipped with AS550s and 30 AH-64As, the latter due to be converted to the more capable AH-64D standard. Fourteen UH-60Ms are also on order.

VIP transport for the Emirates' Sheikhs is provided by no fewer than six Government Flight Services, the most important of which are the Abu Dhabi Amiri Flight (at Bateen), and the Abu Dhabi and the Dubai Air Wing (at Dubai International).

Specifications

Crew: 1
Powerplant: 2 x 97kN (21,834lb) SNECMA M53-P2 turbofan
Maximum speed: 2338km/h (1453mph)
Range: 1480km (920 miles)
Service ceiling: 18,000m (59,055ft)
Dimensions: span 9.13m (29ft 11.5in); length 14.36m (47ft 1.25in); height 5.2m (17ft 0.75in)
Weight: 17,000kg (37,480lb) loaded
Armament: 1 x DEFA 554 cannon; nine external pylons with provision for up to 6300kg (13,889lb) of stores, including air-to-air missiles, rocket launcher pods, and various attack loads, including 454kg (1000lb) bombs

Dassault Mirage 2000-9, Fighter Wing, Al-Dhafra AB

Nos 71 and 76 Fighter Squadrons, based at al-Dhafra AB, operate UAEAF Mirage 2000s alongside F-16s within a mixed Fighter Wing. The UAEAF Mirage fleet includes new-build Mirage 2000 Mk9s, as well as earlier Mirage 2000EAD/DAD/RAD jets that have been upgraded to a similar standard.

UNITED ARAB EMIRATES AIR FORCE

Western Air Command HQ Abu Dhabi

Al Dhafra

1st Shaheen Squadron	F-16E/F
2nd Shaheen Squadron	F-16E/F
3rd Shaheen Squadron	F-16E/F
71 Squadron	Mirage 2000-9EAD/DAD
76 Squadron	Mirage 2000-9EAD/DAD
86 Squadron	Mirage 2000-9EAD/DAD

Al Ain

Khalifa Bin Zayed Air College	Grob 115
Basic Flying Squadron	PC-7
Hawk Squadron	Hawk Mk63
Flying Instructors School	MB339A
SAR Flight	Bell 412, AB 139*

* detachment at Minhad

Bateen

4 Squadron	C-130H
6 Squadron	AB412
CASA Squadron	CN235
Puma Squadron	SA330, IAR-330

Central Air Command HQ Dubai Minhad

102 Squadron	Hawk Mk102

Special Operations Command, HQ Abu Dhabi, Sas al Nakhil

Group 18	CH-47C, Cessna 208, DHC-6

Specifications

Crew: 1–2
Powerplant: 1 x 1342kW (1800hp) Pratt & Whitney Canada PT6T-3B-1 engine
Maximum speed: 259km/h (161mph)
Range: 695km (432 miles)
Service ceiling: 4970m (16,306ft)
Dimensions: rotor diameter 14.02m (46ft); length 12.92m (42ft 4in); height 4.32m (14ft 4in)
Weight: 5397kg (11,900lb) loaded

Agusta-Bell AB412HP, Dubai Interior Ministry Department of Civil Defence

The privatization of SAR duties in the UAE has seen a reduction in the UAEAF fleet of Agusta-Bell AB412s. This former UAEAF example is now operated by the Dubai Interior Ministry for firefighting duties.

Specifications

Crew: 2
Powerplant: 1 x 1996kg (4400lb) Rolls-Royce Viper 680 turbojet
Maximum speed: 898km/h (598mph)
Range: 1760km (1093 miles)
Service ceiling: 14,020m (46,000ft)
Dimensions: span 11.22m (36.8ft); length 11.24m (36.8ft); height 3.9m (12.8ft)
Weight: 6350kg (14,000lb) loaded

Aermacchi MB339A, Flying Instructors School, Al Ain

Half a dozen MB339A advanced trainers are operated by the Flying Instructors School, part of Khalif Bin Zayed Air College. The type is due to be replaced by the Alenia Aermacchi M-346, which will become the UAEAF's standard advanced jet trainer.

Specifications

Crew: 2
Powerplant: 1 x 29kN (6500lbf) Rolls-Royce Adour Mk.861 turbofan with FADEC
Maximum speed: .84 Mach (1028km/h; 638mph)
Range: 2520km (1565 miles)
Service ceiling: 13,565m (44,500ft)
Dimensions: span 9.94m (32ft 7in); length 12.43m (40ft 9in); height 3.98m (13ft 1in)
Weight: 9100kg (20,000lb) loaded
Armament: 4 x 12.7mm (0.5in) M-3 MGs; up to 19,504kg (43,000lb) of bombs

▼ BAe Hawk Mk63C, Hawk Squadron, Al Ain

The Hawk provides the backbone of UAEAF advanced training at Khalif bin Zayed Air College, where several different subversions are in use. First-generation Hawk Mk63s are likely to be phased out in favour of the M-346, although Hawk Mk103s will remain in use at Minhad.

▲ Lockheed Martin F-16E Desert Falcon

Arguably the most capable F-16 variant in service anywhere, the Block 60 Desert Falcon, seen here during a Red Flag training mission in Nevada, is equipped to a notably high standard, with AN/APG-80 active electronically scanned array (AESA) radar, conformal fuel tanks, F110-GE-132 engine, a wide range of air-to-air and offensive weaponry, and the Falcon Edge integrated electronic warfare suite.

Uzbekistan

Uzbekistan Air Force

Uzbekistan has one of the largest armed forces in central Asia, and the air force is relatively well equipped for a Soviet successor state, although some front-line equipment is likely stored.

THE AIR ARM of Uzbekistan includes two brigades located at Karshi-Khanabad and Dzhizak. Front-line equipment includes MiG-29s, Su-24s and Su-27s. Su-17M fighter-bombers are in storage at Chirchik. Transport regiments at Tashkent and Fergana operate Tu-134s, An-12s and An-24/26s and there are helicopter regiments, with Mi-8s and Mi-24s, at Kagan and Verkhnekomsomolsk.

Specifications

Crew: 1
Powerplant: 2 x 81.4kN (18,298lb) Sarkisov RD-33 turbofans
Maximum speed: 2443km/h (1518mph)
Range: 1500km (932 miles)
Service ceiling: 17,000m (55,775ft)
Dimensions: span 11.36m (37ft 3.75in); length (including probe) 17.32m (56ft 10in); height 7.78m (25ft 6.25in)
Weight: 18,500kg (40,785lb) loaded
Armament: 1 x 30mm (1.18in) GSh-30-1 cannon, provision for up to 4500kg (9921lb) of stores, including R-27E (AA-10 'Alamo') and R-77 (AA-12 'Adder') air-to-air missiles

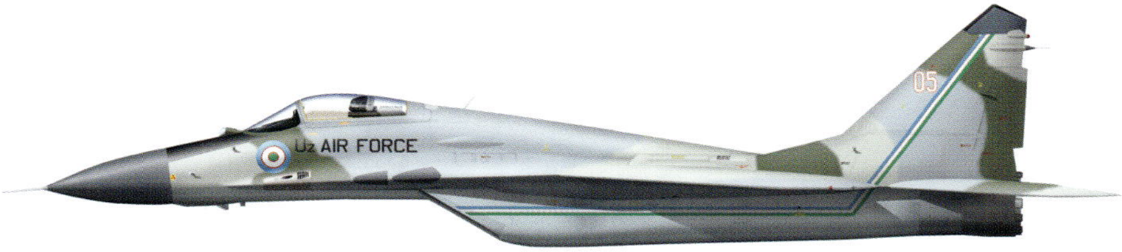

Mikoyan MiG-29, 60th Independent Brigade, Karshi-Khanabad

The Uzbekistan Air Force once operated 39 former Soviet MiG-29s. Most of these have been stored for some years, but several examples have recently been returned to service.

Yemen

Yemen Air Force

Created by the unification of the air arms of the former Yemen Arab Republic Air Force and the South Arabian Air Force, today's Yemen Air Force operates both Eastern and Western aircraft.

Specifications

Crew: 1
Powerplant: 2 x 81.4kN (18,298lb) Sarkisov RD-33 ser.3 turbofans with afterburner
Maximum speed: 2443km/h (1518mph)
Range: 2100km (1305 miles)
Service ceiling: 17,000m (55,775ft)
Dimensions: span 11.36m (37ft 3.75in); length (including probe) 17.32m (56ft 10in); height 7.78m (25ft 6.25in)
Weight: 18,500kg (40,785lb) loaded
Armament: 1 x 30mm (1.18in) GSh-30-1 cannon, provision for up to 4500kg (9921lb) of stores

Mikoyan MiG-29SMT, No. 9 Squadron, Sana'a IAP

All YAF MiG-29s are in service with No. 9 Squadron, based at the military side of Sana'a IAP. The YAF MiG-29 fleet includes SMT-upgraded versions, with a flight-refuelling probe, together with first-generation single-seaters and two-seat MiG-29UB combat trainers.

THE COMBAT EQUIPMENT of the YAF includes MiG-29, MiG-21 Su-22 and F-5B/E fighters, with L-39 and Zlin trainers. Transports include the An-12, An-24/26 and C-130. Helicopters include examples of the Mi-8/17, Mi-14 and Mi-24/35.

CHINA
NORTH KOREA
SOUTH KOREA
JAPAN
PAKISTAN
NEPAL
INDIA
BANGLADESH
MYANMAR
TAIWAN
LAOS
THAILAND
CAMBODIA
VIETNAM
PHILIPPINES
PACIFIC OCEAN
SRI LANKA
MALAYSIA
BRUNEI
SINGAPORE
INDONESIA
INDIAN OCEAN

Chapter 6

South, East and Southeast Asia

Dominated by India in the west and China in the east, the regions of South, East and Southeast Asia are also home to the 'tiger' economies of the Far East, and many nations deploying thoroughly equipped and highly trained air arms. Key flashpoints include Korea, where a considerable U.S. military presence backs up the South Korean forces arranged against the communist North, and Taiwan, which maintains its stand-off against communist China, and which also receives significant U.S. military support. Finally, two nuclear powers, India and Pakistan, maintain a strained relationship, with sporadic outbreaks of warfare. Japan is also home to a major U.S. presence, while the air forces of Indonesia, Malaysia and Singapore have all been recently engaged in high-profile re-equipment programmes for their air forces, creating something of an arms race in the region.

Bangladesh

Bangladesh Air Force

Formed in 1973, the Bangladesh Biman Bahini (BBB) operates a mixture of mainly Chinese and Russian equipment from four major bases: Dhaka, Jessore, Chittagong and Bogra.

The Bangladesh air Force is spearheaded by a squadron of MiG-29 fighters, two squadrons of Chengdu F-7 fighters of various subtypes, and one of Nanchang A-5 attack aircraft, all at Dhaka. Dhaka also houses two helicopter squadrons (with Bell 212s and Mi-17s) and a reduced-size squadron with four C-130B transports. An Air Academy is located at Jessore, with two squadrons flying the Air Academy's T-37s and Bell 206s respectively. Also at Jessore is the transport fleet. Further trainers are at Bogra, in the form of Nanchang FT-6 primary trainers operated by the Air Academy, the only types at this base. A squadron of L-39 jet trainers is stationed at Chittagong, together with further squadrons of An-32s and Mi-17s and a detachment of Bell 212s.

A small Bangladesh Army Aviation arm operates a Cessna 208, and several Mi-17 and Bell 206 helicopters. An aviation wing of the Bangladesh Navy was established in 2010 with an order placed for two AW109 helicopters.

Specifications

Crew: 1
Powerplant: 2 x 81.4kN (18,298lb) Sarkisov RD-33 turbofans
Maximum speed: 2443km/h (1518mph)
Range: 1500km (932 miles)
Service ceiling: 17,000m (55,775ft)
Dimensions: span 11.36m (37ft 3.75in); length (including probe) 17.32m (56ft 10in); height 7.78m (25ft 6.25in)
Weight: 18,500kg (40,785lb) loaded
Armament: 1 x 30mm (1.18in) GSh-30 cannon, provision for up to 4500kg (9921lb) of stores

▼ Mikoyan MiG-29, No. 8 Squadron, Dhaka-Kurmitola (Bashar)

A total of six MiG-29s (plus two twin-seat MiG-29UBs) are operated by No. 8 Squadron from Dhaka. Dhaka actually comprises two bases, Tejgaon (the former international airport) and Kurmitola (the new international airport).

Brunei

Royal Brunei Air Force

The Royal Brunei Air Force, or Angkatan Tentera Udara Diraja Brunei, is the air arm of one of the smallest but wealthiest countries in the world.

As a British protectorate, Brunei hosts a detachment of Royal Air Force Bell 212s at Brunei International Airport. The small local military includes the Royal Brunei Air Force, established in 1991. The Air Force comprises four squadrons, primarily equipped with helicopters based at Brunei International. The current Royal Brunei Air Force rotary-wing fleet consists of two Bell 206s, 10 Bell 212s, one Bell 214, five BO105s and six Sikorsky S-70s. Fixed-wing aircraft comprise four PC-7 trainers and a single CN235 turboprop transport, plus three maritime patrol CN235MPAs.

Specifications

Crew: 2
Powerplant: 2 x 1409kW (1890shp) General Electric T700-GE-701C turboshaft
Maximum speed: 361km/h (224mph)
Range: 463km (288 miles)
Service ceiling: 4021m (13,200ft)
Dimensions: rotor diameter: 16.36m (53ft 8in); length 19.76m (64ft 10in); height 5.33m (17ft 6in)
Weight: 9997kg (22,000lb) loaded

▼ Sikorsky S-70A, 4 Squadron, Royal Brunei Air Force, Brunei International Airport

Brunei operates six S-70s in the medium-lift transport and VIP transport roles. The aircraft comprise four S-70As and two Sikorsky S-70Ls.

Cambodia

Royal Cambodian Air Force

Aircraft of the Royal Cambodian Air Force, or Force Aérienne Royale Cambodge, are based at Phnom Penh and include a small component of jet fighters and jet trainers.

In addition to the major operating base, Royal Cambodian Air Force aircraft may be periodically deployed to satellite bases including Battambang, Kampongchnang, Kohkong, Kompongsom and Siemreap. The modern air arm was re-established in 1993 and now includes a helicopter squadron with Mi-8/17s, and a transport element with two An-24s, two Harbin Y-12s and three Islanders. Six Tecnam Echo microlights serve with a reconnaissance squadron. Jet equipment returned to Cambodia in 1996, with six L-39 trainers. Two Mi-26 heavylift helicopters were acquired in 1998, and these serve in a helicopter squadron. Cambodia hoped to induct 12 Israeli-upgraded MiG-21s, but the deal has been hampered by sanctions and budget constraints. In 2000 a MiG-21bis and a two-seat a two-seat MiG-21UM were delivered from Israel after upgrade. A government-operated VIP transport squadron is also found at Phnom Penh, with a mixed fleet of helicopters, plus an An-24 and a Falcon 20 jet.

Specifications

Crew: 1
Powerplant: 1 x 73.5kN (16,535lb) Tumanskii R-25 turbojet
Maximum speed: 2229km/h (1385mph)
Range: 1160km (721 miles)
Service ceiling: 17,500m (57,400ft)
Dimensions: span 7.15m (23ft 5.5in); length (including probe) 15.76m (51ft 8.5in); height 4.1m (13ft 5.5in)
Weight: 10,400kg (22,925lb) loaded
Armament: 1 x 23mm (0.90in) GSh-23 twin-barrel cannon, provision for about 1500kg (3307kg) of stores

▼ Mikoyan-Gurevich MiG-21bis, 701st Regiment, Pochentong

This is one of 24-28 MiG-21s that were operational with the 701st Regiment at Pochentong in the late 1980s. Attempts to overhaul the fleet in Israel in the early 1990s failed due to a lack of funding.

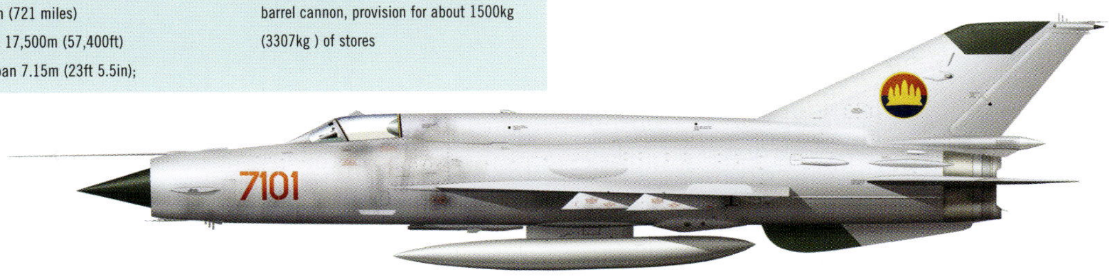

China

PLA Air Force, Navy Air Force and Army Aviation Corps

The airpower of the world's most populous country is vested in the People's Liberation Army Air Force and the PLA Navy Air Force, together with a PLA Army Aviation Corps.

All three Chinese air arms are undergoing a rigorous programme of modernization that has seen older types removed from the inventory, new and upgraded aircraft introduced, and structure rationalized. At the same time, efforts are being made to improve training and increase logistics support.

As the largest of the air arms, the PLAAF and its structure is subordinated to the PLA, which has overall control of the armed forces via a unified command. The seven Air Force Districts are assigned to the seven PLA Military Regions: Beijing, Chengdu, Guangzhou, Jinan, Lanzhou, Nanjing and Shenyang. Every Air Force District consists of a number of divisions, each normally responsible for two or three regiments.

The PLAAF has embraced lessons of recent conflicts and embarked on a widespread re-equipment programme in the last decade, which embraces combined-arms and out-of-area operations, rapid reaction forces, precision-guided munitions and C4ISR. It is estimated that the PLAAF today operates around 1,300 fighters, and 600 bomber/attack aircraft, plus transport and support aircraft, allocated to approximately 32 regiments.

The PLAAF bomber arm continues to rely on the H-6, advanced versions of which remain in use with at least four PLAAF and three PLANAF front-line regiments and now carry cruise missile armament.

Ongoing modernization of the fighter arm is reflected by the fielding of the indigenous J-10. This now complements the J-11/Su-27SK in the air defence role. The 'light' J-10 is gradually replacing the Chengdu J-7, while Su-27 variants displace the Shenyang J-8. Both J-7 and J-8 have been upgraded, however, and continue to serve in large numbers.

Indigenous fighter

The J-10, revealed in 2006, is the PLAAF's latest multi-role fighter, with indigenous weapons and avionics. A two-seat, fully combat-capable J-10S is also available. Initial versions serve with four regiments, while improved J-10A and J-10AS models have been issued to three more regiments, with deliveries continuing. The latest development is the advanced J-10B, revealed in 2009.

First ordered in 1991, 20 Su-27SKs and six two-seat Su-27UBKs were followed by 16 additional Su-27SKs and 34 Su-27UBKs. Licence production of the Su-27 has yielded the J-11 as well as 'indigenous' developments: the improved J-11A and J-11B, the latter with Chinese multi-mode radar. A reported 11 PLAAF and PLANAF fighter regiments operate J-

Specifications

Crew: 2

Powerplant: 2 x 123kN (27,600lbf) Lyulka al-31f turbofans

Maximum speed: Mach 2.0 (2120km/h; 1320mph)

Range: 3000km (1864 miles)

Service ceiling: 17,300m (56,800ft)

Dimensions: span 14.7m (48ft 2.5in); length 21.94m (72in 11in); height 6.36m (20ft 9in)

Weight: 34,500kg (76,100lb) loaded

Armament: 1 x 30mm (1.18n) GSh-3-1 gun, plus air-to-air and air-to-surface missiles

Sukhoi Su-30MK2, 4th Fighter Division/10th Air Regiment, PLANAF, Feidong

The PLANAF received 24 Su-30MK2s ordered in 2003 and delivered in 2004. This example is seen armed with R-77 and R-73 air-to-air missiles, although the type is optimized for naval strike, with the upgraded N001VEP radar used to guide Kh-31A and Kh-59MK anti-ship missiles.

▲ Sukhoi Su-27UBK

Chinese orders for Russian-built Su-27s included a significant proportion of two-seat Su-27UBK combat trainers, including this example, operated by the PLAAF's 1st Fighter Division/1st Air Regiment based at Anshan, Shenyang Military Region.

Specifications

Crew: 1
Powerplant: 1 x 122.5kN (27,557lbf) Saturn-Lyulka AL-31FN or 129.4kN (29,101lbf) WS-10A Taihang turbofan
Maximum speed: Mach 2.2 at altitude (2696km/h; 1675mph)
Combat radius: 550km (341 miles)
Service ceiling: 18,000m (59,055ft)
Dimensions: span 9.7m (31ft 10in); length 15.5m (50ft 10in); height 4.78m (15.7ft)
Weight: 18,500kg (40,785lb) loaded
Armament: 1 x 23mm (0.90in) twin-barrel cannon; 11 hardpoints with a capacity of 6000kg (13,228lb) external fuel and ordnance

▼ Chengdu J-10A, 44th Fighter Division/131st Air Regiment, PLAAF, Luliang

This J-10A is assigned to the Chengdu Military Region. The J-10A is a slightly moderated version with a satellite communications/datalink antenna located behind the canopy and a detachable refuelling probe. The J-10AS is a two-seat version.

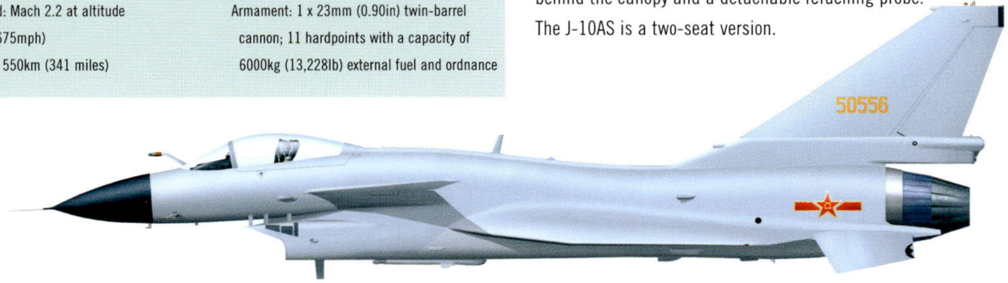

Specifications

Crew: 2
Powerplant: 1 x 122.5kN (27,557lbf) Saturn-Lyulka AL-31FN or 129.4kN (29,101lbf) WS-10A Taihang turbofan
Maximum speed: Mach 2.2 at altitude (2696km/h; 1675mph)
Combat radius: 550km (341 miles)
*NB specifications are for J-10A.
Service ceiling: 18,000m (59,055ft)
Dimensions: span 9.7m (31ft 10in); length 15.5m (50ft 10in); height 4.78m (15.7ft)
Weight: 18,500kg (40,785lb) loaded
Armament: 1 x 23mm (0.90in) twin-barrel cannon; 11 hardpoints with a capacity of 6000kg (13,228lb) external fuel and ordnance

▼ Chengdu J-10B

This aircraft was displayed at Zhuhai in 2009, and is likely the first prototype J-10B. The J-10B features a new, fixed supersonic intake, an infra-red search and track sensor, a new head-up display, underwing electronic warfare pods and a modified tailfin. A re-profiled radome may contain a new active electronically scanned array (AESA) radar.

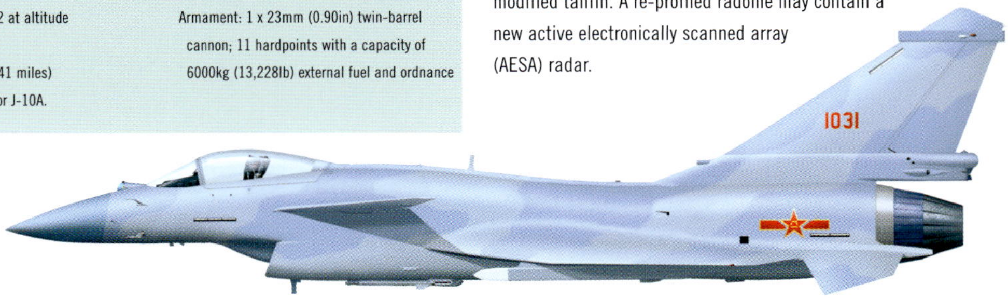

▲ **Chengdu J-10A**

The first front-line PLAAF J-10 unit was established in 2004. Current estimates suggest that units will convert to the new fighter on the basis of one each year, with the J-10 initially replacing older J-7 versions.

11s, or are in the process of conversion. Another Su-27 development, the J-15, is planned as China's first carrier-based fighter, for service on the former Soviet carrier *Varyag*, currently being refurbished at Dalian.

The J-7E equips seven front-line PLAAF and two PLANAF regiments, while the latest J-7G serves with three regiments. Some earlier J-8s have been adapted to become JZ-8 reconnaissance versions, while advanced developments of the J-8II continue in use as long-range interceptors. The upgraded J-8H and the further improved J-8F are used by five operational PLAAF units, and J-8s are also flown by two PLANAF regiments. The J-8G is a defence-suppression version in limited PLAAF use.

The PLA is making efforts to introduce improved airborne early warning and electronic warfare capabilities, manifested in the KJ-2000 AEW platform, and EW versions of the Tu-154, Il-76 and Y-8. Increasing numbers of aircraft, including upgraded H-6s and J-8s, are equipped for aerial

Specifications

Crew: 2
Powerplant: 2 x 632kW (847shp) Turbomeca Arriel-1C1 turboshafts
Maximum speed: 315km/h (195mph)
Range: 1000km (621 miles)
Service ceiling: 6000m (20,000ft)
Dimensions: rotor diameter 11.94m (39ft 2in); length 13.68m (44ft 11in) (with rotors); height 3.47m (11ft 4in)
Weight: 4100kg (9038lb) loaded
Armament: 2 x 23mm (0.90in) fixed cannons; pylon stores for rockets, gun pods, ET52 torpedo, HJ-8 anti-tank missiles, or TY-90 air-to-air missiles

▼ **Harbin Z-9, Hong Kong Garrison, PLA**

A Chinese-built version of the Aérospatiale AS365N Dauphin 2, the Z-9 is in PLA service in army utility, maritime, and attack variants. The Z-9B version features a greater proportion of Chinese-built components, and around 150 are believed to be in PLA service.

refuelling, for which the PLAAF makes use of H-6 tankers, with Il-78 tankers on order.

The fleet of PLA fighter-bombers continues to employ the Nanchang Q-5 attack aircraft, which has also been updated, but the last few PLAAF regiments are now converting to advanced Su-30MKK and Xian JH-7 aircraft. China acquired 76 examples of the Su-30MKK, a two-seat multi-role development of the Su-27, followed by 24 of the maritime Su-30MK2 version for the PLANAF. The JH-7 was developed for the PLANAF as a maritime attack aircraft, but also serves with the PLAAF, equipping three regiments within each arm.

The backbone of the transport fleet is a large number of indigenous Y-5, Y-7 and Y-8 types, with Il-76s on order to provide a genuine strategic airlift capability. Most land-based helicopters are the responsibility of the Army Aviation Corps, where indigenous Z-8, Z-9 and Z-11 transport helicopters and WZ-9 attack helicopters are complemented by Mi-8/17s. Key types unique to the PLANAF include Ka-28 shipboard helicopters, plus Y-8s adapted for maritime patrol. Training is carried out on CJ-6 basic trainers, increasing numbers of JL-8 jet trainers (replacing JJ-5s), and JJ-7 advanced trainers, with the L-15 and JL-9 competing to replace the latter type.

Specifications

Crew: 1
Powerplant: 1 x 65.17kN (14,650lb) thrust Liyang Wopen-13F (R-13-300) afterburning turbojet
Maximum speed: Mach 2.0 limited (2120km/h; 1317mph)
Range: 2230km (1380 miles)
Service ceiling: 18,800m (61,700ft)
Dimensions: span 8.32m (27ft 4in); length 14.89m (48ft 10in); height 4.1m (13ft 5in)
Weight: 7540kg (16,620lb) loaded
Armament: 2 x 30mm (1.18in) Type 30-1 cannon, plus five hardpoints for rockets, air-to-air missiles and bombs

Chengdu J-7GB, 'August 1' Aerial Demonstration Team, PLAAF, Yangcun

An unarmed version of the J-7 fighter, the J-7GB until recently equipped the August 1 (Ba Yi) aerobatic team at Yangcun in the Beijing Military Region. The team has now re-equipped with modified versions of the J-10 designated J-10AY and J-10SY, the latter being a two-seater.

Specifications

Crew: 2
Powerplant: 2 x 1409kW (1890shp) General Electric T700-GE-701C turboshaft
Maximum speed: 361km/h (224mph)
Range: 463km (288 miles)
Service ceiling: 4021m (13,200ft)
Dimensions: rotor diameter: 16.36m (53ft 8in); length 19.76m (64ft 10in); height 5.33m (17ft 6in)
Weight: 9997kg (22,000lb) loaded
Armament: 2 x 7.62mm (0.3in) door guns, AGM-119 Penguin anti-ship missiles, MK46 torpedoes

Sikorsky S-70C-2 Black Hawk, 2nd Army Aviation Regiment, 13th Group of Armies, Chengdu-Feng Huang Shan

Assigned to the Chengdu Military Region, this S-70 is one of 24 purchased for the PLA during the period of Sino-U.S. military cooperation in the mid-1980s. The S-70s are likely to be replaced in future by Mi-17s.

India

Indian Air Force, Naval Aviation and Army Aviation

Facing increasing obsolescence among its fleet of almost 1300 aircraft, the IAF is embarked on a process of modernization, introducing both foreign and indigenous equipment to its ranks.

Modernization has been slowed by economic realities and difficulties encountered by major indigenous defence programmes, typified by the protracted development of the Tejas fighter, planned as a successor to the MiG-21, which once equipped some 20 squadrons. Today, the Su-30MKI is the most important combat aircraft, but large numbers of MiG-21s remain in IAF service, while Jaguars, Mirage 2000s and MiG-27s are all now beginning to show their age. The IAF plans to introduce a new fighter under its Medium Multi-Role Combat Aircraft programme, with at least 126 new aircraft to be acquired. In the meantime, some MiG-21bis have been upgraded to Bison standard, and the MiG-27 is also subject to modernization, while avionics upgrades are being pursued for the Mirage and MiG-29. Licence production of the Su-30MKI is under way, and airborne early warning and aerial refuelling capabilities have been realized with the fielding of the A-50EI and the Il-78MKI, respectively, with six A330 tankers on order. Transport aviation will be overhauled through the induction of six C-130Js.

Specifications

Crew: 1

Powerplant: 2 x 37.3kN (8400lb) Rolls-Royce/Turbomeca Adour Mk 811 turbofans

Maximum speed: 1699km/h (1056mph)

Range: 537km (334 miles)

Service ceiling: Unavailable

Dimensions: span 8.69m (28ft 6in); length 16.83m (55ft 2.5in); height 4.89m (16ft 0.5in)

Weight: 15,700kg (34,613lb) loaded

Armament: 2 x 30mm (1.18in) Aden Mk.4 cannon; provision for 4763kg (10,500lb) of stores

SEPECAT Jaguar IT, 6 Squadron, Jamnagar

Known locally as the Shamsher, this is one of the 35 BAe-built Jaguars delivered to the IAF in the early 1980s. Built by HAL, Indian-made Jaguars wear serials in the 'JS' series. A total of 99 single-seat Jaguars were built by HAL, and these serve with six squadrons.

Specifications

Crew: 2

Powerplant: 2 x 131kN (27,557lbf) Lyulka al-31FP turbofans

Maximum speed: Mach 2.35 (2500km/h; 1533mph)

Range: 5000km (3106 miles)

Service ceiling: 17,300m (56,800ft)

Dimensions: span 14.7m (48ft 2.5in); length 21.94m (72in 11in); height 6.36m (20ft 9in)

Weight: 23,900kg (54,895lb) loaded

Armament: 1 x 30mm (1.18n) GSh-3-1 gun, plus air-to-air and air-to-surface missiles

Sukhoi Su-30MKI, 30 Squadron, Pune

This is the last Su-30MKI Phase II from the fourth batch delivered to India, equipped with canards and thrust-vectoring Saturn AL-31FP engines. The aircraft is seen armed with a Kh-31P anti-radar missile.

BHARATIYA VAYU SENA – INDIAN AIR FORCE FIGHTER UNITS

Central Air Command HQ Allahabad		
1 Squadron	Mirage 2000H/TH	Gwalior
7 Squadron	Mirage 2000H/TH	Gwalior
8 Squadron	Su-30MKI	Bareilly
9 Squadron	Mirage 2000H/TH	Gwalior
16 Squadron	Jaguar IS	Gorakhpur
24 Squadron	Su-30MKI	Bareilly
27 Squadron	Jaguar IS	Gorakhpur
35 Squadron	MiG-21M	Bakshi Ka Talab
TACDE	MiG-27	Gwalior
Eastern Air Command HQ Shillong		
2 Squadron	Su-30MKI	Tezpur
18 Squadron	MiG-27	Kalaikunda
222 Squadron	MiG-27	Hashimara
MOFTU	MiG-21FL	Tezpur
Western Air Command HQ Palam		
3 Squadron	MiG-21 Bison	Ambala
5 Squadron	Jaguar IS	Ambala
14 Squadron	Jaguar IS	Ambala
17 Squadron	MiG-21M	Bhisiana
21 Squadron	MiG-21 Bison	Sirsa
22 Squadron	MiG-27	Halwara
26 Squadron	MiG-21bis	Unknown
31 Squadron	Su-30MKI	Halwara?
37 Squadron	MiG-21M	Unknown
47 Squadron	MiG-29	Adampur
48 Squadron	An-32	Chandigarh
51 Squadron	MiG-21Bison	Srinagar
108 Squadron	MiG-21M	Pathankot
223 Squadron	MiG-29	Adampur
South Western Air Command	**HQ Gandhinagar**	
4 Squadron	MiG-21 Bison	Uttarlai
6 Squadron	Jaguar IM/IS	Jamnagar
10 Squadron	MiG-27	Jodhpur
15 Squadron	MiG-21bis	Bhuj
20 Squadron	Su-30MKI	Pune
23 Squadron	MiG-21 Bison	Suratgarh
28 Squadron	MiG-29	Jamnagar
29 Squadron	MiG-27	Jodhpur
30 Squadron	Su-30MKI	Pune
32 Squadron	MiG-21 Bison	Jodhpur
101 Squadron	MiG-21M	Naliya
224 Squadron	Jaguar IS	Jamnagar

HAL (SEPECAT) Jaguar IS

This Jaguar IS is operated by the IAF's 14 Squadron at Amabala. Alongside the strike-optimized single-seater, the IAF also operates the two-seat Jaguar IB conversion trainer and the radar-equipped single-seat Jaguar IM, which is tailored for the maritime attack mission and equips a single squadron at Jamnagar.

Specifications

Crew: 1
Powerplant: 1 x 73.5kN (16,535lb) Tumanskii R-25 turbojet
Maximum speed: 2229km/h (1385mph)
Range: 1160km (721 miles)
Service ceiling: 17,500m (57,400ft)
Dimensions: span 7.15m (23ft 5.5in); length (including probe) 15.76m (51ft 8.5in); height 4.1m (13ft 5.5in)
Weight: 10,400kg (22,925lb) loaded
Armament: 1 x 23mm (0.9in) GSh-23 twin-barrel cannon in underbelly pack, provision for about 1500kg (3307kg) of stores

Mikoyan MiG-29, 223 Squadron, Adampur

The IAF was the first export operator of the MiG-29, and the surviving fleet of approximately 50 aircraft is now being modernized to extend the fighter's service life by another 15 years, receiving multi-mode Zhuk-ME radar, Klimov RD-33 engines, new avionics, cockpit displays and an in-flight refuelling capability in the process.

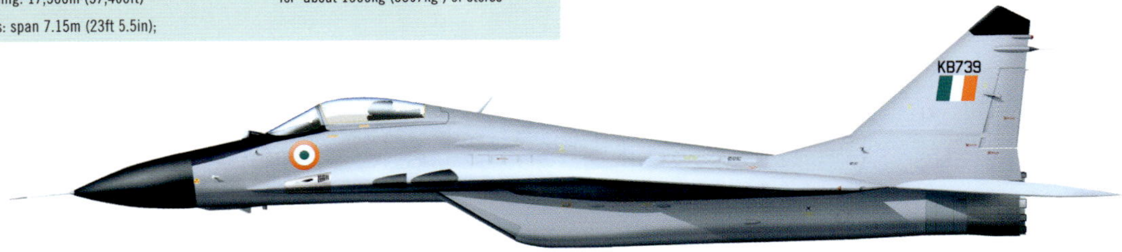

BAE Systems Hawk Mk132

India ordered 66 Hawk advanced trainers, and these entered service in 2008. BAE Systems built the first 24 aircraft, with the remaining 42 assembled locally by Hindustan Aeronautics Limited. Induction of the Hawk is part of an overhaul of IAF training, which will also see introduction of the indigenous HAL HJT-36 jet trainer. Between them, these are due to replace the ageing HJT-16 Kiran MkI and MkII.

The IAF Command is headquartered at Delhi and is led by the Chief of Air Staff. IAF Command is responsible for five operational commands, each headed by an Air Officer Commander-in-Chief. The operational commands are supplemented by Training Command and Maintenance Command.

Largest of the commands is Western Air Command, dominated by air defence and ground-attack squadrons, and responsible for the defence of Delhi, as well as Jammu and Kashmir. It is headquartered at Palam, which is also home to the Air Research Centre and Analysis Wing and the 'Pegasus' Squadron for VIP transport. South Western Air Command is primarily a defensive formation, although it maintains a strike mission. Central Air Command is responsible for most transport assets, and incorporates An-32, Do 228 and Il-76 squadrons, together with helicopter squadrons equipped with the Mi-8/17 and Mi-26. Eastern Air Command includes the areas bordering Bangladesh, Myanmar and Tibet. Headquartered in Kerala, Southern Air Command is the smallest of the operational commands, and lacks combat aircraft.

With headquarters at Yelahanka, Training Command's fleet is being revamped through the addition of 66 Hawk Mk132s acquired under the Advanced Jet Trainer programme, and also involving local production. Between them, the Hawk and the HJT-36 Sitara are planned to replace the HJT-16 Kiran, while the piston-engined HPT-32 Deepak will also require replacement in the near future. The indigenous Dhruv helicopter is also used for training, as well as being introduced by the IAF as a replacement for the ageing Cheetah and Chetak in the utility role. Other IAF helicopter types include the Mi-25/35, in use with two squadrons.

Naval Aviation

Indian Naval Aviation is responsible for land-based maritime aviation, and for providing shipborne detachments, including units that embark aboard the carrier INS *Viraat*. The MiG-29K carrier fighter has entered service in preparation for the commissioning of a new carrier, the INS *Vikramaditya*. *Viraat* embarks Sea Harrier fighters plus a Sea King anti-submarine helicopter, Ka-31 airborne early warning helicopters and Chetak utility helicopters, while smaller warships embark Ka-28s. Land-based patrol aircraft comprise Do 228s, Il-38s, Islanders, and Tu-142s, with eight P-8A Poseidons on order. The Dhruv is also entering Indian Navy service to supersede the Chetak. Naval Aviation training is conducted on the HPT-32 and HJT-16. Major naval aviation facilities are maintained at Arrakonam, Bombay, Cochin, Colaba and Goa-Dablomin.

Indian Army Aviation assets are dominated by the Cheetah and Chetak, although the Dhruv is now being fielded in increasing numbers.

Specifications

Crew: 3
Powerplant: 2 x 1454kW (1950shp) Klimov TV3-117Mt turboshafts
Maximum speed: 260km/h (162mph)
Range: 450km (280 miles)
Service ceiling: 4500m (14,765ft)
Dimensions: rotor diameter 21.29m (69ft 10in); length 18.17m (59ft 7in); height 5.65m (18ft 6in)
Weight: 11,100kg (24,470lb) loaded
Armament: up to 1500kg (3300lb) of disposable stores on six hardpoints

Mil Mi-8, 109 Helicopter Unit, Coimbatore

One of 80 Mi-8s purchased by India in the 1970s and 1980s. In the medium utility role, the Mi-8 (known as Rana) is being replaced by Mi-17s, and in 2008 India and Russia finalized a deal covering the supply of 80 Mi-17V-5s.

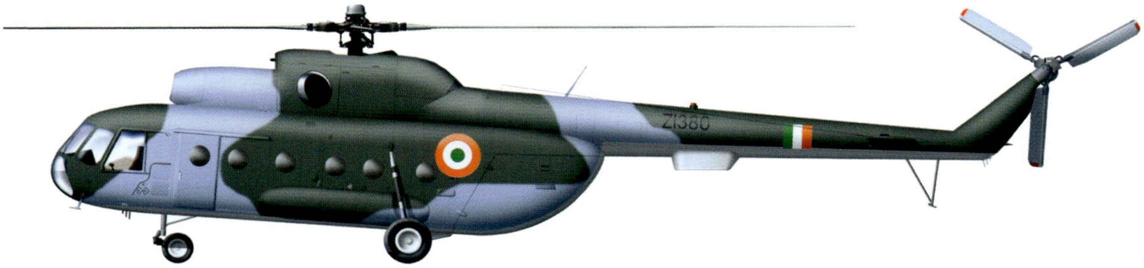

Specifications

Crew: 1
Powerplant: 1 x 73.5kN (16,535lb) Tumanskii R-25 turbojet
Maximum speed: 2229km/h (1385mph)
Range: 1160km (721 miles)
Service ceiling: 17,500m (57,400ft)
Dimensions: span 7.15m (23ft 5.5in); length (including probe) 15.76m (51ft 8.5in); height 4.1m (13ft 5.5in)
Weight: 10,400kg (22,925lb) loaded
Armament: 1 x 23mm(0.9in) GSh-23 twin-barrel cannon in underbelly pack, provision for about 1500kg (3307kg) of stores

HAL (Mikoyan-Gurevich) MiG-21 Bison, 3 Squadron, Ambala

The upgraded Bison has been flown by 3 Squadron 'Cobras' since 2008. The Bison introduces a beyond-visual-range air-to-air capability through the use of the Kopyo multi-mode radar and the R-77 missile. Other advances include an Israeli head-up display, hands on throttle and stick (HOTAS) controls and multi-function cockpit display.

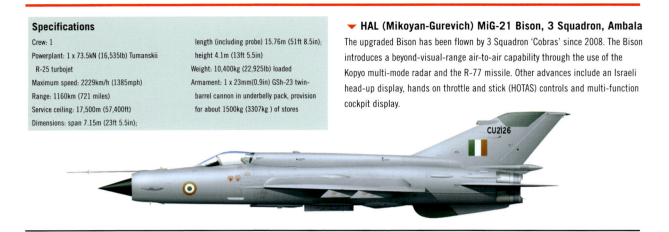

Indonesia

Indonesian Air Force

The largest nation in Southeast Asia, Indonesia's air arm is the Tentara Nasional Indonesia Angkatan Udara, or TNI-AU, which includes two commands covering eastern and western zones.

The pride of the TNI-AU is its fighter arm, which operates 10 F-16A/Bs and a few Su-27SK/Su-30MKs. The latter are arriving slowly, with two Su-27SKs in service (plus three on order), together with four multi-role Su-30MKs from a total of five ordered. The effects of international embargoes mean that the F-16 and F-5 fleets are suffering limited serviceability. Only four F-5Es are reported as active.

Transport is essential in order to cover Indonesia's countless islands, and the TNI-AU calls upon locally built CN235s and C-212s, as well as eight C-130Bs, two KC-130B tankers, and a handful of DHC-5s.

Primary training is conducted on SA 202s and SF260s, before students progress to the KT-1B Wong Bee turboprop trainer, which is replacing the T-34. The Hawk Mk53 advanced trainer is subject to limited availability, with much of the fleet grounded. The Hawk Mk109 trainer fares somewhat better, and the Hawk Mk209 remains in use for counter-insurgency and light attack. Helicopter pilot training relies on the EC120, which is replacing the Bell 47, and locally assembled transport helicopters in use include the Bell 412, BO105, Puma and Super Puma.

Specifications

Crew: 2
Powerplant: 2 x 131kN (27,557lbf) Lyulka al-31FP turbofans
Maximum speed: Mach 2.35 (2500km/h; 1533mph)
Range: 5000km (3106 miles)
Service ceiling: 17,300m (56,800ft)
Dimensions: span 14.7m (48ft 2.5in); length 21.94m (72in 11in); height 6.36m (20ft 9in)
Weight: 23,900kg (54,895lb) loaded
Armament: 1 x 30mm (1.18in) GSh-3-1 gun, plus air-to-air and air-to-surface missiles

Sukhoi Su-30MK, Skadron Udara 11, Hasanuddin

TS-3002 is one of the first two Su-30MKs for Indonesia, delivered in December 2008 as replacements for the A-4 Skyhawk fleet, retired in 2004. SkU 11 is based at Hasanuddin, on the island of Sulawesi.

Japan

Japan Air, Maritime and Ground Self-Defence Forces

Japan's three air arms are the Air Self-Defence Force, Maritime Self-Defence Force and Ground Self-Defence Force. All three are recipients of some of the most advanced aircraft available.

THE SHARP END of the JASDF is provided by 12 fighter squadrons, all under the command of the Air Defence Command (Koku Sotai). Nine of the 12 fighter squadrons are configured as fighter-interceptor units, and three as fighter support squadrons. However, the fighter support units, Dai 3, 6 and 8 Hiko-tai, also maintain air defence alert duties. The fighter squadrons are supported within the Koku Sotai by airborne early warning, reconnaissance and aggressor training units.

The Koku Sota defends Japan on the basis of four regional commands (Hometai), each of which is assigned two fighter wings, with a typical strength of two squadrons each. Being smaller, the Southwestern Air Command is designated as a Composite organization.

The Air Support Command (Koku Sien Shudan), with headquarters at Fuchu, is responsible for transport, SAR and flight-checking units, and maintains the Koku Kyunan-dan (Air Rescue Wing), together with four transport groups: Dai 1 Yuso Koku-tai (1st Tactical Airlift Group) at Komaki AB, Dai 2 Yuso Koku-tai at Iruma AB, Dai 3 Yuso Koku-tai at Miho AB, and the Tokubetu Koku Yuso-tai

Specifications

Crew: 2
Powerplant: 2 x 79.6kN (17,900lb) General Electric J79-GE-17 turbojets
Maximum speed: 2390km/h (1485mph)
Range: 2817km (1750 miles)
Service ceiling: 19,685m (60,000ft)
Dimensions: span 11.7m (38ft 5in); length 17.76m (58ft 3in); height 4.96m (16ft 3in)
Weight: 26,308kg (58,000lb) loaded
Armament: 1 x 20mm (.78in) M61A1 Vulcan cannon and four AIM-7 Sparrow recessed under fuselage or other weapons up to 1370kg (3020lb) on centreline pylon; four wing pylons for stores up to 5888kg (12,980lb)

▼ McDonnell Douglas F-4EJ Phantom II, Dai 8 Hiko-tai, Dai 3 Koku-dan, Misawa AB

27-8306 was flown by Dai 8 Hiko-tai in 2004, although the unit has now re-equipped with the F-2, and this aircraft is now in storage at Misawa. The Kai upgrade outfitted the F-4EF with AN/APG-66J pulse-Doppler radar, for a look-down/shoot-down capability.

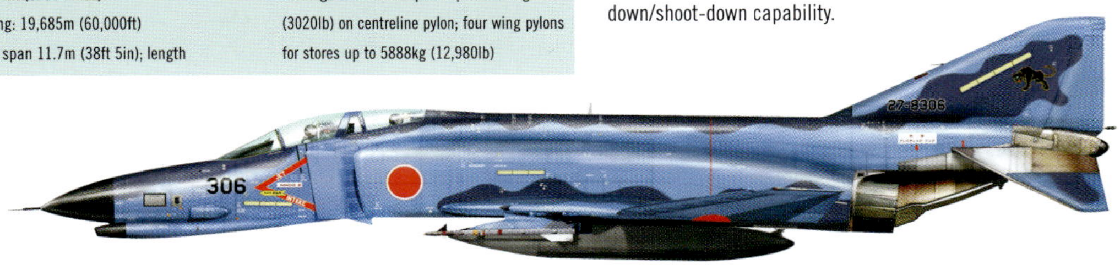

Specifications

Crew: 1
Powerplant: 2 x 105.7kN (23,770lb) Pratt & Whitney F100-PW-220 turbofans
Maximum speed: 2655km/h (1650mph)
Range: 5745km (3570 miles)
Service ceiling: 30,500m (100,000ft)
Dimensions: span 13.05m (42ft 9.75in); length 19.43in (63ft 9in); height 5.63m (18ft 5in)
Weight: 30,844kg (68,000lb) loaded
Armament: 1 x 20mm (0.79in) M61A1 cannon, provision for up to 10,705kg (23,600lb) of stores, including missiles, bombs, tanks, pods and rockets

▼ Mitsubishi (McDonnell Douglas) F-15J Eagle, Dai 305 Hiko-tai, Dai 7 Koku-dan, Hyakuri AB

F-15J 52-8849 is one of 213 F-15J/DJs purchased for the JASDF. The first two F-15Js and the first 14 two-seat F-15DJs were built in the USA, before Mitsubishi took over production.

KOKU SOTAI (AIR DEFENCE COMMAND) HQ FUCHU

Hokubu Koku Hometai (Northern Air Defence Force) HQ Misawa		
Hokubu Sien Hiko-tai (Northern HQ Support Flight)	T-4	Misawa AB
Dai 2 Koku-dan (2nd Air Wing) Chitose AB		
Dai 201 Hiko-tai (201st Squadron)	F-15J/DJ, T-4	Chitose AB
Dai 203 Hiko-tai (203rd Squadron)	F-15J/DJ, T-4	Chitose AB
Dai 3 Koku-dan (3rd Air Wing) Misawa AB		
Dai 3 Hiko-tai (3rd Squadron)	F-2A/B, T-4	Misawa AB
Dai 8 Hiko-tai (8th Squadron)	F-2A/B, T-4	Misawa AB
Hokubu Sien Hiko-han (Northern Air Support Flight)	T-4	Misawa AB
Chubu Koku Hometai (Central Air Defence Force) HQ Iruma		
Dai 6 Koku-dan (6th Air Wing) Komatsu AB		
Dai 303 Hiko-tai (303rd Squadron)	F-15J/DJ, T-4	Komatsu AB
Dai 306 Hiko-tai (306th Squadron)	F-15J/DJ, T-4	Komatsu AB
Dai 7 Koku-dan (7th Air Wing) Hyakuri AB		
Dai 302 Hiko-tai (302nd Squadron)	F-4EJ, T-4	Hyakuri AB
Dai 305 Hiko-tai (305th Squadron)	F-15J/DJ, T-4	Hyakuri AB
Seibu Koku Hometai (Western Air Defence Force) HQ Kasuga		
Seiku Sien Hiko-tai (WADF HQ Support Flight)	T-4	Kasuga
Dai 5 Koku-dan (5th Air Wing) Nyutabaru AB		
Dai 301 Hiko-tai (301st Squadron)	F-15J/DJ, T-4	Nyutabaru AB
Dai 8 Koku-dan (8th Air Wing) Tsuiki AB		
Dai 6 Hiko-tai (6th Squadron)	F-2A/B, T-4	Tsuiki AB
Dai 304 Hiko-tai (304th Squadron)	F-15J/DJ, T-4	Tsuiki AB
Nansei Koku Konsei-Dan (Southwestern Composite Air Division) HQ Naha		
Nansei Sien Hiko-han (SW Support Flight)	T-4	Naha AB
Dai 83 Koku-gun (83rd Air Group) Naha AB		
Dai 204 Hiko-tai (204th Squadron)	F-15J/DJ, T-4	Naha AB
Chokkatu-butai (Direct Reporting Unit)		
Sotai Sireibu Hiko-tai (ADC HQ Flight Group)	T-4, U-4	Iruma AB
Denshisen Sien-tai (ECM Support Unit)	EC-1, YS-11EA	Iruma AB
Denshi Hiko Hiko Sokutei-tai (ELINT Squadron)	YS-11EB	Iruma AB
Teisatu Koku-tai (Tactical Reconnaissance Group) Hyakuri AB		
Dai 501 Hiko-tai (501st Squadron)	RF-4E/EJ, T-4	Hyakuri AB
Hiko Kyodi-tai (Tactical Fighter Training Group)	F-15DJ, T-4	Nyutarau AB
Koku Kyoiku Shudan		
23 Hiko-tai	F-15D/DJ, T-4	Nyutarau AB
Keikai Koku-tai (Airborne Early Warning Group) Misawa AB		
Hiko Keikai Kanshitai (Air Warning Surveillance Squadron)	E-2C	Misawa AB
Hiko Keikai Kanseita (Air Warning Control Squadron)	E-767	Hamamatsu AB

(Special Air Transport Group) at Chitose AB. Headquartered at Iruma AB, the Air Rescue Wing incorporates 11 Akita Kyunan-tai (Air Rescue Squadrons), all being equipped with UH-60J helicopters and fixed-wing U-125A aircraft.

The Air Support Command also includes four Iruma Herikoputa Kuyu-tai (Helicopter Airlift Squadrons), flying the CH-47J. The 1st Tactical Airlift Group) at Komaki AB has a squadron of C-130H transports and one of KC-767 tankers. The 2nd Tactical Airlift Group at Iruma AB has one squadron of C-1s and U-4s. The 3rd Tactical Airlift Group has a squadron of C-1, YS-11P and YS-11NT aircraft at Miho AB, a training squadron of T-400s at Miho AB, and a flight-check squadron with YS-11FC and U-125 aircraft at Iruma AB. Finally, the Special

Air Transport Group at Chitose AB operates a squadron of Boeing 747-47C VIP transports.

Other commands comprise Air Training Command (Koku Kyoiku Shudan) and Aviation Research and Development Command (Koku Kaihatsu Jikken Shudan). Training begins on the T-7 with 11 Hiko Kyoiku-dan or 12 Hiko Kyoiku-dan, while fighter pilots progress to the T-4 jet trainer (13 Hiko Kyoiku-dan and Dai 1 Koku-dan) and transport aircrew to the T-400 (41 Kyoiku Hikotai).

New equipment for the JASDF is to be procured in the form of a replacement for the F-4EJ, for which the F-X requirement has been formulated. A new transport aircraft will arrive in the form of the C-2, which will replace the C-1 and C-130.

Fleet Air Force

The structure of the JMSDF's Fleet Air Force (Koku Shudan), with headquarters at Atsugi AB, is based around Fleet Air Wings (Dai Koku-gun), each of which comprises a number of squadrons. Most operational units are equipped with the P-3C for land-based maritime patrol, or the SH-60J/K, the latter being deployed aboard Japanese Navy warships. P-3s will eventually be replaced by the indigenous P-1. Most Dai Koku-gun also include a base flight equipped with UH-60Js for SAR duties. There are seven Dai Koku-gun, four of which include fixed-wing (P-3C) squadrons at Kanoya AB, Hachinohe AB, Atsugi AB and Naha AB; two are helicopter wings (SH-60J/K, at Tateyama AB and Omura AB), while the remainder, Dai 31 Koku-gun, is a composite wing (with examples of the US-1 and US-2 flying-boat, P-3 of various subtypes, LC-90 King Air, U-36 Learjet, SH-60 and TH-135 training helicopter). There are three further squadrons that function as direct-reporting units. Dai 51 Koku-tai operates P-3s, SH-60s and OH-6s, Dai 61 Koku-tai is equipped with YS-11s and LC-90s, and Dai 111 Koku-tai is a specialist mine countermeasures unit, in the process of replacing its MH-53Es with MCH-101 and CH-101 helicopters.

Aviation units of the JGSDF are allocated according to five military districts. The Regional Army Aviation Groups comprise Northern, Northeastern, Eastern, Central and Western Groups. Each Regional Army Aviation Group (Homen Kokutai) normally includes an Army Air Group HQ Squadron (Homen Kokutai Honbu Zukitai) with fixed-wing LR-1 and LR-2s (Mitsubishi MU-2 and Beech 200s, respectively), an Army Helicopter Squadron (Homen Herikoputatai) with UH-1 and OH-6 helicopters, and an Anti-Tank Helicopter Squadron (Taisensha Herikoputatai) with AH-1S and OH-6D types. Liaison squadrons are in addition attached to each division (Shidan), these typically operating OH-6Ds. New attack helicopters are arriving in the shape of the AH-64DJP, to supplant the AH-1S, while the indigenous OH-1 scout helicopter is also in service as a complement to the OH-6, with deliveries continuing. Helicopter airlift is provided by CH-47Js and medium-lift UH-60Js, which are replacing the KV-107 and UH-1 fleets, respectively.

Specifications

Crew: 2
Powerplant: 2 x 105.4kN (23,700lb) Pratt & Whitney F100-PW-220 turbofans
Maximum speed: 2655km/h (1650mph)
Range: 4631km (2878 miles)
Service ceiling: 30,500m (100,000ft)
Dimensions: span 13.05m (42ft 9.75in); length 19.43in (63ft 9in); height 5.63m (18ft 5in)
Weight: 30,844kg (68,000lb) loaded
Armament: 1 x 20mm (.78in) M61A1 cannon with 960 rounds, external pylons with provision for up to 10,705kg (23,600lb) of stores

Mitsubishi (McDonnell Douglas) F-15DJ Eagle, Dai 304 Hiko-tai, Dai 8 Koku-dan, Tsuiki AB

Japan's F-15D/DJ fleet has undergone a mid-life upgrade that adds licence-built F110-PW-220 engines, an upgraded ejection seat and a modernized radar, known as the AN/APG-63U. The Japanese Eagles can also employ indigenous weapons.

Laos

LAOS PEOPLE'S LIBERATION ARMY AIR FORCE

The Laos People's Liberation Army Air Force is based around a small force of transports and helicopters, with bases at Luang Prabang, Pakse, Savannakhet, Vientiane and Xiengkhouang.

WITH ITS JET fighters now retired from service, the LPLAAF is based around four military regions, with an HQ at Vientiane. Aircraft in use comprise An-2, An-24/26 and a single An-74 transport, plus Mi-8/17, Mi-26 and Z-9 helicopters, and a single Yak-40 for VIP transport duties.

Specifications

Crew: 1
Powerplant: 1 x 60.5kN (13,610lb) thrust Tumanskii R-11F2S-300 afterburning turbojet
Maximum speed: 2229km/h (1385mph)
Range:1670km (1037 miles)
Service ceiling: 19,000m (62,335ft)
Dimensions: span 7.15m (23ft 5.5in); length (including pitot) 14.5m (47ft 7in); height 4.1m (13ft 5.5in)
Weight: 7800kg (17,195lb) loaded
Armament: 1 x 23mm GSh-23 cannon, plus 2 x K-13A (R-3S) AAM or 2 x 500g (1102lb) of stores

Mikoyan-Gurevich MiG-21PFM, Interceptor Regiment, Vientiane

Formerly operated by the LPLAAF, this was one of 15 MiG-21PFMs and two-seat MiG-21US trainers, as well as 15 improved MiG-21bis fighters, acquired from the USSR in the mid-1980s.

Malaysia

ROYAL MALAYSIAN AIR FORCE

Possessing a modern fleet of combat and support aircraft of varied origin, the RMAF (Tentera Udara Diraja Malaysia – TUDM) operates from bases on the Malayan Peninsula and Borneo.

THE COMBAT FLEET of the RMAF comprises 18 Su-30MKMs, 10 MiG-29s, eight F/A-18Ds, seven F-5E/Fs, 13 Hawk Mk208s for ground attack, and two RF-5Es for reconnaissance. MB339s and Hawk Mk108s provide advanced training, while a transport capability rests primarily with C-130s and CN235s. Most numerous helicopter is the S-61A Nuri.

Specifications

Crew: 2
Powerplant: 2 x 131kN (27,557lbf) Lyulka al-31FP turbofans
Maximum speed: Mach 2.35 (2500km/h; 1533mph)
Range: 5000km (3106 miles)
Service ceiling: 17,300m (56,800ft)
Dimensions: span 14.7m (48ft 2.5in); length 21.94m (72in 11in); height 6.36m (20ft 9in)
Weight: 23,900kg (54,895lb) loaded
Armament: 1 x 30mm (1.18n) GSh-3-1 gun, plus air-to-air and air-to-surface missiles

Sukhoi Su-30MKM, No. 11 Squadron, Gong Kedak

One of 18 Su-30MKMs ordered for the RMAF in 2003 and delivered from 2007. These multi-role fighters include equipment of French, Indian and Israeli origin.

Myanmar

Myanmar Air Force

The Tamdaw Lay, or Myanmar Air Force, operates a growing combat and support fleet, with equipment coming primarily from China and Russia, while Poland has provided helicopters.

THE MAJOR COMBAT types are Chinese-supplied, comprising A-5 attack jets, and J-6 and F-7 fighters. The fighters are being in the process of replacement by MiG-29s. G-4 Super Galebs and K-8s provide advanced training, while major helicopter types in use are the Mi-2, Mi-17, UH-1 and W-3.

Specifications

Crew: 1
Powerplant: 2 x 81.4kN (18,298lb) Sarkisov RD-33 turbofans
Maximum speed: 2443km/h (1518mph)
Range: 1500km (932 miles)
Service ceiling: 17,000m (55,775ft)
Dimensions: span 11.36m (37ft 3.75in); length (including probe) 17.32m (56ft 10in); height 7.78m (25ft 6.25in)
Weight: 18,500kg (40,785lb) loaded
Armament: 1 x 30mm (1.18in) GSh-30 cannon, provision for up to 4500kg (9921lb) of stores

Mikoyan MiG-29, Myanmar Air Force, Shante

This is one of 10 MiG-29s from the original batch acquired, Myanmar since having ordered additional MiG-29SMTs. The MiG-29s are operated by an unknown unit based at Shante, near Meiktila.

Nepal

Nepal Army Aviation

Lacking an air force, the Himalayan kingdom of Nepal's army maintains an aviation element primarily equipped with helicopters. These are operated by the 11th Brigade (Army Air Wing).

THE ARMY AIR Wing bases its aircraft at Kathmandu-Tribhuvan, although as many as 36 satellite airfields are available. Types in use include AS350, Bell 206, Cheetah/Lancer, Chetak, Dhruv and Mi-17 helicopters, and small numbers of fixed-wing HS748, Islander, M-28 and Y-7 aircraft.

Specifications

Crew: 3
Powerplant: 2 x 1545kW (2225shp) Klimov TV3-117VM turboshafts
Maximum speed: 250km/h (156mph)
Range: 950km (594 miles)
Service ceiling: 6000m (19,690ft)
Dimensions: rotor diameter 21.35m (69ft 10in); length 18.42m (60ft 5in); height 4.76m (15ft 7in)
Weight: 11,100kg (24,470lb) loaded
Armament: Capable of carrying up to 1500kg (3300lb) of bombs, rockets and gunpods on six hardpoints

Mil Mi-171MTV-5, 11th Brigade, Kathmandu

Nepal purchased its first two Mi-171MTV-5s in January 2002. At total of four or six have since been acquired over the time, at least one of which was written off under unknown circumstances.

North Korea

Democratic People's Republic of Korea Air Force

One of the world's most secretive air arms, the DPRKAF is mainly equipped with Chinese, Soviet and Russian aircraft, and is headquartered at Pyongyang, with at least 25 operational airfields.

ALTHOUGH IT OPERATES a large number of aircraft, current levels of serviceability are unclear. Combat types delivered include the F-5, F-6, F-7 and MiG-21, MiG-23, MiG-29, Q-5, Su-7 and Su-25 jets, together with transport aircraft and trainers.

Specifications

Crew: 1
Powerplant: 2 x 81.4kN (18,298lb) Sarkisov RD-33 turbofans
Maximum speed: 2443km/h (1518mph)
Range: 1500km (932 miles)
Service ceiling: 17,000m (55,775ft)
Dimensions: span 11.36m (37ft 3.75in); length (including probe) 17.32m (56ft 10in); height 7.78m (25ft 6.25in)
Weight: 18,500kg (40,785lb) loaded
Armament: 1 x 30mm (1.18in) GSh-30 cannon, provision for up to 4500kg (9921lb) of stores

Mikoyan MiG-29, 55th Air Regiment, Sunchon

The DPRKAF received an unknown number of MiG-29s. These are operated by a single squadron of the 55th Air Regiment, part of the 1st Air Combat Division.

Philippines

Philippine Air Force

The combat potential of the Philippine Air Force has been reduced following the retirement of its F-5 combat jets. The current fleet is optimized for counter-insurgency, transport and training.

OPERATING WITH A USAF-style structure, the Philippine Air Force includes OV-10s and armed MD520 helicopters for COIN work, C-130, F27, Islander and Nomad transports and maritime patrol aircraft, and S-70, S-76 and UH-1H helicopters. Training is conducted on S211 jets, preceded by SF260s and T-41s. Also on order are W-3 helicopters.

Specifications

Crew: 1
Powerplant: 2 x 18.1kN (4080lb) General Electric J85-GE-13 turbojetsWhitney F100-PW-220 turbofans
Maximum speed: 1487km/h (924mph)
Range: 314km (195 miles)
Service ceiling: 15,390m (50,500ft)
Dimensions: span 7.7m (25ft 3in); length 7.7m (25ft 3in); height 4.01m (13ft 2in)
Weight: 9374kg (20,667lb) loaded
Armament: 2 x 20mm (0.79in) M39 cannon; provision for 1996kg (4400lb) of stores (missiles, bombs, cluster bombs, rocket launcher pods)

Northrop F-5A Freedom Fighter, 6th Tactical Fighter Squadron, 5th Fighter Wing, Basa

This is one of 19 F-5As delivered to the Philippines in 1966 (together with three two-seat F-5Bs) that served until the mid-1990s. The type has meanwhile been withdrawn from service and the unit disbanded.

Pakistan

Pakistan Air Force, Army Aviation Corps and Naval Aviation

The Pakistan Fiza'ya (Pakistan Air Force) is divided into Central, Northern and Southern Air Command, each of which contains two or three wings and their respective squadrons.

IN ADDITION TO the regional air commands, the PAF includes an Air Force Academy, headquartered at Risalpur, and a composite transport wing, 35 Wing, which reports directly to PAF headquarters. 35 Wing has three squadrons, all based at Chaklala. One operates the force of C-130/L-100 transports, one has the VIP fleet (F27, Falcon 20, Boeing 707 and Gulfstream IV and 350), and one comprises Cessna 172, Piper PA-34 and Y-12 liaison types. The Air Force Academy operates MFI-17 Mushshak primary trainers (Primary Flying Training Wing) and T-37 and K-8 jet trainers (Basic Flying Training Wing).

Central Air Command includes two wings. 34 Wing at Rafiqui has one squadron of F-7P/FT-7P fighters, two of Mirage III/5s, one of Mirage 5s, and a squadron of Alouette III helicopters. 38 Wing at Mushaf maintains two squadrons of F-16A/Bs, one of Falcon 20s outfitted for electronic warfare, and one squadron of Alouettes.

The largest of the three regional air commands, Northern Air Command, is equipped mainly with fighters and attack aircraft. 33 Wing at Kamra has a squadron each of F-7P/FT-7P and Mirage III/5 fighters, one squadron of Alouettes, and a test unit equipped with the new JF-17 Thunder fighter. 36 Wing, based at Peshawar, is optimized for attack and has one squadrons of A-5C attack aircraft, one of JF-17s and two of Alouettes. At Miawali, 37 (Combat Training) Wing operates two operational conversion units of F-7P/FT-7P jets, one of FT-5 jet trainers, and one squadron of Alouettes.

Southern Air Command's 31 Wing is based at Quetta, but includes one squadron – with F-7P/FT-7P jets at Rafiqui. The two Quetta-based squadrons fly F-7P/FT-7Ps, and are joined by a squadron of Alouettes. 32 Wing is the largest PAF wing, with five squadrons. Three of these are equipped with Mirage III/5s, one with F-7P/FT-7Ps, and one with Alouettes and Mi-171s. All 32 Wing units are located at Masroor. Most bases maintain station flights equipped with MFI-17s.

Army and Navy

The Pakistan Army Aviation Corps operates AH-1F/S, Alouette II/III, AS350, Bell 206, Bell 412, Mi-17, Puma and UH-1H helicopters, MFI-17s, Y-12s and a handful of VIP types. Pakistan Naval Aviation includes Atlantic, Defender, F27 and P-3C maritime patrol aircraft, and Alouette III and Sea King Mk45 helicopters, all shore-based at Sharea Faisal, otherwise known as PNS *Mehran*, near Karachi.

Specifications

Crew: 1

Powerplant: either 1 x 105.7kN (23,770lb) Pratt & Whitney F100-PW-200 or 1 x 128.9kN (28,984lb) General Electric F110-GE-100 turbofan

Maximum speed: 2142km/h (1320mph)

Range: 925km (525 miles)

Service ceiling: 15,240m (50,000ft)

Dimensions: span 9.45m (31ft); length 15.09m (49ft 6in); height 5.09m (16ft 8in)

Weight: 16,057kg (35,400lb) loaded

Armament: 1 x General Electric M61A1 20mm (0.79in) multi-barrelled cannon, wingtip missile stations; provision for up to 9276kg (20,450lb) of stores

General Dynamics F-16A Fighting Falcon, 38 Wing, Sargodha

F-16A 81-0921 was operated by 38 Wing until written off in June 1991. The fighter displayed two kill markings denoting victories scored against Afghan fighters in the 1980s. The PAF is in the process of receiving 24 advanced new Block 50/52 F-16C/Ds.

Singapore

Republic of Singapore Air Force

One of the economic powerhouses of Southeast Asia, the island of Singapore's air arm is suitably equipped and proficiently trained, and also maintains permanent detachments overseas.

The most important combat type flown by the RSAF is the F-16C/D, in its advanced Block 52 variant, and this is soon to be joined by 24 F-15SG strike aircraft. Remaining F-5 jets have been upgraded locally to F-5S/T and RF-5S standard, and both F-5s and F-16s are supported by KC-135R tankers and E-2C airborne early warning aircraft.

A number of RSAF assets are based overseas for training, including F-15s, F-16s, AH-64s and CH-47s in the US, S211 jet trainers and Puma helicopters in Australia, and A-4SU/TA-4SU trainers in France.

Maritime patrol is the responsibility of Fokker 50MPAs, while ground forces are supported by a fleet of 20 AH-64D attack helicopters and CH-47SDs and S-70Bs for transport. Training is conducted using a fleet of EC120 and AS550 helicopters, with fixed-wing pilots provided with S211s and PC-21s. Transport assets comprise Cougar and Super Puma helicopters, C-130Hs, KC-130B/H tanker/transports and Fokker 50s.

Specifications

Crew: 2
Powerplant: 2 x 131kN (29,400lb) General Electric F110-GE-129 thrust engines
Maximum speed: 2655km/h (1650mph)
Range: 3900km (2400 miles)
Service ceiling: 18,200m (60,000ft)
Dimensions: span 13.05m (42ft 9.75in); length 19.43in (63ft 9in); height 5.63m (18ft 5in)
Weight: 36,700kg (81,000lb) loaded
Armament: 1 x 20mm (0.79in) M61A1 cannon, provision for up to 11,000kg (24,250lb) of external stores, including missiles, bombs, tanks, pods and rockets

Boeing F-15SG Strike Eagle, 149 Squadron, Paya Lebar

06-0007 was introduced to service in 2010. The F-15SG features F110-129 engines, AN/APG-63 active electronically scanned array radar, helmet-mounted sight, sniper targeting and infra-red search and track pod and a range of precision-guided weapons.

Specifications

Crew: 1
Powerplant: 1 x 126.7kN (28,500lb) thrust Pratt & Whitney F100-PW-229 afterburning turbofan
Maximum speed: 2177km/h (1353mph)
Range: 3862km (2400 miles)
Service ceiling: 15,240m (49,000ft)
Dimensions: span 9.45m (31ft); length 15.09m (49ft 6in); height 5.09m (16ft 8in)
Weight: 19,187kg (42,300lb) loaded
Armament: 1 x GE M61A1 20mm (0.79in) multi-barrelled cannon, seven external hardpoints with provision for up to 9276kg (20,450lb) of stores

Lockheed Martin F-16D Fighting Falcon, 143 Squadron 'Phoenix', Tengah

96-5030 is one of Singapore's two-seat Block 52 Fighting Falcons, these featuring an extended spine housing electronic warfare equipment.

South Korea

Republic of Korea Air Force, Naval Aviation

The RoKAF's raison d'être is to maintain a defensive posture against North Korea, and as a result the air arm pursues a constant programme of upgrades and acquisition of new equipment.

Specifications

Crew: 1
Powerplant: 1 x 126.7kN (28,500lb) thrust Pratt & Whitney F100-PW-229 afterburning turbofan
Maximum speed: 2177km/h (1353mph)
Range: 3862km (2400 miles)
Service ceiling: 15,240m (49,000ft)
Dimensions: span 9.45m (31ft); length 15.09m (49ft 6in); height 5.09m (16ft 8in)
Weight: 19,187kg (42,300lb) loaded
Armament: 1 x General Electric M61A1 20mm (0.79in) multi-barrelled cannon, wingtip missile stations; seven external hardpoints with provision for up to 9276kg (20,450lb) of stores

Lockheed Martin F-16C Fighting Falcon, 20th Fighter Wing, Sosan AB

01-515 is a Block 52 F-16C, part of a total of 180 aircraft that were acquired. This particular aircraft was part of the Peace Bridge III programme, covering 20 aircraft delivered during 2003-4.

THE MOST SIGNIFICANT recent acquisition for the RoKAF is the F-15K strike aircraft, 60 of which are on order. These are joining a combat fleet dominated by the F-16C/D, the F-5E/F – both of which were produced under licence – and the F-4D/E. Other new equipment under contract includes 44 indigenous A-50 light attack aircraft and four Boeing 737 airborne early warning aircraft. RoKAF helicopters include HH-47Ds and UH-60Ps for combat SAR. The trainer fleet includes indigenous KT-1s, while Hawk jet trainers are being joined by locally built T-50s. Armed KO-1 versions of the KT-1 serve in the forward airborne controller role.

The primary equipment of RoK Naval Aviation are two squadrons of Lynx Mk99 anti-submarine helicopters, complemented by smaller numbers of Alouette IIIs, UH-1Hs and UH-60Ps. P-3Cs serve in the land-based maritime patrol role.

Army Aviation

The RoK Army's Aviation Operations Command includes two aviation brigades equipped with AH-1S and MD500 Defender attack helicopters, CH-47D and locally assembled UH-60P transport helicopters, and BO105 utility helicopters.

HANKOOK KONG GOON – REPUBLIC OF KOREA AF

Air Force Operations Command		
5th Tactical Air Transport Wing		**Gimhae AB**
251st Tactical Air Support Squadron	C-130H	Gimhae AB
256th Tactical Air Transport Squadron	CN235	Gimhae AB
258th Tactical Air Transport Squadron	UH-60P	Gimhae AB
259th Tactical Air Support Squadron	C-130H	Gimhae AB
15th Composite Wing	**Seongnam AB**	
251st Tactical Control Squadron	KO-1	Seongnam AB
255th Special Operations Squadron	C-130H	Seongnam AB
257th Tactical Air Transport Squadron	C-130H	Seongnam AB
35th Combined Group*		
296th VIP Squadron	Boeing 737, VH-60P, CN235	Seongnam AB

* subordinate to 15th Composite Wing.

Air Force Northern Combat Command		
8th Fighter Wing	**Wongju AB**	
103rd Fighter Squadron	F-5E/F	Wongju AB
203rd Fighter Squadron	F-5E/F	Wongju AB
207th Fighter Squadron	F-5E/F	Wongju AB
238th Fighter Squadron	A-37B	Wongju AB
239th Special Flying Squadron 'Black Eagles'	A-37B	Wongju AB
10th Fighter Wing	**Suwon AB**	
101st Fighter Squadron	F-5E/F	Suwon AB
201st Fighter Squadron	F-5E/F	Suwon AB
38th Fighter Group*		
111th Fighter Squadron	F-5E/F	Gunsan AB
* subordinate to 10th Fighter Wing.		
39th Tactical Reconnaissance Group*		
125th Tactical Reconnaissance Squadron	Hawker 800	Seongnam AB
131st Tactical Reconnaissance Squadron	RF-4C	Suwon AB
132nd Tactical Reconnaissance Squadron	RF-5A, F-5A/B	Suwon AB
* subordinate to 15th Composite Wing.		
17th Fighter Wing	**Chongju AB**	
152nd Fighter Squadron	F-4E	Chongju AB
153rd Fighter Squadron	F-4E	Chongju AB
156th Fighter Squadron	F-4E	Chongju AB
29th Tactical Development and Training Group *		
191st Tactical Development and Training Squadron	F-16C/D	Chongju AB
192nd Tactical Development and Training Squadron	F-16C/D	Chongju AB
* subordinate to 17th Fighter Wing.		
6th Search and Rescue Group*		
233rd Combat Search and Rescue Squadron	HH-60P, AS332, Bell 412	Chongju AB
235th Search and Rescue Squadron	HH-47D, HH-32	Chongju
* subordinate to 17th Fighter Wing.		

18th Fighter Wing	**Gangneung AB**	
105th Fighter Squadron	F-5E/F	Gangneung AB
112th Fighter Squadron	F-5E/F	Gangneung AB
205th FTS	F-5E/F	Gangneung AB
19th Fighter Wing	**Yungwon AB**	
161st Fighter Squadron	F-16C/D	Yungwon AB
162nd Fighter Squadron	F-16C/D	Yungwon AB
155th Fighter Squadron	F-16C/D	Yungwon AB
159th Fighter Squadron	F-16C/D	Yungwon AB
20th Fighter Wing	**Sosan AB**	
120th Fighter Squadron	F-16C/D	Sosan AB
121st Fighter Squadron	F-16C/D	Sosan AB
123rd Fighter Squadron	F-16C/D	Sosan AB
157th Fighter Squadron	F-16C/D	Sosan AB

Air Force Southern Combat Command		
1st Fighter Wing	**Kwangju AB**	
102nd Fighter Squadron	F-15K	Daegu AB
122nd Fighter Squadron	F-15K	Daegu AB
206th Fighter Squadron	F-5E/F	Kwangju AB
11th Fighter Wing	**Taegu AB**	
110th Fighter Squadron	F-4D	Taegu AB
151st Fighter Squadron	F-4D	Taegu AB
16th Fighter Wing	**Yechen AB**	
115th FTS	T-38A, T-50	Yechen AB
189th FTS	T-38A, T-50	Yechen AB
202nd Fighter Squadron	F-5E/F	Yechen AB
216th FTS	Hawk Mk67	Yechen AB

Air Force Education and Training Command		
Air Force Academy		
208th FTS	CAP 10B	Seongmu AB
212th FTS	Il-103	Seongmu AB
3rd Training Wing		
213rd FTS	KT-1	Saechon AB
215th FTS	KT-1	Saechon AB
217th FTS	KT-1	Saechon AB
236th FTS	KT-1	Saechon AB
52nd Test Evaluation Group		
281 Test Evaluation Squadron	KT-1, T-50	Saechon AB

Sri Lanka

Sri Lankan Air Force

In recent years the SLAF has been waging a campaign against the Tamil Tigers guerrilla movement, and its air arm has inducted increasingly potent combat types as a result.

Specifications

Crew: 1
Powerplant: 1 x 79.41kN (17,860lb thrust) (with afterburner) IAI/General Electric licence-built J79-JIE turbojet engine
Maximum speed: 2440km/h (1516mph)
Range: 548miles (882km)
Service ceiling: 17,690m (58,038ft)
Dimensions: span 8.22m (26.97ft); length 15.65m (51.35ft); height 4.55m (14.93ft)
Weight: 16,500kg (36,376lbs) loaded
Armament: 2 x 30mm (1.18in) Rafael DEFA 533 cannons plus cluster bombs and missiles

▼ IAI Kfir C7, No. 10 Fighter Squadron, Katunayake

CF717 is one of the fleet of nine single-seat Kfirs operated from Katunayake, on the military side of Colombo-Bandaranaike international airport. A pair of two-seat Kfir TC2 trainers are also in service.

AIR BASES USED by the SLAF include Katunayake, Ratmalana, Trincomalee, Minneriya and Vavuniya. The fighting in Sri Lanka included a guerrilla attack against Katunayake Airport in 2001 that claimed part of the SLAF destroyed.

Katunayake is home to three combat squadrons with Kfirs, F-7s of various subtype, and MiG-27s. It is expected that the air defence types will be replaced by MiG-29s, with reported orders for five examples. Two transport squadrons are stationed at Ratmalana, with An-32s, Cessna 421s, C-130s, MA60s and Y-12s. Four helicopter squadrons utilize a number of bases around the country, operating Bell 206s, Bell 212s, Bell 412s, Mi-17s and Mi-24/35s.

The SLAF's basic training element is found at Trincomalee, where students fly the CJ-6 before moving on to the K-8 at Katunayake.

A small Sri Lankan Navy aviation component operates Chetak and Dauphin helicopters.

Specifications

Crew: 1
Powerplant: 1 x 103.4kN (23,353lb) Tumanskii R-29B-300 turbojet
Maximum speed: 1885km/h (1170mph)
Combat radius on lo-lo-lo mission 540km (335 miles)
Service ceiling: 14,000m (45,900ft)
Dimensions: span 13.97m (45ft 10in spread, 7.78m (25ft 6.25in) swept; length 17.07m (56ft 0.75in); height 5m (16ft 5in)
Weight: 20,300kg (44,750lb) loaded
Armament: 1 x 23mm (0.9in) GSh-6-30 cannon, provision for up to 4000kg (8818lb) of stores

▲ Mikoyan-Gurevich MiG-27M, No. 5 Jet Squadron, Katunayake

Sri Lanka began purchasing MiG-27Ms from Ukraine in 2000. Over time the type became the most important strike asset for the SLAF, and played a dominant role during the final battle against the Tamil Tiger rebellion in northeast Sri Lanka in early 2009.

Taiwan

Republic of China Air Force, Naval Aviation and Army Aviation

The organization of the RoCAF is based aonlong USAF lines, with a Combat Air Command responsible for aircraft that are deployed within eight wings, plus training and support units.

Of the eight wings, five are designated as 'pure' Tactical Fighter Wings (TFW), one as a Composite TFW (TCW), one as a TFW/Tactical Training and Development Centre (TTDC) and one as a Transport and Early Warning Wing (T/EWW).

Three main types are integrated within the fighter force: the indigenous F-CK-1 Ching-Kuo; the Mirage 2000-5; and the F-16A/B. The F-16 has replaced most F-5E/Fs, although the latter continue with one wing in upgraded form, and with the TTDC, with which they also operate as aggressors. Adapted F-16s serve alongside RF-5Es converted locally for the reconnaissance role.

The relatively small transport arm is based around the C-130H, serving with two squadrons. The operating wing is also responsible for the E-2Ts that provide an airborne early warning and control capability, and a C-130H modified for the electronic warfare role. Beech 1900Cs operate in the navaid calibration role. Other transport aircraft are based at Sungshan as the Presidential Flight Section, equipped with Boeing 737 and Fokker F27s VIP transports.

The rescue Squadron conducts RoCAF search and rescue, flying S-70C Blue Hawk helicopters (similar to USAF HH-60A). The S-70Cs are also detached to other bases. Major training assets in use are the indigenous AT-3 jet trainer and the T-34C, with Beech 1900s available for training multi-engine aircrew.

RoC Naval Aviation maintains bases at Hualien and Pingtung South and operates both fixed- and rotary-wing equipment. The S-2Ts operated in the anti-submarine role are due to be replaced by 12 P-3Cs. Anti-submarine helicopters comprise the MD500 and S-70C Thunderhawk, both of which embark on warships of the RoC Navy.

Army helicopters

RoC Army Aviation includes two attack helicopter wings, as well as communications and training units, based at Longtang-Tao Yuan and Kuejien-Tainan. The offensive capability is provided by 62 AH-1W attack helicopters, with 30 AH-64Ds on order. Also operated are CH-47SD transports, OH-58D scout helicopters, UH-1Hs for utility and TH-67s for helicopter training.

Specifications

Crew: 1

Powerplant: either 1 x 105.7kN (23,770lb) Pratt & Whitney F100-PW-200 or 1 x 128.9kN (28,984lb) General Electric F110-GE-100 turbofan

Maximum speed: 2142km/h (1320mph)

Range: 925km (525 miles)

Service ceiling: 15,240m (50,000ft)

Dimensions: span 9.45m (31ft); length 15.09m (49ft 6in); height 5.09m (16ft 8in)

Weight: 16,057kg (35,400lb) loaded

Armament: 1 x General Electric M61A1 20mm (0.79in) multi-barrelled cannon, provision for up to 9276kg (20,450lb) of stores

General Dynamics F-16A Fighting Falcon, 5th TFW, Hualien

Taiwan's Fighting Falcon fleet includes this F-16A Block 20, 93-0774, part of a total of 150 ordered under the Peace Fenghuang programme, with deliveries between 1997 and 2001. Taiwan has expressed interest in acquiring 66 more 66 F-16C/D Block 52 aircraft in the future.

Dassault Mirage 2000-5Ei
Serving with the 2nd TFW at Hsinchu, Taiwan's fleet of Mirage 2000-5 fighters comprises 46 single-seat 2000-5Ei versions and 11 two-seat 5Di conversion trainers, survivors from an original order for 60 aircraft. These can be armed with Mica and Magic 2 air-to-air missiles, and have also been noted carrying indigenously developed air-to-ground weapons. AF was one of the last C-model aircraft in service.

TA CHUN KUO KUNG CHUANG — REPUBLIC OF CHINA AF

1st TFW (433rd TFW)*

1st TFG	F-CK-1A/B	Tainan
3rd TFG	F-CK-1A/B	Tainan
9th TFG	F-CK-1A/B	Tainan

* periodic F-CK-1A/B detachments to Makung.

2nd TFW (499th TFW)

41st TFG	Mirage 2000-5Ei/Di	Hsinchu
42nd TFG	Mirage 2000-5Ei/Di	Hsinchu
48th TFG	Mirage 2000-5Ei/Di	Hsinchu

3rd TFW (427th TFW)*

7th TFG	F-CK-1A/B	Ching Chuan Kang
28th TFG	F-CK-1A/B	Ching Chuan Kang

* periodic F-CK-1A/B detachments to Makung.

4th TFW, Hualien (455th TFW)

21st TFG	F-16A/B	Chia Yi
22nd TFG	F-16A/B	Chia Yi
23rd TFG	F-16A/B	Chia Yi
Rescue Squadron	S-70C	Chia Yi

5th TFW (401st TCW)

12th TRS	RF-5E, RF-16A	Hualien
17th TFG	F-16A/B	Hualien
26th TFG	F-16A/B	Hualien
27th TFG	F-16A/B	Hualien

6th T/EWW (439th CW)

10th TAG

101st TCS	C-130H	Pingtung North
102nd TCS	C-130H	Pingtung North
20th EWG		
2nd Early Warning Squadron	E-2T	Pingtung North
6th Electronic Warfare Squadron	C-130H(EW)	Pingtung North

7th TFW (737th TFW)

44th TFS	F-5E/F	Taitung
45th TFS	F-5E/F	Taitung
Tactical Training and Development Centre		
46th TFS	F-5E/F	Taitung

Sungshan Air Base Command

Special Transport Squadron	Beech 1900C, Fokker F27	Sunghsan
Presidential Flight Section	Boeing 737, Fokker F27	Sungshun

Air Force Academy

Basic Training Group	T-34C	Kangshan
Fighter Training Group	AT-3	Kangshan
Transport Training Group	Beech 1900C	Kangshan

Thailand

Royal Thai Air Force, Navy Air Division and Army Air Division

The RTAF (Kongtap Agard Thai) is organized as four regional Air Divisions and a Flying Training School, and is backed up by a significant Royal Thai Navy Air Division.

THE FOUR AIR Divisions of the RTAF are responsible for the Bangkok area (1st AD), eastern Thailand (2nd AD), the central-northern provinces (3rd AD) and the south (4th AD). Each Air Division is responsible for two or three wings (for a total of 10), these being equipped with flying squadrons.

The RTAF's latest and most significant acquisitions are six JAS39C/D Gripen fighters. These will operate in conjunction with a SAAB 340 configured for airborne early warning and control. Fighters currently in service comprise the F-16A/B and F-5E/F. Transport aircraft in use are the A310, AU-23, C-130H, G222 and HS748. A significant VIP fleet includes Airbus A319, ATR-72, and Boeing 737 aircraft. Training is conducted on CT-4 Airtrainer and DA42 Twin Star primary trainers, and PC-9 basic trainers, with Alpha Jets and L-39s employed on advanced training and secondary light attack duties. The rotary-wing inventory includes Bell 412s and UH-1s.

The Royal Thai Navy Air Division includes the air wing for the carrier HTMS *Chakri Naruebet*, although the AV-8S Harriers once operated are no longer active. Bell 212s, Lynx Mk300s and S-70Bs serve in the anti-submarine role, with MH-60S on order. Shore-based Do 228, F27, Nomad and P-3 aircraft conduct maritime patrol.

The Royal Thai Army Air Division maintains a large and varied fleet, including AH-1F attack helicopters, Beech 200/350s for transport and surveillance, Bell 206/212 and UH-1H utility helicopters, CH-47D and S-70/UH-60 transports (and Mi-17s on order), plus training and VIP assets.

Specifications

Crew: 1

Powerplant: either 1 x 105.7kN (23,770lb) Pratt & Whitney F100-PW-200 or 1 x 128.9kN (28,984lb) General Electric F110-GE-100 turbofan

Maximum speed: 2142km/h (1320mph)

Range: 925km (525 miles)

Service ceiling: 15,240m (50,000ft)

Dimensions: span 9.45m (31ft); length 15.09m (49ft 6in); height 5.09m (16ft 8in)

Weight: 16,057kg (35,400lb) loaded

Armament: 1 x General Electric M61A1 20mm (0.79in) multi-barrelled cannon, provision for up to 9276kg (20,450lb) of stores

General Dynamics F-16A Fighting Falcon, 102 Squadron 'Starfighters', Korat

This ex-USAF F-16A Block 15G aircraft is one of a total of 54 F-16A/Bs ordered by Thailand. The RTAF received a further seven F-16A/B aircraft, donated by Singapore.

Northrop F-5 Tiger II

The RTAF continues to maintain a significant fleet of F-5s. In addition to around two dozen single-seat F-5Es that serve in the air defence role, a handful of two-seat F-5Fs are used for operational conversion training. Three F-5E air defence squadrons are found at Bangkok-Don Muang, Ubon Ratchathani and Surat Thani.

Vietnam

VIETNAM PEOPLE'S AIR FORCE

Of almost entirely Soviet and Russian origin, aircraft of the VPAF are a blend of new and old, but recent procurement of new fighters suggests that a programme of overhaul is under way.

THE ORGANIZATIONAL STRUCTURE of the VPAF is based around three divisions, each of which has a specific role, and maintains squadrons at different bases. The 370th Division, headquartered at Da Nang, was formerly responsible for two squadrons of MiG-21bis fighters and one of Su-22M4 attack aircraft, and is now the recipient of the VPAF's latest fighter, the multi-role Su-30MK2V, which serves at Phan Rang, previously known as a Su-22M4 base. The 371st Division (HQ at Noi Bai) previously operated three squadrons of MiG-21bis, but may also have partly re-equipped with Su-27SK interceptors. The 372 Division operated three squadrons, flying the Su-22M and the MiG-21bis, and has headquarters at Tho Xuan.

VPAF transport arm

A Transport Brigade maintains at least three squadrons, operating Mi-8/17 and Mi-24 helicopters alongside An-2, An-24/26/30, An-38 and M-28 transports. Identified transport bases include Hoa Lac, Tan Son Nhut and Gia Lam. A quantity of UH-1H helicopters inherited from the former South Vietnamese Air Force are also believed to remain in use. The VPAF Air Force Academy operates L-39 advanced trainers from Hoa Lac (910 'Julius Fucik' Squadron) as well as MiG-21bis and MiG-21UMs for conversion training at Phu Cat. Operated on behalf of the Navy are Ka-25/27 anti-submarine helicopters, based at Kien An and Da Nang.

▲ **Sukhoi Su-30MK2V**

The most potent asset within the VPAF inventory is the handful of Su-30MK2V multi-role fighters delivered to date. The MK2 version is a further upgrade of the Su-30MKK developed for China, with improved avionics and expanded weaponry.

Specifications

Crew: 2
Powerplant: 2 x 123kN (27,600lbf) Lyulka al-31F turbofans
Maximum speed: 2120km/h (1320mph)
Range: 3000km (1900 miles)
Service ceiling: 17,300m (56,800ft)
Dimensions: span 14.7m (48ft 2.5in); length 21.94m (72in 11in); height 6.36m (20ft 9in)
Weight: 24,900kg (54,900lb) loaded
Armament: 1 x 30mm (1.18in) GSh-3-1 gun, plus air-to-air and air-to-surface missiles

▲ **Sukhoi Su-30MK2V, 370th Fighter Division, Phan Rang**

One of two Su-30MK2Vs delivered to Vietnam in 2006. Today, the VPAF operates four Su-30MK2Vs, with another eight on order. These will complement 12 earlier Su-27SKs and three two-seat Su-27UBKs.

TUNISIA
MOROCCO
ALGERIA
LIBYA
EGYPT
MAURITANIA
MALI
NIGER
CHAD
SUDAN
ERITREA
SENEGAL
THE GAMBIA
GUINEA-BISSAU
GUINEA REPUBLIC
BURKINA FASO
BENIN
TOGO
NIGERIA
ETHIOPIA
SIERRA LEONE
COTE D'IVOIRE
GHANA
LIBERIA
CENTRAL AFRICAN REPUBLIC
CAMEROON
EQUATORIAL GUINEA
UGANDA
KENYA
GABON
CONGO
DEM. REP. OF CONGO
RWANDA
BURUNDI
TANZANIA
ANGOLA
ATLANTIC OCEAN
ZAMBIA
MOZAMBIQUE
ZIMBABWE
MADAGASCAR
NAMIBIA
BOTSWANA
SOUTH AFRICA

Chapter 7

Africa

Befitting a continent of its diversity, Africa is host to air forces that range greatly in terms of size and combat potential. In the north, air arms are typically larger and well equipped, and provide balanced capabilities. East Africa has seen its air arms take part in various conflicts in recent years, notably in Eritrea, Ethiopia and Sudan. West Africa's air forces are generally small and comparatively poorly equipped – armed trainers often form the backbone of the combat inventory – and a number suffer from the effects of low serviceability. In Central Africa, years of conflict have left their mark on the region's air arms, although most nations have at least token combat forces, in some cases supplementing combat helicopters with small fleets of jets. With the exception of South Africa and Zimbabwe, Southern Africa's air forces are generally small and have seen only limited combat since the end of the 'bush wars' that characterized much of the Cold War era.

Algeria

Algerian Air Force

Established in 1962 after Algeria won independence from France, the Algerian Air Force (al-Quwwat al-Jawwiya al-Jaza'eriya – QJJ) is an increasingly well-equipped air arm.

ORGANIZED ON THE basis of nine wings, each of which has a designated task, the QJJ also maintains a number of independent squadrons that report directly to air force headquarters. Wings have varying numbers of squadrons attached and occupy more than one air base. While squadrons have 'official' permanent bases, their aircraft can frequently be found operating from alternative locations.

QJJ wings comprise the 1st Combat Helicopter Regiment, 2nd Tactical Transport and Logistics Wing, 3rd Air Defence Wing, 4th Attack and Penetration Wing, 5th Reconnaissance Wing, 6th Transport Helicopter Regiment, 7th Transport and Refuelling Wing, 8th Training Wing and the 9th Helicopter Training Wing.

The Su-30MKA is now replacing the MiG-25 and supplementing three squadrons of Su-24MKs in the strike role. Other combat equipment includes three active MiG-29 air defence squadrons, MiG-25R, Su-24MR and Seeker UAV reconnaissance aircraft, and Il-76/78, C-130H and CN235 transports. Primary helicopters are the Mi-17/171 and Mi-24 MkIII.

Specifications

Crew: 2

Powerplant: 2 x 74.5kN (16,750lbf) AL-31FL low-bypass turbofans

Maximum speed: Mach 2.0 (2120km/h; 1320mph)

Range: 3000km (1864 miles)

Service ceiling: 17,300m (56,800ft)

Dimensions: span 14.7m (48ft 2.5in); length 21.94m (72in 11in); height 6.36m (20ft 9in)

Weight: 24,900kg (54,900lb) loaded

Armament: 1 x30mm (1.18n) GSh-3-1 gun, plus air-to-air and air-to-surface missiles

Sukhoi Su-30MKA, 120e Escadron de Chasse, Ain Beida

The 120e Escadron de Chasse is receiving the multi-role Su-30MKA to replace the unit's remaining few MiG-25PDS interceptors. Another QJJ Su-30MKA squadron has been established at Oum el-Boughi.

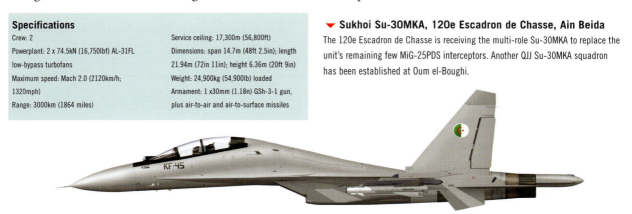

Egypt

Arab Republic of Egypt Air Force

Traditionally among most the powerful and best-equipped air arms on the continent, the Arab Republic of Egypt Air Force maintains a large inventory of both Western and Eastern equipment.

SUCCESSIVE ACQUISITION PROGRAMMES have provided Egypt with 220 F-16s, and the Fighting Falcon now spearheads the air arm, despite the continued use of older Soviet and Chinese aircraft.

Air Defence Command includes the 102nd Tactical Fighter Wing (TFW) with two squadrons of Shenyang F-7Bs at Mersa Matruh and the 103rd and 104th TFWs at Aswan and el-Mansourah, respectively, each wing operating two MiG-21MF squadrons. Two further F-7B squadrons are the responsibility of the 282nd TFW at Fayid, this expanded wing also having two F-16C/D squadrons.

Tactical Command comprises the 222nd TFW at Cairo West, with two squadrons of F-4Es co-located with an E-2C squadron. The F-16 is in use with the 232nd TFW at Inchas, the 242nd TFW at Bani Swayf and the 262nd TFW at Abu Suweir (two squadrons each), while the 272nd TFW at Giancalis maintains three F-16C/D squadrons. Mirage wings are the 236th TFW at Birma/el-Tanta (two Mirage 5 squadrons) and the 252nd TFW at Gabel al-Basur (a squadron each of Mirage 5s and Mirage 2000s).

Helicopter units include brigades at Hurghada (Mi-8/17), Qwaysina (Gazelle), Khutamiya (Gazelle and AH-64D) and Abu Hammad (AH-64D).

Arab Republic of Egypt Air Force Transport and Training Commands each operate at least two brigades together with constituent squadrons.

Specifications

Crew: 1
Powerplant: 1 x 126.7kN (28,500lb) thrust Pratt & Whitney F100-PW-229 afterburning turbofan
Maximum speed: 2177km/h (1353mph)
Range: 3862km (2400 miles)
Service ceiling: 15,240m (49,000ft)
Dimensions: span 9.45m (31ft); length 15.09m (49ft 6in); height 5.09m (16ft 8in)
Weight: 19,187kg (42,300lb) loaded
Armament: 1 x GE M61A1 20mm (0.79in) multi-barrelled cannon, seven external hardpoints with provision for up to 9276kg (20,450lb) of stores

Lockheed Martin F-16C Fighting Falcon, Arab Republic of Egypt Air Force

Operated by an unknown unit, F-16C Block 40 96-0096 was delivered under the Peace Vector V programme, which was signed in 1996 and provided Egypt with 21 newly built F-16C/D aircraft. The Block 40 aircraft as flown by Egypt have provision for the AGM-88 HARM missile used for the defence-suppression mission.

Ethiopia

Ethiopian Air Force

Although not one of the biggest African air arms, the Ethiopian Air Force has been one of the most active in recent years, its aircraft having seen air-to-air combat against those of Eritrea.

With all remaining MiG-21s, MiG-23BNs and Su-25s now stored, Ethiopia relies on the Su-27s of No. 5 Squadron to provide the sharp end of its air force. In addition, there are at least two units flying helicopters and two more operating fixed-wing transport aircraft. Helicopters include Mi-35s, while transports include An-12s, An-26s and C-130s.

Specifications

Crew: 1
Powerplant: 1 x 73.5kN (16,535lb) Tumanskii R-25 turbojet
Maximum speed: 2229km/h (1385mph)
Range: 1160km (721 miles)
Service ceiling: 17,500m (57,400ft)
Dimensions: span 7.15m (23ft 5.5in); length (including probe) 15.76m (51ft 8.5in); height 4.1m (13ft 5.5in)
Weight: 10,400kg (22,925lb) loaded
Armament: 1 x 23mm (0.90in) GSh-23 twin-barrel cannon in underbelly pack, provision for about 1500kg (3307kg) of stores

Mikoyan-Gurevich MiG-21bis, Ethiopian Air Force, Debre Zebit

One of more than 150 MiG-21s delivered to Ethiopia from 1977, these aircraft were mainly operated from Debre Zebit, and saw extensive service in the wars with Eritrea in the 1980s, and again between 1998–2001.

Libya

Libyan Arab Air Force

The LARAF has undergone significant change in the last decade, with older types being retired, and the government looking to acquire new types to replace generally ageing equipment.

A NUMBER OF older LARAF types have been withdrawn altogether, while others, such as the MiG-25, are now mainly in storage.

Most modern combat equipment is the Mirage F1, flown by two squadrons at Okba Ibn Nafa. The MiG-23 remains numerically the most important fighter, however, serving between five and seven squadrons. The MiG-21, in contrast, is now only operated by a single unit. Ground-attack assets comprise the Su-22M3 (two squadrons, one possibly non-operational), Su-22M4 (one unit) and Su-24MK (one unit, but with only a handful of aircraft operational). The MiG-23BN fleet is likely retired.

In terms of helicopter squadrons, these include units equipped with examples of the CH-47, Mi-2, Mi-8, Mi-14 and Mi-24. Transport equipment includes the An-26, C-130H, Falcon 20 and 50, Gulfstream (perhaps retired), Il-76 and L-410.

Specifications

Crew: 1

Powerplant: 2 x 100kN (22,487lb) Tumanskii R-15B-300 turbojets

Maximum speed: 2974km/h (1848mph)

Combat radius: 1130km (702 miles)

Service ceiling: over 24,385m (80,000ft)

Dimensions: span 14.02m (45ft 11.75in); length 23.82m (78ft 1.75in); height 6.1m (20ft 0.5in)

Weight: 37,425kg (82,508lb) loaded

Armament: 2 x R-40 and 4 x R-60 air-to-air missiles

Mikoyan-Gurevich MiG-25PD, 1015 Squadron, Sirte/Ghurdabiyah

Libya purchased almost 80 MiG-25s of various subtypes in the late 1970s and the early 1980s, and the type formed the backbone of the LARAF interceptor fleet until its retirement from service in 2004. Despite this move, around 60 MiG-25s are retained in storage in an airworthy condition.

Morocco

Royal Moroccan Air Force

The Royal Moroccan Air Force (Al-Quwwat al-Jawwiya al-Malakiya Marakishniya – QJMM) is a Western-influenced air arm with a balanced fleet of fighter, transport and training assets.

THE STRUCTURE OF the QJMM divides assets among Fighter Aviation Command, Transport Aviation Command, Helicopter Command and Training Command, with squadrons distributed across numbered bases.

Fighter Aviation Command is responsible for air defence, with two squadrons of F-5E/Fs at Meknes and two of Mirage F1s at Sidi Slimane, the Mirage units being allocated air defence and ground-attack roles respectively. A Fighter Pilot School is co-located at Meknes, this being equipped with Alpha Jets.

Workhorse of Transport Aviation Command is the C-130H, while other squadrons operate Boeing 707 tanker/transports and CN235s. Transport assets are based at Kénitra. Rabat-Sale is centre of rotary-wing operations, with types including the SA330, Bell 205,

CH-47C and SA342. A wide variety of trainers at Marrakech include AS 202s, T-34s and T-37s. Transport pilots are schooled on the Beech 200 and helicopter pilots on the Bell 205/206 and SA342. Gulfstreams and Falcons are available for VIP flights.

Specifications

Crew: 1
Powerplant: 2 x 22.2kN (5000lb) General Electric J85-GE-21B turbojets
Maximum speed: 1741km/h (1082mph)
Range: 306km (190 miles)
Service ceiling: 15,790m (51,800ft)
Dimensions: span 8.13m (26ft 8in); length 14.45m (47ft 4.75in); height 4.07m (13ft 4.25in)
Weight: 11,214kg (24,722lb) loaded
Armament: 2 x two 20mm (.78in) cannon; five external pylons with provision for 3175kg (7000lb) of stores

Northrop F-5E Tiger II, Escuadron de Chasse, Meknes-Bassatine (2nd Air Base)

Morocco received a total of 24 F-5E/Fs over the years. At least two were lost in clashes with the Polisario Front in the 1980s. The survivors are operated by the Escadrones de Chasse 'Chahine' and 'Borak'. Morocco plans to replace its F-5s with 24 F-16C/Ds.

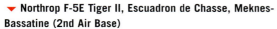

Sudan

Sudanese Air Force

Changing political allegiances have seen the Sudanese Air Force (Silakh al Jawwiya As'Sudaniya) receive aircraft from a variety of sources, and these have seen significant combat.

ALTHOUGH UNCONFIRMED, the probable order of battle of the Sudanese Air Force is based around three combat squadrons, three helicopter squadrons and a single fixed-wing transport squadron. In the last decade or so, oil revenues have allowed Sudan, Africa's largest country, to begin acquiring new, and more modern military aircraft.

No. 1 Squadron flies Nanchang A-5C attack aircraft (and FT-6 trainers), No. 2 Squadron is equipped with MiG-29 fighters, and No. 3 Squadron is reported to have a mixed fleet of MiG-21s (12 of which may have been acquired from Ukraine) and MiG-23s (although these may have been retired). Sudan received 11 Su-25s from Belarus in 2008. Helicopters include around 24 Mi-25/35s, and a smaller number of Mi-17s. Training is conducted on Chinese-supplied CJ-6As and K-8s. The most modern fixed-wing transports are five An-74s.

Specifications

Crew: 1
Powerplant: 2 x 81.4kN (18,298lb) Sarkisov RD-33 turbofans
Maximum speed: 2443km/h (1518mph)
Range: 1500km (932 miles)
Service ceiling: 17,000m (55,775ft)
Dimensions: span 11.36m (37ft 3.75in); length (including probe) 17.32m (56ft 10in); height 7.78m (25ft 6.25in)
Weight: 20,000kg (44,090lb) loaded
Armament: 1 x 30mm (1.18in) GSh-30 cannon, provision for up to 4500kg (9921lb) of stores

Mikoyan MiG-29SE, No. 2 Fighter Squadron, Wadi Sayyidna

This is one of between 12 and 24 MiG-29s delivered to Sudan to date. The type saw some combat service against JEM rebels, in Darfur, and one is known to have been lost during a rebel attack on Wadi Sayyidna, in May 2009.

Smaller North & East African states

Eritrea, Kenya, Tanzania and Tunisia

While Tunisia has long been among the most stable African states, in East Africa, Eritrea has been plagued by conflict. Kenya and Tanzania both maintain modest air arms, albeit with jet equipment.

Compared to other North African air forces, that of Tunisia is small, and receives military aid from France and the USA. In East Africa, Eritrea has turned to Russia to provide combat aircraft, while Tanzania procures Chinese jets. Kenya's air arm traditionally maintains links with the UK.

Eritrean Air Force

With all operations based out of Asmara, the Eritrean Air Force consists of eight numbered squadrons. Equipment includes Westwinds and CL-601s for VIP transport, L-90 Redigo trainers, Mi-8/17 and Mi-35 helicopters, MB339 jet trainers (although these may no longer be operational), a squadron each of MiG-29 and Su-27 fighters, Bell 412 helicopters and Y-12 transports.

Kenyan Air Force

Based around a fighter force of F-5E/Fs and Hawk Mk52 trainers, the Kenyan Air Force schools its pilots on Bulldog and Tucano trainers. Helicopters include armed MD500s and Z-9s, SA330s and Gazelles. DHC-5, DHC-8, Fokker 70 and Y-12 aircraft provide transport capacity.

Specifications

Crew: 1
Powerplant: 2 x 81.4kN (18,298lb) Sarkisov RD-33 turbofans
Maximum speed: 2443km/h (1518mph)
Range: 1500km (932 miles)
Service ceiling: 17,000m (55,775ft)
Dimensions: span 11.36m (37ft 3.75in); length (including probe) 17.32m (56ft 10in); height 7.78m (25ft 6.25in)
Weight: 18,500kg (40,785lb) loaded
Armament: 1 x 30mm (1.18in) GSh-30 cannon, provision for up to 4500kg (9921lb) of stores

Mikoyan MiG-29, No. 5 Squadron, Eritrean Air Force, Asmara

This is an example from the first batch of four MiG-29s delivered to Eritrea from Ukraine in 1998. Two aircraft from this batch were lost during the subsequent war with Ethiopia.

Specifications

Crew: 1
Powerplant: 2 x 31.9kN (7165lb) Shenyang WP-6 turbojets
Maximum speed: 1540km/h (957mph)
Range: 1390km (864 miles)
Service ceiling: 17,900m (58,725ft)
Dimensions: span 9.2m (30ft 2.25in); length 14.9m (48ft 10.5in); height 3.88m (12ft 8.75in)
Weight: 10,000kg (22,046lb) loaded
Armament: 3 x 30mm (1.18in) NR-30 cannon; four external hardpoints with provision for up to 500kg (1102lb) of stores

Shenyang F-6C, Tanzanian Air Force

One of only a handful of F-6Cs that remain operational with the Tanzanian AF, this aircraft was originally delivered in the early 1980s. The J-6s were stored for many years before being returned to service with Chinese assistance some time after 2005.

Tanzanian Air Force

This consists of one squadron of F-6C fighters, plus single helicopter and transport squadrons, the latter with Y-8s and Y-12s. A training squadron flies CJ-6s.

Tunisian Republic Air Force

Using a structure of squadrons and flights, most aircraft are based at Bizerte/Sidi Ahmed, Gafsa, Bizerte/La Karouba and Sfax. The sharp end of the Tunisian air arm is provided by a squadron of F-5E/Fs, supported by armed L-59s and MB326s. Basic and primary training is conducted on SF260s. Rotary-wing types include the AB205, AB412, Alouette II and III, Ecureuil, HH-3E and UH-1H. Transport assets include ex-USAF C-130Bs and newly built C-130Hs, as well as G222s and L-410s.

Specifications

Crew: 1
Powerplant: 2 x 22.2kN (5000lb) General Electric J85-GE-21B turbojets
Maximum speed: 1741km/h (1082mph)
Range: 306km (190 miles)
Service ceiling: 15,790m (51,800ft)
Dimensions: span 8.13m (26ft 8in); length 14.45m (47ft 4.75in); height 4.07m (13ft 4.25in)
Weight: 11,214kg (24,722lb) loaded
Armament: 2 x 20mm (.78in) cannon; two air-to-air missiles, five external pylons with provision for 3175kg (7000lb) of stores

▼ Northrop F-5E Tiger II, 15 Squadron, Tunisian Republic Air Force, Bizerte/Sidi Ahmed

Tunisia began to receive 24 Tiger IIs in 1985. The surviving aircraft are now used for dual air defence and ground attack duties with 15 Squadron.

Angola

National Air Force of Angola

Angola's air arm emerged from the costly civil war of the 1980s and has now made some efforts to re-equip as well as reportedly adopting the new official title National Air Force of Angola.

ALTHOUGH DETAILS REMAIN scarce, the Angolan Air Force is understood to consist of a Transport Command (based in Luanda, together with a helicopter flight) a Military Air Training School (in Lobito), an Advanced Pilot Training Regiment (Catumbela), a Fighter Regiment (Lubango) and a Fighter-Bomber Regiment (Catumbela).

Specifications

Crew: 1
Powerplant: 2 x 122.5kN (27,557lb) Lyul'ka AL-31M turbofans
Maximum speed: 2150km/h (1335mph)
Range: 500km (930 miles)
Service ceiling: 17,500m (57,400ft)
Dimensions: span 14.7m (48ft 2.75in); length 21.94m (71ft 11.5in); height 6.36m (20ft 10.25in)
Weight: 30,000kg (66,138lb) loaded
Armament: 1 x one 30mm (1.18in) GSh-3101 cannon with 149 rounds; 10 external hardpoints with provision for 6000kg (13,228lb) of stores

▼ Sukhoi Su-27UB, Regimento de Caças (Fighter Regiment), Lubango

Only one Su-27UB and one Su-27 entered Angolan service; the single-seater was later written off in a crash. The two-seat aircraft was last seen in 2009, and is reportedly still operational at Lubango.

Smaller West African states

Burkina Faso, Cameroon, Equatorial Guinea, Gabon, Ghana, Guinea Republic, Ivory Coast, Mali, Nigeria, Senegal and Togo

The smaller air arms of West Africa typically fly just a handful of armed trainers or combat helicopters, although most maintain assets to undertake transport, liaison and training duties.

THE FOLLOWING PROVIDES details of the most important of the smaller West African air arms. It should be noted that Benin, Cape Verde, Mauritania, Niger and Sierra Leone all maintain air arms, although most consist of little more than half a dozen helicopters and light transport types, and among them only Sierra Leone maintains credible combat equipment, in the form of a small number of Mi-24 assault helicopters. Gambia is another exception. It has obtained jet equipment, in the form of the Su-25 attack aircraft, though to date only a single example is in use with the Gambian National Army, and there is as yet no separate air arm branch. The air force of Guinea-Bissau retired almost its entire combat fleet in the early 1990s, and is likely now left with two Mi-24 assault helicopters and a small collection of transport. After years of civil war, Liberia's air arm has yet to be re-established.

Burkina Faso Air Force

Traditionally, the air force was based around two units, both based at Ouagadougou, and comprising the Escadron de Transport and the Escadron d'Helicopteres, followed by an Escadron de Chasse. The Force Aérienne de Burkina Faso now divides its assets between two districts, each with one air base: Ouagadougou and Bobo Dioulasso. Aircraft are assigned to a single air brigade, which may have just one squadron. The most potent equipment is the SF260WP Warrior armed trainer, acquired from sources in Bolivia, Italy and Libya, with Libyan financial backing, but these are now stored. Also withdrawn are the MiG-21 fighters supplied by Libya. Otherwise, a range of transport and liaison types (including a single CN235) and helicopters (AS350, Mi-8/17, Mi-35 and SA365) are on strength.

Cameroon Air Force

The Armée de l'Air Cameroun operates from bases at Garoua, Koutaba, Yaoundé, Douala and Bamenda. Four Alpha Jets provide a light attack and advanced training capability, supported by four ex-South African Air Force Impala Mk2s (light attack) and a pair of Impala Mk1 jet trainers. Aravas, C-130Hs, DHC-4s, DHC-5s and Do 28s are the major transport types. Helicopters include examples of the Alouette II/III, Bell 206, Bell 412EP, SA330 and SA342. A single Do 128 is used for maritime patrol.

Specifications

Crew: 1
Powerplant: 1 x Lycoming 194kW (260hp) IO540 D4A5
Maximum speed: 441km/h (276mph)
Range: 2050km (1274 miles)
Service ceiling: 5790m (19,000ft)
Dimensions: span 8.35m (27ft 5in); length 7.10m (23ft 4in); height 2.41m (7ft 11in)
Weight: 1102kg (2430lb) loaded
Armament: 2 or 4 hardpoints for 7.62mm (0.3in) machine guns or general-purpose and practice bombs and one or two photo-reconnaissance pods or auxiliary drop tanks

SIAI-Marchetti SF260W Warrior, Force Aérienne de Burkina Faso, Bobo Dioulasso

Burkina Faso received six ex-Philippine Air Force SF260s in mid-1986, before these were sold on to a Belgian dealer in 1993. The air force also received four more SF260s acquired as new from the manufacturer.

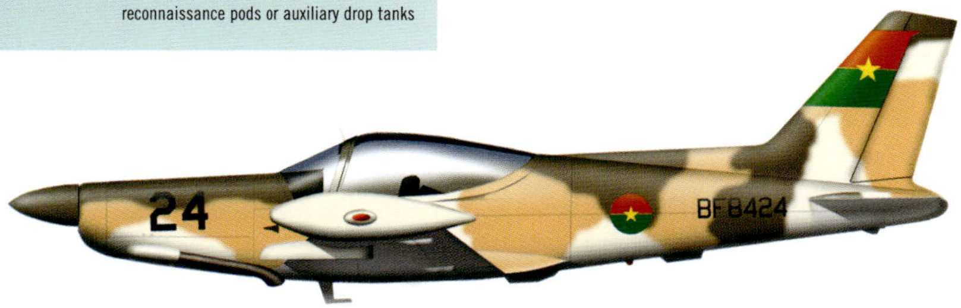

Specifications

Crew: 2
Powerplant: 2 x SNECMA/Turbomeca Larzac 04-C6 each rated at 13.24kN (2976lb thrust)
Maximum speed: 1000km/h (621mph)
Range: 670km (415 miles)
Service ceiling: 14,630m (48,000ft)
Dimensions: span 9.11m (30ft); length 11.75m (38ft); height 4.19m (14ft)
Weight: 8000kg (17,600lb) loaded
Armament: 1 x 30mm (1.18in) DEFA 553 cannon pod; up to 2500kg (5500lb) of bombs, rockets or drop-tanks

▼ Dassault-Dornier Alpha Jet MS2, Armée de l'Air Cameroun, Garoua

One of seven Alpha Jets purchased by Cameroon, these aircraft are stationed at Garoua from where they are reportedly flown only sporadically. Two examples have been lost in accidents.

Equatorial Guinea National Guard

Previously equipped only with a handful of transport types, the Ala Aérea de Guardia Nacional (Air Wing of the National Guard) is developing a useful combat arm, benefiting from its status as third-biggest oil producer in sub-Saharan Africa. The air arm is based on between four and six Mi-24 assault helicopters and four single-seat Su-25 attack jets flown and is maintained by mainly Ukrainian mercenaries. Mercenaries also provide local pilots with instruction on two L-39 jet trainers and three or four two-seat Su-25UB combat trainers. A number of types also in use as VIP transports, comprise examples of the A109, Boeing 737, ERJ-145, Falcon 50, Mi-172 and S-92. Single examples of the An-32 and An-72 are used for military transport. The main operating base is Malabo, with a detachment of Mi-24s at Bata.

Gabonese Air Force

The Forces Aériennes Gabonaises structure has traditionally included No. 1 Transport Squadron, No. 2 Fighter Squadron (equipped with Mirages), No. 5 Advanced Training Squadron, No. 11 Transport-Reconnaissance Squadron (EMB-110 and EMB-111, the latter also used for maritime patrol) and No. 12 Heavy Transport Squadron (C-130H). Other types in use include ATR-42 and CN235 transports, Alouette II, Bell 412 and SA330 helicopters, and Magister and T-34C trainers. The Gabonese Army has a separate air arm, flying SA330 and SA342 helicopters.

Ghana Air Force

Ghana plans to upgrade its air arm – after past funding shortages – with four C-27J tactical transports and six Twin Star maritime patrol aircraft.

Specifications

Crew: 2
Powerplant: 1 x 16.87kN (3792lbf) Ivchenko AI-25TL turbofan
Maximum speed: 750km/h (466mph)
Range: 1100km (683 miles)
Service ceiling: 11,000m (36,100ft)
Dimensions: span 9.46m (31ft 0.5in); length 12.13m (39ft 9.5in); height 4.77m (15ft 7.75in)
Weight: 4700kg (10,362lb) loaded
Armament: External bomb load up to 284kg (626lb)

▼ Aero L-39C Albatross, Ala Aérea de Guardia Nacional (Equatorial Guinea National Guard), Malabo

This is one of two L-39s delivered to Equatorial Guinea from the Ukraine between 2004 and 2006. Together with Su-25s, they are based at Malabo. All recent combat aircraft acquired by Equatorial Guinea (comprising L-39s, Mi-24s and Su-25s) were provided by Ukraine.

Specifications

Crew: 1
Powerplant: 1 x 100kN (15,873lb) SNECMA Atar 9K-50 turbojet
Maximum speed: 2350km/h (1460mph)
Range: 900km (560 miles)
Service ceiling: 20,000m (65,615ft)
Dimensions: span 8.4m (27ft 7in); length 15m (49ft 2.25in); height 4.5m (14ft 9in)
Weight: 15,200kg (33,510lb) loaded
Armament: 2 x internal DEFA 30mm (1.18in) cannons, plus usually 6 x MK81 or MK82 bombs, 2 x Kentron Kukri V3b or V3c missiles on wingtip rails

Dassault Mirage F1AZ, No. 2 Fighter Squadron, Forces Aériennes Gabonaises, Libreville

This is one of the first two (of an eventual four) ex-South African Air Force Mirage F1ZAs, upgraded by Aerosud, and acquired by Gabon in 2006.

Current structure is reported to be based around No. 1 Squadron flying patrol aircraft, No. 2 Squadron (helicopters), No. 3 Squadron (transports) and No. 4 Squadron (with four MB339s and four K-8s used for advanced training). The latter unit likely also operates two armed L-39 jets. Other types include A109, Alouette III, Bell 412, Mi-2 and Mi-17 helicopters, plus Fokker 27, Fokker 28 and Islander transports.

Guinea Republic Air Force

The backbone of the Force Aérienne de Guinée (the air arm of Guinea Republic, otherwise known as Guinea-Conakry) was formerly a single fighter squadron with MiG-21s at Conakry. These fighters were delivered by the USSR and were operated with the assistance of Soviet advisors. Attrition replacements were also received from Ukraine. The MiG-21 unit has apparently disbanded, leaving an inventory comprising three L-29 jet trainers, plus An-12, An-14 and An-24 transports, and a handful of AS350, MD500 Defender, Mi-8, SA330 and SA342 helicopters. A number of Yak-18s may remain in use for basic training.

Cote D'Ivoire Air Force

Successive military coups, in 1999 and 2001, followed by a civil war that began in September 2002, have left the air arm of the Ivory Coast in a parlous state. During the unrest, however, the government turned to Eastern Europe and assembled a relatively potent force of combat jets. Until 2004, the Force Aérienne de la Côte d'Ivoire kept a small combat element based around four Su-25s obtained from Belarus in 2002, plus two ex-Botswana Strikemasters and a pair of

Specifications

Crew: 2
Powerplant: 1 x 16.01kN (3600lb) Garrett TFE731-2A-2A turbofan
Maximum speed: Mach 0.75 (800km/h; 498mph)
Range: 2250km (1398 miles)
Service ceiling: 13,000m (42,651ft)
Dimensions: span 9.63m (31ft 7in); length 11.6m (38ft); height 4.21m (13ft 9in)
Weight: 4330kg (9546lb) loaded
Armament: 1 x 23mm (0.9in) cannon pod, 5 hard-points carrying up to 1000kg (2205lb) external fuel and ordnance

Hongdu K-8, No. 4 Squadron, Ghana Air Force, Accra

G913 is one of the aircraft from the second batch of K-8s delivered to Ghana in 2008. Four examples are currently in use for advanced training, with another two on order.

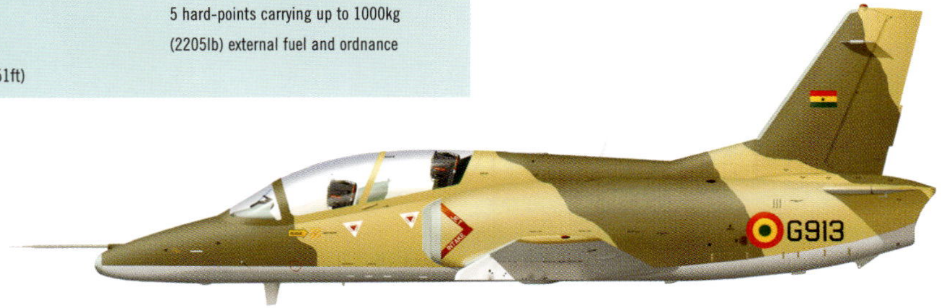

Strikemasters and a pair of former Bulgarian MiG-23MLD interceptors. The Su-25s (which included two two-seat Su-25UB models) were flown primarily by mercenaries until put out of action by French commandos in 2004, while the MiG-23s were impounded in Togo. At the same time, the Alpha Jet Cs were also abandoned, and most of the air force's helicopters were likewise rendered non-operational. Today, the air force mainly relies on leased and chartered aircraft in order to fulfil transport services.

Mali Air Force

The aircraft of the Force Aérienne de la République du Mali are stationed at two air bases (Bamako and Gao) that act as wings, and are responsible for one fighter and one helicopter squadron. Fighter equipment comprises MiG-17s and MiG-21MFs, plus L-29 jet trainers. For transport, the air force can call upon a force of An-2, An-24/26 and BT-67 aircraft. AS350, Mi-8 and Mi-24 helicopters are also in service in small numbers. Mali has used its air force in successive combat operations against Burkina Faso over the disputed Agacher Strip, in order to put down Tuareg rebellion and, most recently, against rebels operating from bases in Niger. Known air bases of the FARMA include Base Aérienne 100 in Bamako (no longer in use), Base Aérienne 101 in Bamako-Senou and Base Aérienne 102 in Mopti-Sévaré.

Nigerian Air Force and Naval Air Arm

Dominating the region, Nigeria once possessed the most capable air arm in West Africa, although at the time of writing only a portion of its inventory remains serviceable. Formerly spearheaded by three combat wings (including Nos 1 and 2 Squadrons with MiG-21s and Alpha Jets at Kano, followed by

Specifications

Crew: 1
Powerplant: 1 x 73.5kN (16,535lb) Tumanskii R-25 turbojet
Maximum speed: 2229km/h (1385mph)
Range: 1160km (721 miles)
Service ceiling: 17,500m (57,400ft)
Dimensions: span 7.15m (23ft 5.5in); length (including probe) 15.76m (51ft 8.5in); height 4.1m (13ft 5.5in)
Weight: 10,400kg (22,925lb) loaded
Armament: 1 x 23mm (0.9in) GSh-23 twin-barrel cannon in underbelly pack, provision for about 1500kg (3307kg) of stores

Mikoyan-Gurevich MiG-21, Guinea Republic Air Force, Conakry

Only three or four MiG-21s remain operational in Guinea Republic (Guinea Conakry). The survivors have been overhauled in Ukraine and are all based at the military side of Conakry international airport.

Specifications

Crew: 1
Powerplant: 2 x 44.1kN (9921lb) Tumanskii R-195 turbojets
Maximum speed: 975km/h (606mph)
Range: 750km (466 miles)
Service ceiling: 7000m (22,965ft)
Dimensions: span 14.36m (47ft 1.5in); length 15.53m (50ft 11.5in); height 4.8m (15ft 9in)
Weight: 17,600kg (38,800lb) loaded
Armament: 1 x 30mm (1.18in) GSh-30-2 cannon; eight external pylons with provision for up to 4400kg (9700lb) of stores

Sukhoi Su-25, Escadrille de Chasse, Force Aérienne de la Côte d'Ivoire, Abidjan

One of two single-seat Su-25s received by the FACI's Escadrille de Chasse (Fighter Flight) in February 2003. The fleet has not been operational since November 2004, when most of the air arm was disabledby French troops.

Specifications

Crew: 1
Powerplant: 1 x 73.5kN (16,535lb) Tumanskii R-25 turbojet
Maximum speed: 2229km/h (1385mph)
Range: 1160km (721 miles)
Service ceiling: 17,500m (57,400ft)
Dimensions: span 7.15m (23ft 5.5in); length (including probe) 15.76m (51ft 8.5in); height 4.1m (13ft 5.5in)
Weight: 10,400kg (22,925lb) loaded
Armament: 1 x 23mm (0.9in) GSh-23 twin-barrel cannon in underbelly pack, provision for about 1500kg (3307kg) of stores

Mikoyan-Gurevich MiG-21bis, Force Aérienne de la République du Mali, Bamako

Mali received 12 MiG-21bis and four MiG-21UMs directly from the USSR in the mid-1970s. One MiG-21UM crashed in 1989 and the rest of the fleet was subsequently stored at Bamako, even though some were sporadically flown in the following years. The MiG-21bis have since been replaced by ex-Czech Air Force MiG-21MFs.

wings at Makurdi, Maiduguri and Kainji), all of these units' aircraft are now non-operational. However, in 2010 Nigeria had begun to induct the first of 15 new Chengdu F-7 fighters purchased from China. The F-7 fleet will eventually include 12 F-7NI single-seat interceptors and three FT-7NI two-seat trainers, and these are to be delivered together with PL-9 air-to-air missiles, rockets and bombs. The F-7s will be based at Makurdi. The only MiG-21 unit of the NAF to have been identified was No. 21 Operational Conversion Unit, part of the 64th Air Defence Group at Makurdi, and it is expected that the latter formation will be responsible for the F-7s.

An Air Transport Group consists of 221 Wing, with one Transport (C-130H-30 and G222), one Helicopter (AS332 and BO105), one Special Operations (Mi-24), and one VIP Squadron (BAe 125s and Falcon 900s). Training Command once had three squadrons (one flying PC-7s, one with L-39s and one with Mi-34s), but most of its assets are now likely not in service. Other types within the inventory include Alpha Jet trainers, ATR-42MP Surveyor maritime patrol aircraft, Fokker 27 transports, Air Beetle and Bulldog basic trainers, Do 27, 28 and Do 228 light transports, and MB339 jet trainers, though availability of these types remains questionable. The VIP transport fleet also includes civil-registered examples of the AW139, Boeing 727, Boeing 737, Cessna 550, Fokker 28 and Gulfstream IV/V. Other rotary-wing equipment includes the Mi-8 and Mi-24/35 assault helicopters.

A separate Nigerian Naval Air Arm operates Lynx Mk89s (obtained in order to serve on the Navy's single frigate) and A109s, although these are also reportedly mainly inactive.

Specifications

Crew: 2
Powerplant: 2 x SNECMA/Turbomeca Larzac 04-C6 each rated at 13.24kN (2976lb thrust)
Maximum speed: 1000km/h (621mph)
Range: 670km (415 miles)
Service ceiling: 14,630m (48,000ft)
Dimensions: span 9.11m (30ft); length 11.75m (38ft); height 4.19m (14ft)
Weight: 8000kg (17,600lb) loaded
Armament: 1 x 30mm (1.18in) DEFA 553 cannon pod; up to 2500kg (5500lb) of bombs, rockets or drop-tanks

Dassault-Dornier Alpha Jet N, Nigerian Air Force

Nigeria purchased 25 Alpha Jets from Dornier (rather than from Dassault-Breguet, as was the norm), between 1981 and 1986. Four of these saw some combat in Sierra Leone in the 1990s. No fewer than nine have been lost in various mishaps.

Senegal Air Force

The Armée de l'Air du Senegal consists of a single air group (the 1st Senegalese Air Group) equipped with mainly transport types and helicopters. The most capable aircraft in the inventory are the F27 tactical transports, delivered in the mid-1970s, as well as two Mi-35 assault helicopters and two Mi-171 transport helicopters acquired more recently. Magister jet trainers have been retired, leaving training in the hands of a fleet of Epsilons, as well as Rallye 235s, the latter being outfitted as armed trainers. The air force operates from Dakar International Airport, although detachments are maintained elsewhere in the country. In 2008 Senegal received two UH-1Hs and two C-212s that were a donation from Spain. Other helicopter types in use include the AS355 and Mi-2.

Togo

The Force Aérienne Togolaise is split between two main air bases, Niamtougou and Lomé. Niamtougou has a fighter squadron with six Brazilian-supplied EMB-326GB Xavantes, and a training squadron flying Epsilons. The air force is reportedly interested in overhauling and returning to service the Alpha Jets once flown by the fighter squadron. Lomé supports a transport squadron, with DHC-5s and helicopters, and a presidential squadron, which includes a Boeing 707, a Fokker 28 and an SA365 Alpha Jets formerly flown by the fighter squadron. Lomé supports a transport squadron, with DHC-5s and helicopters, and a presidential squadron of a Boeing 707, a Fokker 28 and an SA365.

Specifications

Crew: 3	Dimensions: rotor diameter 21.35m (69ft 10in); length 18.42m (60ft 5in); height 4.76m (15ft 7in)
Powerplant: 2 x 1545kW (2225shp) Klimov TV3-117VM turboshafts	Weight: 11,100kg (24,470lb) loaded
Maximum speed: 250km/h (156mph)	Armament: Capable of carrying up to 1500kg (3300lb) of stores on six hardpoints
Range: 950km (594 miles)	
Service ceiling: 6000m (19,690ft)	

Mil Mi-171Sh, Armée de l'Air du Senegal, Ouakam

Acquired as part of a recent modernization effort on the part of the Senegal Air Force, this Mi-171Sh is one of two examples operated from Ouakam (on the military side of the Léopold Sédar Senghhor international airport).

Specifications

Crew: 2	Dimensions: span 9.11m (30ft); length 11.75m (38ft); height 4.19m (14ft)
Powerplant: 2 x SNECMA/Turbomeca Larzac 04-C6 each rated at 13.24kN (2976lb thrust)	Weight: 8000kg (17,600lb) loaded
Maximum speed: 1000km/h (621mph)	Armament: 1 x 30mm (1.18in) DEFA 553 cannon pod; up to 2500kg (5500lb) of bombs, rockets or drop-tanks
Range: 670km (415 miles)	
Service ceiling: 14,630m (48,000ft)	

Dassault/Dornier Alpha Jet E, Force Aérienne Togolaise, Niamtougou

Togo was the first export customer for the Alpha Jet, ordering five in May 1977. Only three examples remained in service in 2000, when the fleet was put into storage at Niamtougou.

Smaller Central African states

Burundi, Chad, Congo Brazzaville, DR Congo, Madagascar, Rwanda and Uganda

The years of conflict that have afflicted Central Africa have left their mark on the region's air arms, and the armed forces of Rwanda and Uganda have both been drawn into the fighting in the Democratic Republic of Congo (as the former Zaïre was re-named in 1997).

In addition to the air arms outlined, the region includes the Central African Republic, with its small Escadrille Centreafricaine. This has been in a parlous state since unrest in the country in the 1990s, but does include a single C-130, three helicopters, as well as a handful of AL-60 light transports.

Burundi

The Armée National de Burundi maintains a small air arm centred on a single helicopter squadron, equipped with two to four SA342s, at least two Mi-8MTV-5s and one or two Mi-24 assault helicopters.

Chad National Flight

Operating from N'Djamena international airport and Abéché, the Escadrille Nationale Tchadienne includes single fighter, helicopter and transport squadrons. By 2008 Chad had acquired three Su-25s from Ukraine (from six reportedly on order). An-26s and C-130Hs

▲ Mil Mi-24, Armée National de Burundi, Bujumbura

An unknown unit from Bujumbura international airport operates this Mi-24. The Mi-24 serves alongside SA342L Gazelles and Mi-8s and possibly a small number of surviving SA316B Alouette IIIs.

Specifications

- Crew: 2–3
- Powerplant: 2 x 1600kW (2200hp) Isotov TV3-117 turbines
- Maximum speed: 335km/h (208mph)
- Range: 450km (280 miles)
- Service ceiling: 4500m (14,750ft)
- Dimensions: span 6.5m (21ft 3in); length 17.5m (57ft 4in); height 6.5m (21ft 3in)
- Weight: 12,000kg (26,500lb) loaded
- Armament: 1 x 12.7mm (0.5in) Yakushev-Borzov gun, 4 x S-8 80mm (3.15in) of rocket pods or up to 3460kg (7612lb) rockets or missiles

▼ Sukhoi Su-25, Escadrille Nationale Tchadienne (Chad National Flight), N'Djamena

TT-QAI is the only Chadian single-seat Su-25 identified so far (the air arm has also received a pair of two-seat Su-25UBs).

Specifications

- Crew: 1
- Powerplant: 2 x 44.1kN (9921lb) Tumanskii R-195 turbojets
- Maximum speed: 975km/h (606mph)
- Range: 750km (466 miles)
- Service ceiling: 7000m (22,965ft)
- Dimensions: span 14.36m (47ft 1.5in); length 15.53m (50ft 11.5in); height 4.8m (15ft 9in)
- Weight: 17,600kg (38,800lb) loaded
- Armament: 1 x 30mm (1.18in) GSh-30-2 cannon, eight external pylons with provision for up to 4400kg (9700lb) of stores

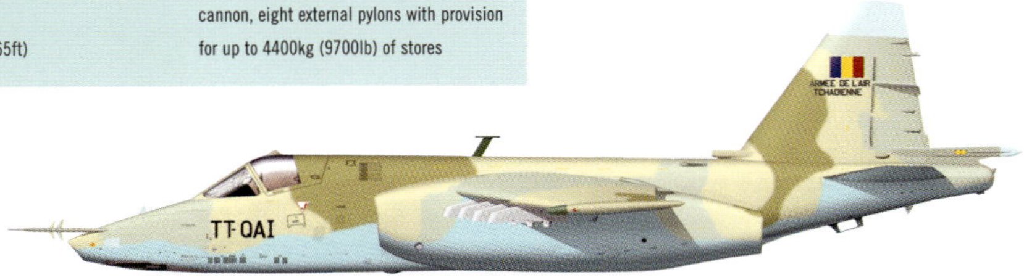

provide the mainstay of the transport squadron, while helicopters in use include the Alouette III, AS550, Mi-8/17/171 and Mi-35. A Beech 1900 and a DC-9 serve as VIP transports. Other types in use in small numbers comprise the Cessna 337, PC-6, PC-7, PC-9 and SF260W.

Congolese Air Force

No unit structure is known for the air force of Congo (also known as Congo-Brazzaville), although in the 1990s it was based on French-supplied helicopters, and Soviet-built fighters and transports. By 2001, most of the surviving aircraft had been grounded.

Specifications

Crew: 1
Powerplant: 1 x 73.5kN (16,535lb) Tumanskii R-25 turbojet
Maximum speed: 2229km/h (1385mph)
Range: 1160km (721 miles)
Service ceiling: 17,500m (57,400ft)
Dimensions: span 7.15m (23ft 5.5in); length (including probe) 15.76m (51ft 8.5in); height 4.1m (13ft 5.5in)
Weight: 10,400kg (22,925lb) loaded
Armament: 1 x 23mm (0.9in) GSh-23 twin-barrel cannon in underbelly pack, provision for about 1500kg (3307kg) of stores

▼ Mikoyan-Gurevich MiG-21bis, Congolese Air Force, Pointe Noire

Wearing the markings of Congo Brazzaville, this MiG-21bis was one of the last two operational MiG-21s reported as such in September 1999, when they were stationed at Pointe Noire air base.

Specifications

Crew: 1
Powerplant: 2 x 44.1kN (9921lb) Tumanskii R-195 turbojets
Maximum speed: 975km/h (606mph)
Range: 750km (466 miles)
Service ceiling: 7000m (22,965ft)
Dimensions: span 14.36m (47ft 1.5in); length 15.53m (50ft 11.5in); height 4.8m (15ft 9in)
Weight: 17,600kg (38,800lb) loaded
Armament: 1 x 30mm (1.18in) GSh-30-2 cannon, eight external pylons with provision for up to 4400kg (9700lb) of stores

▲ Sukhoi Su-25, Air Force of the DR Congo, N'Djili

This Su-25 is one of four delivered in November 1999. Since then, two have crashed and the two survivors, both stationed at the military side of N'Djili international airport, are rarely flown.

Specifications

Crew: 1
Powerplant: 1 x 73.5kN (16,535lb) Tumanskii R-25 turbojet
Maximum speed: 2229km/h (1385mph)
Range: 1160km (721 miles)
Service ceiling: 17,500m (57,400ft)
Dimensions: span 7.15m (23ft 5.5in); length (including probe) 15.76m (51ft 8.5in); height 4.1m (13ft 5.5in)
Weight: 10,400kg (22,925lb) loaded
Armament: 1 x 23mm (0.9in) GSh-23 twin-barrel cannon, provision for 1500kg (3307kg) of stores

▼ Mikoyan-Gurevich MiG-21bis, Armée de l'Air Malgache (Malagasy Air Force), Ivato

In common with the majority of the entire air force (with the exception of a few helicopters), all Malagasy MiG-21bis have been withdrawn from service and dumped at Ivato air base.

Air Force of the Democratic Republic of Congo

Since the late 1990s, the air arm of the Democratic Republic of Congo has been in a state of disarray. All combat aircraft (including MB326s and MiG-23s) are now believed to be stored, with only a few Mi-35s remaining operational. Congo acquired four Su-25s from Georgia in 1999, although only two now remain. Transport types reported include the An-26, C-47, C-130, DHC-5 and Islander. AS332, Mi-26, SA316 and SA330 helicopters have also been noted.

Madagascar – Malagasy Air Force

All combat aircraft (including MiG-17s and MiG-21s) and most transports formerly operated by the Armée de l'Air Malgache went into storage at Ivato during the mid-1990s, and were reportedly disposed of as scrap in 2008. Surviving types likely include Mi-8 helicopters and perhaps a number of light fixed-wing aircraft.

Rwandan Air Force

After the country's years of civil war in the 1990s, the Force Aérienne Rwandaise is today believed to consist of two operational squadrons, one equipped with a pair of Mi-24 assault helicopters, the other with around eight Mi-8/17 transport helicopters. Single examples of the AS355 and SA365 utility helicopters may also remain in use.

Uganda People's Defence Force

The sharp end of the Ugandan air force is provided by a single fighter squadron, equipped with six MiG-21s, and a helicopter squadron (Mi-8/17s and a single Mi-24). Other assets comprise a small number of Bell 206s, three L-39s and an SF260 trainer, and a pair of Y-12 transports.

▼ Mil Mi-24, Combat Squadron, Rwandan Air Force, Kigali

Operated by the Combat Squadron (apparently this is an official designation; the unit is also sometimes cited as the Mi-24 Squadron), this aircraft is based on the military side of Kigali international airport.

Specifications

Crew: 2–3	Dimensions: span 6.5m (21ft 3in); length 17.5m (57ft 4in); height 6.5m (21ft 3in)
Powerplant: 2 x 1600kW (2200hp) Isotov TV3-117 turbines	Weight: 12,000kg (26,500lb) loaded
Maximum speed: 335km/h (208mph)	Armament: 1 x 12.7mm (0.5in) Yakushev-Borzov gun, 4 x S-8 80mm (3.15in) rocket pods or up to 3460kg (7612lb) of rockets or missiles
Range: 450km (280 miles)	
Service ceiling: 4500m (14,750ft)	

Specifications

Crew: 1	Dimensions: span 7.15m (23ft 5.5in); length (including probe) 15.76m (51ft 8.5in); height 4.1m (13ft 5.5in)
Powerplant: 1 x 73.5kN (16,535lb) Tumanskii R-25 turbojet	Weight: 10,400kg (22,925lb) loaded
Maximum speed: 2229km/h (1385mph)	Armament: 1 x 23mm (0.9in) GSh-23 cannon, provision for 1500kg (3307kg) of stores
Range: 1160km (721 miles)	
Service ceiling: 17,500m (57,400ft)	

▼ Mikoyan-Gurevich MiG-21bis, Uganda People's Defence Force

This aircraft is one of six MiG-21s purchased from Poland via Israel, and overhauled by IAI. Three have been lost in accidents to date, and additional examples have been acquired from Ukraine.

South Africa

South African Air Force

With capabilities unmatched in sub-Saharan Africa, the SAAF is combat proven and well equipped, and is in the process of introducing a number of advanced new types to its inventory.

Originally established in 1920, today's SAAF operates on a much smaller budget than in previous years, but has nevertheless made efforts to maintain its edge in the region. It is now spearheaded by the first of 28 Gripen fighters. Other new equipment includes 24 Hawk Mk120s, four Super Lynx 300s, and 30 A109 utility helicopters, while older types have been withdrawn, and certain bases closed down in a process of rationalization.

The sole fighter unit now active is 2 Squadron at Makhado, flying the Gripen. Eleven Rooivalk attack helicopters are operated by 16 Squadron at Bloemspruit. Transport aircraft are centred at Waterkloof, with 28 Squadron's C-130BZs; C-212s, CN235s and Cessna 185s of 44 Squadron; Beech 200/300s, Cessna 208s and PC-12s of 41 Squadron, and the mixed VIP fleet of 21 Squadron. The turboprop-powered C-47TP survives in the maritime patrol role, with 35 Squadron at Ysterplaat.

Training syllabus

Before progressing to the Hawks of 85 Combat Flying School at Makhado, trainee pilots fly the PC-7 of the Central Flying School at Langebaanweg, also home to the Silver Falcons display team. Helicopter pilots are schooled by 87 Helicopter Flying School, flying A109s, BK117s and Oryx from Bloemspruit.

▲ Denel AH-2 Rooivalk

The Rooivalk project began in 1984 and led to a first flight in 1990. The attack helicopter suffers from limited operational capability and, to date, only 12 production examples have been completed for the SAAF.

Ysterplaat-based 22 Squadron is a mixed helicopter unit, with the maritime-configured Super Lynx and Oryx. With flights maintained at Durban and Port Elizabeth, 15 Squadron operates Oryx and BK117s. 17 and 19 Squadrons are both equipped with A109s and Oryx, and are based at Hoedspruit and Waterkloof. The SAAF also maintains a Test Flight and Development Centre, flying various types from the test ranges at Overberg.

Specifications

Crew: 1	Dimensions: span 8m (26ft 3in); length 14.1m (46ft 3in); height 4.7m (15ft 5in)
Powerplant: 1 x 80.5kN (18,100lb) Volvo Flygmotor RM12 turbofan	Weight: 12,473kg (27,500lb) loaded
Maximum speed: more than Mach 2	Armament: 1 x 27mm (1.06in) Mauser BK27 cannon, plus rockets, cluster bombs and missiles
Range: 3250km (2020 miles)	
Service ceiling: 15,240m (50,000ft)	

▼ SAAB JAS39C Gripen, 2 Squadron, Makhado

The first of two single-seat Gripens delivered to the SAAF in November 2009. The type has replaced the Cheetah C/D as the SAAF's front-line fighter, with orders placed for 17 JAS39Cs and nine two-seat JAS39Ds.

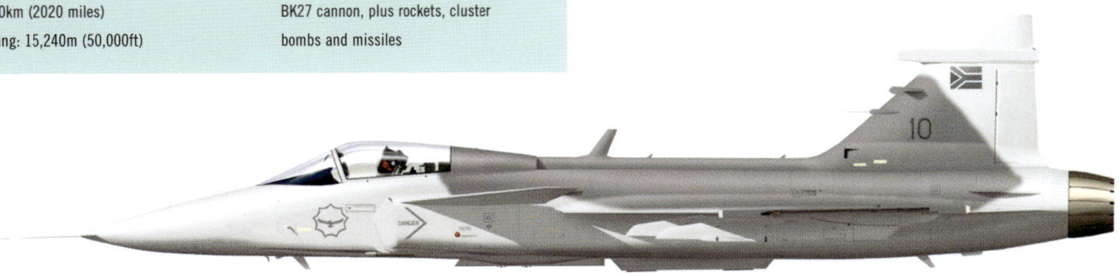

Smaller Southern African states

BOTSWANA, NAMIBIA, ZAMBIA AND ZIMBABWE

Although relatively peaceful today (the once powerful Mozambique air arm has effectively disbanded) the volatile situation in Zimbabwe ensures that neighbours remain on their guard.

THE SMALLER NATIONS in Southern Africa typically maintain proportionally sized air wings. However, while the air wings of Lesotho and Swaziland are equipped with small fleets for mainly paramilitary duties, those of their neighbours in the region include jet equipment of various types.

Botswana Defence Force Air Wing

The Botswana Defence Force Air Wing was created in 1977. The most important base is Molepolole, although Gaborone and Francistown are also used. Main combat equipment is Z28 Squadron's ex-Canadian CF-5A/Ds, 13 of which were ordered in 1996, followed by another five in 2000. Transport capacity is provided by C-212, CN235 and C-130B aircraft of Z10 Squadron and the Islanders of Z1 and Z12. Helicopters consist of the AS350 and Bell 412 (Z21 and Z23). Training is conducted on PC-7s of Z7, while O-2As (Z3) are used for anti-poaching operations. VIP transport at Molepolole consists of a Bell 412, a Beech 200 and a Gulfstream IV.

Namibia Defence Force

Namibia's Air Squadron includes a privately run basic flying school and a jet flying school that was established with Chinese assistance and operates K-8s. A fighter squadron equipped with 12 Chengdu F-7s is still in the process of establishment, although a helicopter squadron (Mi-8, Mi-35 and SA315/316) and a transport squadron (An-12, An-26 and Y-12) are active. A VIP flight is also operational.

Zambia Air Force and Air Defence

Zambia's single fighter squadron (once equipped with MiG-19s and MiG-21s) is now defunct, leaving a jet training squadron with K-8s, a transport squadron with two Y-12s, and a helicopter squadron equipped with AB205, AB212 and Mi-8 types, and reportedly a single Mi-24. The Zambian VIP flight is apparently no longer operational.

Air Force of Zimbabwe

The AFZ, which has been involved in the conflict in the Democratic Republic of Congo since the late 1990s, is primarily based at two locations: Gweru-Thornhill and Harare-Manyame. The most capable combat type is the Chengdu F-7, 20 of which are in service, including two twin-seat FT-7s, and these were deployed operationally during the fighting in the Congo. Training is conducted on around 30

Specifications

Crew: 1–2
Powerplant: 2 x 13.0kN (2925lbf) (dry thrust) Orenda-built GE J85-15 turbojet
Maximum speed: 1575km/h (978mph)
Range: 1400km (660 miles)
Service ceiling: 12,000m (41,000ft)
Dimensions: span 7.87m (25ft 10in); length 14.38m (47ft 2in); height 4.01m (13ft 2in)
Weight: 9249kg (20,390lb) loaded
Armament: 2 x 20mm (0.787in) Pontiac M39A2 cannons in nose, 2 x AIM-9 Sidewinder Air-to-air missiles and 3200kg (7000lb) payload

Canadair CF-5A Freedom Fighter, Z28 Squadron, Botswana Defence Force Air Wing, Molepolole

Designated as CF-5s, Botswana's Freedom Fighters are actually ex-Canadian Forces CF-116s. Deliveries began in 1996, and the aircraft had been previously upgraded to serve as lead-in trainers for the Hornet.

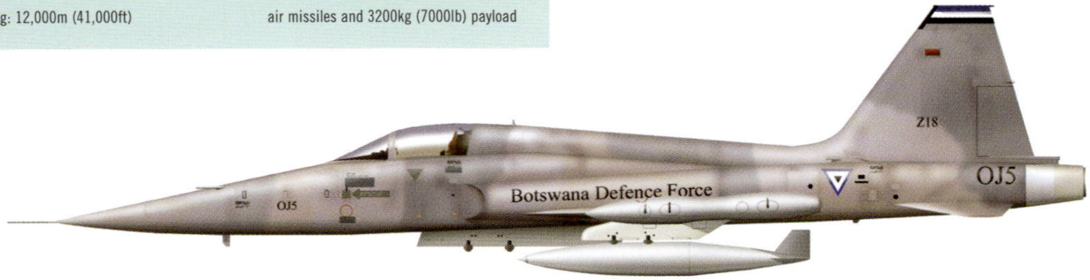

SF260s and 11 K-8s, the latter replacing the now-grounded Hawks. The AFZ transport fleet is based at Harare and includes single examples of the An-12 and Il-76, plus C-47TPs, C-212s and Islanders. Around 15 FTB-337G Skymaster light transports survive. A helicopter fleet relies on AB412s and Alouette IIIs, together with six Mi-24/35s, the latter having seen combat in the Congo. For VIP transport, the AFZ operates two AS532 helicopters, a BAe 146 and possibly a number of surviving Yak-40s.

Specifications

Crew: 2
Powerplant: 1 x 16.01kN (3600lb) Garrett TFE731-2A-2A turbofans
Maximum speed: Mach 0.75 (800km/h; 498mph)
Range: 2250 km (1398 miles)
Service ceiling: 13,000m (42,651ft)
Dimensions: span 9.63m (31ft 7in); length 11.6m (38ft); height 4.21m (13ft 9in)
Weight: 4330kg (9546lb) loaded
Armament: 1x 23mm (0.90in) cannon pod, 5 hardpoints with a capacity of 1000kg (2205lb)

Hongdu K-8, Namibia Defence Force, Windhoek

It appears that Namibia received only four K-8 jet trainers, even though sources indicate deliveries of up to 12. The Chinese influence on the Namibia Defence Force is clear, with pilot graduates progressing from the K-8 to the Chengdu F-7 fighter.

Specifications

Crew: 2
Powerplant: 1 x 16.01kN (3600lb) Garrett TFE731-2A-2A turbofans
Maximum speed: Mach 0.75 (800km/h; 498mph)
Range: 2250 km (1398 miles)
Service ceiling: 13,000m (42,651ft)
Dimensions: span 9.63m (31ft 7in); length 11.6m (38ft); height 4.21m (13ft 9in)
Weight: 4330kg (9546lb) loaded
Armament: 1x 23mm (0.90in) cannon pod, 5 hardpoints with a capacity of 1000kg (2205lb)

Hongdu K-8, Zambia Air Force and Air Defence, Ndola

Zambia purchased a total of eight K-8s, and this was the first example to enter service with an unknown training unit, based at Ndola in northern-central Zambia. Another former customer of Soviet equipment, Zambia's air arm is now turning increasingly to China.

Specifications

Crew: 1
Powerplant: 1 x 66.7kN (14,815lb) thrust Liyang Wopen-13F afterburning turbojet
Maximum speed: 2229km/h (1385mph)
Range: 1160km (721 miles)
Service ceiling: 17,500m (57,400ft)
Dimensions: span 7.15m (23ft 5.5in); length (including probe) 15.76m (51ft 8.5in); height 4.1m (13ft 5.5in)
Weight: 10,400kg (22,925lb) loaded
Armament: 1 x 23mm (0.9in) cannon, provision for about 1500kg (3307kg) of stores

Chengdu F-7NI, 5 Squadron, Air Force of Zimbabwe, Gweru

This is one of only a few F-7NIs delivered to Zimbabwe, the majority of the AFZ's F-7Ns being of the NII sub-variant (differing in having four underwing hardpoints). Zimbabwe also purchased two FT-7BZs. All are operated by 5 Squadron 'Arrow' from Gweru air base.

PACIFIC
OCEAN
AUSTRALIA
NEW
ZEALAND
SOUTHERN OCEAN

Chapter 8

Australasia

Australia and New Zealand maintain the only significant air arms in their region, with aviation elements of the Australian Defence Force (ADF) providing a powerful bulwark against possible aggression from countries in Southeast Asia. Both countries are aligned with the USA under the ANZUS defence agreement, and support UN peacekeeping missions in the Pacific. The Royal New Zealand Air Force has been active in Timor-Leste in recent years, while major ADF operational commitments include support of Operation Enduring Freedom and Iraqi Freedom and the UN mission in East Timor, together with smaller assignments in Africa and Oceania.

Australia

Royal Australian Air Force, Navy Fleet Air Arm and Army Aviation

Australia's island status and huge coastline demand a robust defence, and the three air arms of the Australian Defence Force (ADF) play a key role in preserving sovereignty.

Among significant new equipment, the ADF is introducing six Wedgetail Airborne Early Warning and Control (AEW&C) platforms and the F/A-18F strike fighter as a replacement for the F-111. Both are almost certain to be joined by around 100 F-35s, which will replace 'legacy' F/A-18s from 2012.

New transport capacity is represented by four C-17As that provide a Responsive Global Airlift capability, and can be used to deploy ADF Chinook, MRH90 and Tiger helicopters. The five KC-30A tankers provide a refuelling capability, replacing 707s, and can also operate as strategic airlifters.

Rotary-wing modernization for the ADF is represented by 46 MRH90 transport helicopters, which will ultimately replace Army S-70As, UH-1Hs and, in navalized form, the Sea King. A new maritime helicopter to replace the S-70B will be selected from the MRH90 or MH-60R. The RAAF's first UAV is the Heron 1, acquired in conjunction with the Canadian Armed Forces and used in Afghanistan.

ROYAL AUSTRALIAN AIR FORCE

HQ Air Command, Glenbrook

Direct Reporting Unit		
Aerospace Operational Support Group	F/A-18A/B, PC-9/A, P-3C	Edinburgh

Air Combat Group — Williamtown

78 Wing,	**Williamtown**	
76 Squadron	Hawk Mk127	Williamtown
79 Squadron	Hawk Mk127	Pearce
2 OCU	F/A-18A/B	Williamtown
81 Wing,	**Williamtown**	
3 Squadron	F/A-18A/B	Williamtown
75 Squadron	F/A-18A/B	Tindal
77 Squadron	F/A-18A/B	Williamtown
82 Wing	**Amberley**	
1 Squadron	RF/F-111C, F/A-18F	Amberley
6 Squadron	F-111C, F/A-18F	Amberley

Note: F/A-18F will replace F-111s with 1 and 6 Squadrons from 2010.

Forward Air Control Development Unit	PC-9/A	Williamtown

Surveillance and Response Group

42 Wing	**Williamtown**	
2 Squadron	Wedgetail	Williamtown

Air Lift Group Richmond

84 Wing	**Richmond**	
32 Squadron	Beech 350	East Sale
33 Squadron	KC-30A	Amberley
34 Squadron	Boeing 737-BBJ, CL-604	Canberra International Airport
86 Wing	**Richmond**	
36 Squadron	C-17A	Amberley
37 Squadron	C-130H/J	Richmond

Maritime Patrol Group

92 Wing	**Edinburgh**	
10 Squadron	AP-3C	Edinburgh
11 Squadron	AP-3C	Edinburgh
292 Squadron	AP-3C	Edinburgh

Training Command Williams

Central Flying School	PC-9/A	East Sale
2 FTS	PC-9/A	Pearce

Specifications

Crew: 2
Powerplant: 2 x 97.90kN (22,000lb) thrust General Electric F414-GE-400 afterburning turbofan engines
Maximum speed: 1190 km/h (1190mph)
Range: 722km (449 miles)
Service ceiling: 15,000m (50,000ft)
Dimensions: span 13.62m (60ft 1in); length 13.62m (44ft 9in); height 4.88m (16ft)
Weight: 29,900kg (66,000lb) loaded
Armament: 1 x 20mm (.78in) M61A1 Vulcan cannon; 11 external hardpoints for up to 8050kg (17,750lb) of stores

Boeing F/A-18F Super Hornet, 1 Squadron, RAAF Base Amberley

The latest combat equipment for the RAAF is the two-seat F/A-18F. It has been procured as a successor to the F-111. Deliveries of the 24 aircraft began in 2010.

Order of battle

RAAF organization divides assets among the Air Combat Group (ACG), Surveillance and Response Group (SRG), Air Lift Group (ALG), together with training units, the latter including the Roulettes aerobatic team, equipped with PC-9/A trainers.

Australian Army Aviation Corps is spearheaded by the Tiger Armed Reconnaissance Helicopter (ARH), 22 of which are on order. Primary air mobility assets are six CH-47Ds and 35 S-70As, while the MRH90 is also now arriving in service, allowing retirement of the UH-H. The Army's 171 Squadron is used for anti-terrorist operations. AAAvn and RAN instructor training is handled by the School of Army Aviation.

Lockheed AP-3C Orion

The parent unit of the AP-3C fleet is the Maritime Patrol Group, but the Orion is increasingly used by the RAAF for overland missions. The upgraded AP-3C has new mission equipment, including multi-mode radar and electro-optical sensors.

The Royal Australian Navy's airborne activities are centred at Nowra (HMAS *Albatross*), the sole naval air station. S-70Bs operate from RAN frigates. The Sea King maritime support helicopter will be replaced by the MRH90. AS350s and A109s are used for lead-in pilot, observer and aircrew training, and occasional shipborne utility duties.

ROYAL AUSTRALIAN NAVY FLEET AIR ARM		
723 Squadron	AS350, A109	Nowra
816 Squadron	S-70B	Nowra
817 Squadron	Sea King Mk50A/B	Nowra

AUSTRALIAN ARMY AVIATION CORPS		
1st Aviation Regiment		
161(R) Squadron	Bell 206B/CA-32, Tiger ARH	Darwin
162(R) Squadron	Bell 206B/CA-32, Tiger ARH	Townsville
171(GS) Squadron	S-70A	Holsworthy
173(GS) Squadron	Beech 350, Beech 200	Oakey
5th Aviation Regiment		
A Squadron	MRH90	Townsville
B Squadron	S-70A	Townsville
C Squadron	CH-47D	Lavarack Barracks/ Townsville
School of Army Aviation		
Bell 206B/CA-32, Tiger ARH, S-70A		Oakey

Specifications

Crew: 2
Powerplant: 2 x 1409kW (1890shp) General Electric T700-GE-701C turboshaft
Maximum speed: 361km/h (224mph)
Range: 463km (288 miles)
Service ceiling: 4021m (13,200ft)
Dimensions: rotor diameter: 16.36m (53ft 8in); length 19.76m (64ft 10in); height 5.33m (17ft 6in)
Weight: 9997kg (22,000lb) loaded
Armament: 2 x 7.62mm door guns, AGM-119 Penguin anti-ship missiles, MK46 torpedoes

Sikorsky S-70B-2 Seahawk, 816 Squadron, HMAS Anzac

Seen here armed with AGM-119 Penguin anti-ship missiles, this S-70B-2 is one of 16 examples shore-based at Nowra when not embarked on Royal Australian Navy warships. Other weapons include 7.62mm (0.3in) door guns and Mk46 torpedoes.

Specifications

Crew: 2
Powerplant: 2 x 1160kW (1171hp) MTU/Rolls-Royce/Turboneca MTR 390 turboshafts
Maximum speed: 280km/h (175mph)
Battle endurance: 2 hours 50 min
Initial climb rate: more than 600m/min (1900fpm)
Dimensions: rotor diameter 13m (42ft 7in); length 14m (46ft); height 4.32m (14ft 1in)
Weight: 6000kg (13,225lb) loaded
Armament: 4 wing stations for Hellfire II air-to-ground missiles and 4 air-to-air missiles

Eurocopter Tiger ARH, 161(R) Squadron, 1st Aviation Regiment, Roberts Barracks, Darwin

Armed with Hellfire II air-to-ground missiles, this is one of 22 Tigers acquired under the ARH programme to equip 161(R) and 162(R) Squadrons, replacing the Bell 206B/CA-32 as well as the UH-1H gunships, which are now retired.

Lockheed C-130H Hercules

The RAAF's No. 37 Squadron, stationed at RAAF Base Richmond, near Sydney, is equipped with the C-130H, introduced in 1978, as well as the latest C-130J model, which arrived in 1999. The C-130s are used for troop transport, airdropping of paratroops and cargo, and special forces insertion.

New Zealand

Royal New Zealand Air Force

Tasked with, among others, defence of one of the world's largest Exclusive Economic Zones, the RNZAF fleet is based around maritime patrol, transport and helicopter elements.

THE THREE FORCE elements of the RNZAF are the Maritime Patrol Force, Fixed Wing Transport Force and the Rotary Wing Transport Force. The Maritime Patrol Force is comprised of No. 5 Squadron, with six P-3Ks, based at RNZAF Auckland. No. 40 Squadron, also at Auckland, provides the Fixed Wing Transport element, and is equipped with five C-130H and two 757-200 transports. The Rotary Wing Transport Force is at RNZAF Base Ohakea, and is assigned the UH-1H helicopters of No. 3 Squadron.

No. 42 Squadron, responsible for multi-engine pilot training, uses five King Air 200s. This unit is based at Ohakea alongside the Helicopter Conversion Flight (a branch of No. 3 Squadron). As well as using UH-1Hs as required, the Helicopter Conversion Flight has five of its own Sioux helicopters for conversion training. Also at Ohakea are the CT-4 Airtrainers of the Pilot Training Squadron and the Central Flying School. The PTS and CFS share the fleet of 13 Airtrainers, the CFS being responsible for the Flying Instructors Course, and also providing the Red Checkers aerobatic display team.

The RNZAF is acquiring eight NH90s to replace the UH-1H fleet, while the Sioux will be superseded by five A109 Light Utility Helicopters.

Five SH-2Gs are operated on behalf of the Navy as No. 6 Squadron, a joint RNZAF/RNZN-manned unit. Flying from RNZN vessels, the Seasprites are based at RNZAF Base Auckland in Whenuapai.

▲ Kaman SH-2G Seasprite

No. 6 Squadron's Seasprites are operated by Navy and Air Force personnel, but are flown by Navy pilots, trained by the RNZAF. The helicopters deploy onboard the frigates HMNZ *Te Mana* and *Te Kaha*.

Specifications

Crew: 11 + 4
Powerplant: 4 x 4910 SHP Allison T56-A-14
Maximum speed: 815km/h (508mph)
Range: 7670km (4766 miles)
Service ceiling: 9296m (30,500ft)
Dimensions: span 30.38m (99ft 8in);
length 35.61m (116ft 10in);
height 10.29m (33ft 9in)
Weight: 57,834kg (127,500lb) loaded
Armament: Bombload of 9000kg (20,000lb), missiles, torpedoes, mines and depth charges

▲ Lockheed P-3K Orion, No. 5 Squadron, RNZAF Auckland

The RNZAF operates six P-3K Orions. The first five examples were acquired as P-3Bs in 1966, with a further P-3B transferred to the inventory from the RAAF in 1985. All six Orions received an avionics upgrade in the early 1980s, leading to the revised P-3K designation. P-3Ks have served operationally in the Persian Gulf, and a detachment supported Coalition forces during Operation Enduring Freedom between May 2003 and February 2004.

Glossary

AAC	Army Air Corps
AAF	Army Airfield
AAM	Air-to-Air Missile
AASF	Army Aviation Support Facility
AB	Air Base
ACC	Air Combat Command
ACS	Air Cavalry Squadron
ADV	Air Defence Variant (of the Tornado)
AEF	Air & Space Expeditionary Force
AETC	Air Education and Training Command
AEW	Airborne Early Warning
AFB	Air Force Base
AFGSC	Air Force Global Strike Command
AFMC	Air Force Material Command
AFRC	Air Force Reserve Command
AFSOC	Air Force Special Operations Command
AFSPC	Air Force Space Command
AHB	Assault Helicopter Battalion
AMC	Air Mobility Command
AMRAAM	Advanced Medium-Range Air-to-Air Missile
AP	Airport
ARB	Attack Reconnaissance Helicopter Battalion
ARB	Air Reserve Base
ARNG	Army National Guard
ARS	Attack Reconnaissance Helicopter Squadron
ASF	Aviation Support Facility
ASTOR	Airborne STand-Off Radar
ASW	Anti-Submarine Warfare
AVN	Aviation
AVN CO	Aviation Company
AWACS	Airborne Warning and Control System
CAB	Command Aviation Battalion
CAP	Combat Air Patrol
CAV	Cavalry Regiment or Cavalry Squadron
CSAR	Combat Search and Rescue
Det	Detachment
ECCM	Electronic Counter-Countermeasures: measures taken to reduce the effectiveness of ECM by improving the resistance of radar equipment to jamming
ECM	Electronic Countermeasures: systems designed to confuse and disrupt enemy radar equipment
ECR	Electronic Combat Reconnaissance: a variant of the Panavia Tornado optimized for electronic warfare
ELINT	Electronic Intelligence. Information gathered through monitoring enemy electronic transmissions by specially equipped aircraft, ships or satellites
EW	Electronic Warfare
FAA	Federal Aviation Administration
FAA	Fleet Air Arm
FAC	Forward Air Controller. A battlefront observer who directs strike aircraft on to their targets near the front line
FLIR	Forward-Looking Infra-Red. Heat-sensing equipment fitted in an aircraft that scans the path ahead to detect heat from objects such as vehicle engines
FRS	Fleet Readiness Squadron
GPS	Global Positioning System. A system of navigational satellites
GSAB	General Support Aviation Battalion
HM	Helicopter Mine Countermeasures Squadron
HOTAS	Hands on Throttle and Stick. A system whereby the pilot exercises full control over his aircraft in combat without the need to remove his hands from the throttle and control column to operate weapons selection switches or other controls
HQ	Headquarters
HS	Helicopter Anti-Submarine Squadron
HSC	Helicopter Sea Combat Squadron
HSL	Helicopter Anti-Submarine Light Squadron
HSM	Helicopter Maritime Strike Squadron
HUD	Head-Up Display. A system in which essential information is projected on to a cockpit windscreen so that the pilot has no need to look down at his instrument panel
IAP	International Airport
ICBM	Intercontinental Ballistic Missile
IFF	Identification Friend or Foe. An electronic pulse emitted by an aircraft to identify it as friendly on a radar screen
INS	Inertial Navigation System. An on-board guidance system that steers an aircraft or missile over a pre-determined course by measuring factors such as the distance travelled and reference to 'waypoints' (landmarks) en route

IR	Infra-Red
ISTAR	Intelligence, Surveillance, Targeting and Reconnaissance
JFTB	Joint Forces Training Base
JHC	Joint Helicopter Command
JNGS	Joint National Guard Station
JRB	Joint Reserve Base
JSTARS	Joint Surveillance and Target Attack Radar System. An airborne command and control system that directs air and ground forces in battle
MAD	Magnetic Anomaly Detection. The passage of a large body of metal, such as a submarine, through the earth's magnetic field, causes disturbances that can be detected by special equipment, usually housed in an extended tail boom, in an anti-submarine warfare aircraft
MCAF	Marine Corps Air Facility
MCAS	Marine Corps Air Station
MCB	Marine Corps Base
NAF	Naval Air Facility
NAS	Naval Air Station
NATO	North Atlantic Treaty Organization
NBC	Nuclear, Chemical and Biological (warfare)
NVG	Night Vision Goggles. Specially designed goggles that enhance a pilot's ability to see at night
PACAF	Pacific Air Forces
Phased-Array Radar	A warning radar system using many small aerials spread over a large flat area, rather than a rotating scanner. The advantage of this system is that it can track hundreds of targets simultaneously, electronically directing its beam from target to target in microseconds (millionths of a second)
Pulse-Doppler Radar	a type of airborne interception radar that picks out fast-moving targets from background clutter by measuring the change in frequency of a series of pulses bounced off the targets. This is based on the well-known Doppler Effect, an apparent change in the frequency of waves when the source emitting them has a relative velocity towards or away from an observer.

RAF	Royal Air Force
RAS	Regimental Aviation Squadron
RWR	Radar Warning Receiver. A device mounted on an aircraft that warns the pilot if he is being tracked by an enemy missile guidance or intercept radar
SAM	Surface-to-Air Missile
SHAPE	Supreme Headquarters Allied Powers Europe
SIGINT	Signals Intelligence. Information on enemy intentions gathered by monitoring electronic transmissions from his command, control and communications network
SLAM	Stand-off Land Attack Missile
SLAR	Side-Looking Airborne Radar. A type of radar that provides a continuous radar map of the ground on either side of the aircraft carrying the equipment
SSB	Security and Support Battalion
	Stealth Technology: technology applied to aircraft to reduce their radar signatures
STOVL	Short Take-off, Vertical Landing
TAB	Theater Aviation Battalion
USAF	United States Air Force
USAFE	United States Air Force in Europe
UAV	Unmanned Aerial Vehicle
UCAV	Unmanned Combat Aerial Vehicle
USARC	United States Army Reserve Command
USMC	United States Marine Corps
USN	United States Navy
USNR	United States Naval Reserve
VAQ	Electronic Attack Squadron
VAW	Carrier Airborne Early Warning Squadron
VFA	Strike Fighter Squadron
VFC	Fighter Composite Squadron
VP	Patrol Squadron
VQ	Fleet Air Reconnaissance Squadron
VR	Fleet Logistic Support Squadron
VRC	Fleet Logistic Support Squadron (Composite)

Index

Page numbers in *italics* refer to illustrations.